Humana Festival 2018
The Complete Plays

About the Humana Foundation

The Humana Foundation was established in 1981 as the philanthropic arm of Humana Inc., one of the nation's leading health and well-being companies. Located in Louisville, Kentucky, the Foundation seeks to co-create communities where leadership, culture, and systems work to improve and sustain positive health outcomes. For more information, visit www.HumanaFoundation.org.

Humana and the Humana Foundation are dedicated to Corporate Social Responsibility. Our goal is to ensure that every business decision we make reflects our commitment to improving the health and well-being of our members, our associates, the communities we serve, and our planet.

Humana Festival 2018
The Complete Plays

Edited by
Amy Wegener and Jenni Page-White

Lanham • Boulder • New York • London

Published by Limelight Editions
An imprint of The Rowman & Littlefield Publishing Group, Inc.
4501 Forbes Boulevard, Suite 200, Lanham, Maryland 20706
www.rowman.com

6 Tinworth Street, London SE11 5AL, United Kingdom

Copyright © 2020 by The Rowman & Littlefield Publishing Group, Inc.

All rights reserved. No part of this book may be reproduced in any form or by any electronic or mechanical means, including information storage and retrieval systems, without written permission from the publisher, except by a reviewer who may quote passages in a review.

British Library Cataloguing in Publication Information Available

Library of Congress Cataloging-in-Publication Data

ISSN 1935-4452
ISBN 978-1-5381-3318-7 (pbk. : alk. paper)
ISBN 978-1-5381-3635-5 (electronic)

Contents

About the Humana Festival of New American Plays xi

Do You Feel Anger? by Mara Nelson-Greenberg 1

Evocation to Visible Appearance by Mark Schultz 57

we, the invisibles by Susan Soon He Stanton. .111

Marginal Loss by Deborah Stein 175

God Said This by Leah Nanako Winkler. 253

You Across from Me
   by Jaclyn Backhaus, Dipika Guha,
   Brian Otaño, and Jason Gray Platt. 309

Acknowledgments

The editors wish to thank the following people for their invaluable assistance in compiling this volume:

Vivian Barnes
John Cerullo
Jelani Cornick
Allison Epperson
Robert Barry Fleming
Elizabeth Greenfield
Mary Kate Grimes
Carrie Hagovsky
Melissa Hines
Laura Humble
Jane B. Jones
Steve Knight
Meredith McDonough
Meghan McLeroy
Zachary Meicher-Buzzi
Erin Meiman
Kevin E. Moore
Hannah Rae Montgomery
Jessica Reese
Jeffrey S. Rodgers
Joan Sergay
Charlotte Stephens
Michael Tan
Emily Tarquin
Les Waters
Paul Werner

Beth Blickers
Emma Feiwel
Michael Finkle
Leah Hamos
Olivier Sultan
Rachel Viola
Alexis Williams
Derek Zasky

Actors Theatre of Louisville Staff 2018 Humana Festival

ARTISTIC DIRECTOR, Les Waters
MANAGING DIRECTOR, Kevin E. Moore

ARTISTIC

Associate Artistic Director . . . . Meredith McDonough
Artistic Producer . . . . Emily Tarquin
Artistic Manager . . . . Zachary Meicher-Buzzi
Company Manager . . . . Dot King

Literary

Literary Director . . . . Amy Wegener
Literary Manager . . . . Jenni Page-White
Resident Dramaturg . . . . Hannah Rae Montgomery
Literary Associate . . . . Jessica Reese

Education

Education Director . . . . Jane B. Jones
Education Manager . . . . Betsy Anne Huggins
Education Associate . . . . Janelle Renee Dunn
Teaching Artists . . . . Liz Fentress, Keith McGill,
Talleri McRae, Letitia Usher

ADMINISTRATION

General Manager . . . . Jeffrey S. Rodgers
Human Resources Manager . . . . Marie Tull
Systems Manager . . . . Dottie Krebs
Executive Assistant . . . . Janelle Baker
Administrative & IT Services Coordinator . . . . Alan Meyer

AUDIENCE SERVICES & SALES

Ticket Sales Director . . . . Kim McKercher
Season Tickets Manager . . . . Julie Gallegos
Patron Services Managers . . . . Steve Clark, Kristy Kannapell
Patron Services Associates . . . . LaShana Avery, Matthew Brown,
Kristine Farley, Marty Huelsmann, Kala Lewis

Volunteer and Audience Relations

Director . . . . Allison Hammons
House Managers . . . . Tiffany Bush, Elizabeth Cooley,
Rachel Downs, Jordan Kelch,
Bridget Kojima, Abigail Rogers

Lobby Manager. . . . . Tiffany Walton
Coat Check Supervisor . . . . Tanisha Johnson
Coat Check Attendants . . . . Nathan Hewitt, Stevie Lipps

DEVELOPMENT

Director of Development. . . . . Mark Warner
Director of Community Partnerships . . . . Carrie Syberg
Director of Individual Giving. . . . . Katherine Lander
Donor Relations Coordinator. . . . . Susan Bramer

FINANCE

Director . . . . Peggy Shake
Accounting Coordinator . . . . .Jason Acree
Accounting Assistant. . . . . Dara Tiller

MARKETING & COMMUNICATIONS

Director . . . . Steve Knight
Marketing Manager. . . . . Melissa Hines
Festival & Events Manager. . . . . Erin Meiman
Public Relations Manager . . . . Elizabeth Greenfield
Marketing & Communications Coordinator. . . . . .Laura Humble
Graphic Designer . . . . Mary Kate Zihar
Website & Graphic Design Assistant . . . . Jen Williams
Group Sales Manager . . . . Sarah Peters
Outbound Customer Service Representative. . . . . David Meredith

OPERATIONS

Director of Operations . . . . .Carlo Stallings
Operations Manager . . . . .Barry Witt
Building Services Supervisor . . . . Ricky Baldon
Building Services . . . . Deonta Burns, Cassandra Smith,
Jeramaine Spain

PRODUCTION

Production Manager . . . . Paul Werner
Associate Production Manager. .Michael DeWhatley
Production Stage Manager. . . . . Paul Mills Holmes
Resident Stage Managers. . . . . Stephen Horton, Jessica Kay Potter,
Katie Shade
Resident Production Assistants. . . . . Leah Pye, Katherine Thesing

Scenic

Technical Director. . . . . Justin Hagovsky
Associate Technical Director . . . . Braden Blauser

Scenic Charge Artist . . . . Rachael Claxton
Scene Shop Manager. . . . . Javan Roy-Bachman
Master Carpenter . . . . Alexia Hal
Scenic Carpenters . . . . Andrew Boucher, Elliot Cornett,
Matthew Krell, Brooke McPherson
Jacob Turner, Pierre Vendette
Assistant Scenic Charge. . . . . Colleen Doty
Deck Carpenters . . . . Gracie Lawson, Peter Regalbuto

Costumes

Costume Director . . . . Mike Floyd
Crafts Master . . . . Shari Cochran
Wig and Makeup Supervisor . . . . Jehann Gilman
Draper/Tailor . . . . Jeffery Park
First Hands . . . . Rachel Gregory, Natalie Maynard
Stitchers . . . . Faith Brown, Christina Marcantonio
Costume Design Assistants . . . . Isabel Martin, Adrienne Nixon
Wig and Makeup Assistant . . . . Rebecca Traylor
Wardrobe Manager . . . . Anna Jenny
Wardrobe Assistants . . . . Ashlynne Abraham,
Chloe Hixson, Audrey Morton
Wardrobe Technician . . . . Brady Irwin

Lighting

Supervisor . . . . Jason E. Weber
Assistant Lighting Supervisor . . . . Dani Clifford
Electrics Shop Manager . . . . Steve Burdsall
Pamela Brown Lighting Technician . . . . Wylder Cooper
Bingham Lighting Technician . . . . Oliver Kassenbrock
Swing Lighting Technician. . . . . Tyler Warner
Lighting Technicians . . . . Nichole Marquez, Christian Bowyer,
Ashley Raper, Paige Johnson

Sound

Supervisor . . . . Paul Doyle
Assistant Sound Supervisor . . . . Lindsay Burdsall
Sound Technicians . . . . Marion Ayers, Jesús Rivera

Properties

Director . . . . Mark Walston
Associate Properties Master . . . . Heather Lindert
Assistant Properties Master . . . . Katelin Ashcraft
Carpenter Artisan . . . . Ben Herrera
Soft Goods Artisan . . . . Jessie Combest

General Artisan . . . . Bradley Baute
Properties Artisan . . . . Erin Brandt

Video

Media Technologist . . . . Philip Allgeier

PROFESSIONAL TRAINING COMPANY

Director . . . . Michael Legg
Artistic Coordinator . . . . Jonathan Ruiz
Acting . . . . Andrea Abello, Calum Bedborough,
Bear Brummel, Sergio Caetano, Satya Chavez,
Nayib Felix, Brandon Fox, Rigel Harris, Alaina Kai,
Emily Kaplan, Emily Kleypas, Jerardo Larios,
Joseph Miller, Tim Peters, Marika Proctor,
Omer Abbas Salem, Jack Schmitt,
Suzy Weller, Karoline Xu, Jenna Zhu
Communications . . . . Laurel C. Henning
Company & Artistic Management . . . . Bridget Kojima
Costumes . . . . Emma Kravig
Development . . . . Nathan Hewitt
Directing . . . . Jelani Cornick, Joan Sergay
Dramaturgy/Literary Management . . . . Vivian Barnes, Meghan McLeroy
Education/Teaching Artist . . . . Abigail Miskowiec, Zoe Rosenfeld
Festival & Events Management . . . . Gabriela De La Rosa
Lighting . . . . Jessie Lynn Smith
Marketing . . . . Tory Parker
Producing & Casting Management . . . . Jordan Bean
Production Management . . . . Shannon Csorny
Properties . . . . Connor M. O'Leary
Scenic Painting . . . . Corey Umlauf
Sound . . . . Dwaine Jihaad Potts
Stage Management . . . . Kevin J. P. Hanley, Kelly Jonske,
Jess Kemp, Margaret Rial

USHER CAPTAINS

Dolly Adams, Shirley Adkins, Marie Allen, Terryl Allen, Katherine Austin, June Blair, Libba & Chuck Bonifer, Tanya Briley, Brenda Cease, Maleva Chamberlain, Donna Conlon, Terry Conway, Laurie Eiden, Doris Elder, Joyce French, Bee Gravatte, Carol Halbleib, LuAnn & Tom Hayes, Candace Jaworski, Holly Kissel, Barbara Nichols, Teresa Nusz, Dalen Payton, Judy Pearson, Beth Phipps, Nancy Rankin, Bob Rosedale, Tim Unruh

Actors Theatre's Company Doctor

Dr. Andrew Mickler, F.A.C.S.

About the Humana Festival of New American Plays

For more than four decades, Actors Theatre of Louisville has been home to the internationally acclaimed Humana Festival of New American Plays, which has introduced over 450 plays and launched hundreds of subsequent productions around the world. Every year, producers, critics, artists, and theatre lovers of all kinds gather in Louisville to encounter groundbreaking world premieres, all fully designed and produced in rotating repertory. It's an invigorating annual celebration of the art form, and its success has marked the Humana Festival as one of the nation's preeminent powerhouses for new play development. Plays first brought to life in Louisville include three Pulitzer Prize winners, as well as multiple Pulitzer finalists and winners of the Obie Award, Kesselring Prize, Steinberg/ATCA New Play Award, Yale Drama Series Prize, Susan Smith Blackburn Prize, and many other prestigious honors. More than 400 Humana Festival plays have been published in anthologies and individual acting editions, making Actors Theatre a vital force in building the American dramatic repertoire.

Beyond its far-reaching impact, the Humana Festival is also good fun. The sense of excitement is palpable when these brand-new plays meet their audiences for the first time. Actors Theatre's buildings buzz with creative energy as boldly imagined worlds come to life onstage, and theatregoers mingle with a fiercely talented company of artists and staff in the lobbies. Louisville is a vibrant cultural destination, known not only for its horse racing and bourbon, but also for its bustling arts scene and spirit of curiosity. The city thrives on innovation and embraces difference, so it's no wonder that the Humana Festival has taken root in Louisville, where an adventurous ethos guides both the audience and the curation of each season. Year after year, the festival champions the extraordinary breadth of American playwriting by seeking out and amplifying new voices and diverse viewpoints. Each spring's lineup offers a dynamic mix of styles, stories, and theatrical vocabularies—tales that whisk you to other worlds or move you to consider the one you know with fresh eyes.

The enduring influence of Actors Theatre's decades-long commitment to the full production of new work—and the philosophical shift it helped catalyze—is immeasurable. When the festival began in 1977, it gained widespread renown within a few short seasons, and found a generous, visionary sponsor in the Humana Foundation. In the years that followed, this venture would help change the ecology of American theatre, leading a movement among the nation's regional theatres to discover and support playwrights. The Humana

Festival's significance has continued to be concretely demonstrated in the work itself: year after year, extraordinary plays spark lively conversations both in Louisville and in their lives beyond our stages, making these exciting world premieres the crucial first chapters of much longer stories.

DO YOU FEEL ANGER?
by Mara Nelson-Greenberg

Copyright © 2018 by Mara Nelson-Greenberg. All rights reserved. CAUTION Professionals and amateurs are hereby warned that *Do You Feel Anger?* is subject to a royalty. It is fully protected under the copyright laws of the United States of America and of all countries covered by the International Copyright Union (including the Dominion of Canada and the rest of the British Commonwealth), the Berne Convention, the Pan-American Copyright Convention, and the Universal Copyright Convention, as well as all countries with which the United States has reciprocal copyright relations. All rights, including professional, amateur stage rights, motion picture, recitation, lecturing, public reading, radio broadcasting, television, video or sound recording, all other forms of mechanical or electronic reproduction, such as CD-ROM, CD-I, information storage and retrieval systems and photocopying, and the rights of translation into foreign languages, are strictly reserved. Particular emphasis is laid upon the matter of readings, permission for which must be secured from the Author's agent in writing.

Required royalties must be paid every time this play is performed before any audience, whether or not it is presented for profit and whether or not admission is charged.

All inquiries concerning rights, including amateur rights, should be addressed to: United Talent Agency, 888 Seventh Avenue, 9th Floor, New York, NY 10106. ATTN: Rachel Viola, Viola_R@unitedtalent.com.

ABOUT *DO YOU FEEL ANGER?*

> *This article first ran in the* Limelight Guide to the 42nd Humana Festival of New American Plays, *published by Actors Theatre of Louisville, and is based on conversations with the playwright before rehearsals for the Humana Festival production began.*

Sofia truly believes that everyone is capable of exercising deep, radical empathy towards one another, if they're just given the chance to learn how. But when she starts her new job as an empathy coach at a debt collection agency, her conviction is stretched to its limit. These employees are spectacularly clueless when it comes to compassionate listening. (In fact, they spend more time *swearing* at debtors than listening to them during collection calls.) And their tone-deaf phone demeanor is just the tip of the iceberg; things are much worse in the office. Eva, the sole woman on staff, is getting mugged in the kitchen with alarming frequency—and no one but Eva seems to care. Can Sofia really help her clients understand other people's emotions, if they can barely identify what an emotion *is*?

In her outrageous new comedy *Do You Feel Anger?*, Mara Nelson-Greenberg draws a portrait of an absurdly toxic workplace environment, where genuine concern for other humans is in short supply. According to the playwright, the impulse for this sharp satire sprang from the emotionally fraught 2016 presidential election, and the tenor of public discourse that followed it. "Everyone was saying, 'We just have to love one another right now,' and 'It's just about listening right now,'" she recalls. And though the author shared those sentiments, she recognized how easy it would be to neglect following through on good intentions. "I think it's easy to say, 'I'm a good listener; I'm empathetic,'" she muses. "But the real challenge lies in holding yourself accountable on the micro-level to practice the things you say you want to practice. I think we're really good at self-deception."

The play was also inspired by the empathy training classes Nelson-Greenberg's mother and sister took as part of their medical studies. Clinical empathy, once casually dismissed as "good bedside manner," is increasingly considered an essential skill. Workshops offering step-by-step techniques designed to improve compassionate listening are part of a growing trend—not only in hospitals, but also in corporations and business schools. Nelson-Greenberg's curiosity was piqued when she researched course outlines online and found a practical how-to approach. "Treating feelings like something you need to problem-solve, almost like a math problem, was really fascinating to me," says the playwright. The suggested exercises are simple but effective, she explains, giving an example: "Someone stands up and tells a story about something that happened to them, and then someone else has to identify the feelings that person must have experienced when they went through it."

Many of these exercises appear in *Do You Feel Anger?*—but Nelson-Greenberg has imagined them unfolding with hilariously awful results. Howie and Jordan, two employees at the debt collection agency, are astonishingly inept at identifying feelings; when pressed, they just make up words. Sofia's attempts to help Howie and Jordan expand their emotional vocabulary are met with seething anger (which happens to be one of the few feelings they can identify). Meanwhile, poor Eva is wound so tightly that she'll say just about anything to avoid upsetting her colleagues. As she immerses herself in the agency's workplace culture, Sofia discovers a fundamental challenge to her work: some people in this office have permission to feel anger; others don't.

"For me, anger is one of the scarier emotions to get fully in touch with," shares Nelson-Greenberg. "Anger is a really policed feeling. And that's interesting to me." The characters in *Do You Feel Anger?* all have very different relationships to the titular emotion: Eva, for example, seems terrified to even say the word, but Howie's volatile temper has been tacitly endorsed by the boss since day one. In Sofia's empathy exercises, Howie wields his rage like a weapon when he reaches the limits of his ability to express himself. With surprising sensitivity and nuance in an otherwise outlandish comedy, *Do You Feel Anger?* illuminates the complicated gender politics that discourage men from exploring a full range of emotional expression. "Anger can become a catch-all for other unarticulated feelings," reflects the author. "It can be used as a weapon, but it can also be a prison. I think a lot of people—and many men in particular—are prisoners of their own anger." And of course, anger demands immediate attention. It can suck up all the oxygen in the room, while other issues (such as Eva's legitimate concerns about her own safety) simply get ignored.

As Sofia leads these emotionally stunted coworkers towards some sort of enlightenment, her progress is painstakingly slow. And ironically, her own emotions are proving just as unwieldy. She's been wrestling with some complicated feelings ever since she learned about her father's betrayal of the family. But when Sofia's mother reaches out to her on the phone—again and again and again—Sofia prefers to silence the call. "I've been thinking about how these larger social issues play out on a personal level in many families as well," says Nelson-Greenberg.

In *Do You Feel Anger?*, the problem is that some people's feelings matter more than others'. The implications of that dynamic emerge as the play unfolds, revealing a kind of danger that's hilarious until it isn't. And that's precisely how Nelson-Greenberg wants it: "My goal is to keep the audience laughing until they realize it's too late."

—Jenni Page-White

BIOGRAPHY

Mara Nelson-Greenberg's work has been developed at Clubbed Thumb, Playwrights Horizons, Ensemble Studio Theatre, A Contemporary Theatre and Dixon Place, among others. Her play *Do You Feel Anger?* premiered at the 42nd Humana Festival of New American Plays and received its New York premiere at The Vineyard Theatre in Spring 2019. Her play *Hamlet by Mia Fefferman* was a finalist for the 2017 Relentless Award. She is a member of Youngblood at Ensemble Studio Theatre and an alumna of Clubbed Thumb's Early Career Writers' Group. She is currently pursuing her MFA at the University of California, San Diego, under Naomi Iizuka.

ACKNOWLEDGMENTS

Do You Feel Anger? premiered at the Humana Festival of New American Plays in March 2018. It was directed by Margot Bordelon with the following cast:

JORDAN	Bjorn DuPaty
JON	Dennis William Grimes
EVA	Megan Hill
OLD MAN	Jon Huffman
SOFIA'S MOTHER/JANIE	Lisa Tejero
SOFIA	Tiffany Villarin
HOWIE	Amir Wachterman

and the following production staff:

Scenic Designer	Arnulfo Maldonado
Costume Designer	Jessica Pabst
Lighting Designer	Isabella Byrd
Sound Designer	M. L. Dogg
Stage Manager	Katie Shade
Dramaturg	Jenni Page-White
Casting	Michael Cassara, CSA
Properties Master	Heather Lindert
Production Assistant	Michael Donnay
Directing Assistant	Allison Epperson
Assistant Dramaturg	Vivian Barnes

Special thanks to Sarah Lunnie, Michael Legg, RJ Tolan, Graeme Gillis, Maggie Burrows, and all of the great minds at WildWind Performance Lab and in Youngblood at Ensemble Studio Theatre for their help in developing this play.

CHARACTERS

SOFIA, late 20s
EVA, early 30s
JON, late 40s
HOWIE, early 30s
JORDAN, late 20s
SOFIA'S MOTHER, mid-50s
JANIE, any age (may be doubled with Sofia's Mother)
OLD MAN, 130

Prerecorded:
DONNA, 60s; MAN'S VOICE, any age

This play deals with power, violence, and complicity, so please be aware of the story you are telling based on the actors you cast in each role.

Everything in this world should move quickly, and the actors should play against the menace rather than leaning into it. For example, when Howie says he'd like to have sex with Sofia, it should sound more like he'd like to grab a coffee with her than being an aggressive come-on.

SETTING

Most of the stage is a conference room with glass walls. It is attached to a phone bank just offstage, and people cross behind the room every so often

In the conference room there is one chair that stays empty the whole time. A cardigan hangs over the back of the chair, and a cup of coffee sits on the table in front of it.

Toward the very end of the play, bathroom stalls appear onstage.

Megan Hill
in *Do You Feel Anger?*

42nd Humana Festival of New American Plays
Actors Theatre of Louisville, 2018
Photo by Bill Brymer

DO YOU FEEL ANGER?

SCENE ONE

SOFIA'S MOTHER *is leaving* SOFIA *a voice message.*

SOFIA'S MOTHER. Hi, dear. Just checking in. I know you're starting your new assignment today, and you must be very busy, but… I just wanted to say hi and wish you luck! Not that you *need* my luck… I realize that I'm talking to the person who once taught a broker without tear ducts how to cry out of his *mouth…*

(*Pause.*)

Anyways—I hope you're okay. I haven't heard from you since—well, since your father wrote you, so… I just wanted to see how you're doing.

(*Pause.*)

And let's see… what else. Oh! Sherry told me about this beautiful island called Compass Point with these gorgeous views, and sea creatures that talk to you and keep you company as you swim. And so… maybe we can go together after your job!

(*Pause.*)

I know you must be processing some… *complicated* feelings right now, so… I just wanted to let you know that… I'm here if you want to talk. I love you my little spider. Okay—bye bye.

(SOFIA *is in the conference room, setting up a tape recorder and some papers.* EVA *enters.*)

EVA. Hi! I'm Eva.

SOFIA. Hi, Eva. I'm Sofia.

EVA. You're here to try and help us scream less at people on the phone?

SOFIA. Yes. I'm an empathy coach.

EVA. To be honest, I don't think I need lessons on empathy. But everyone else in the office does, so.

(*She laughs.*)

You're going to love it here. I know you hear "debt collection agency," and you think everyone in this office must be really mean, but you're right. It's a very small, insular community here, and everyone *is so* outgoing and mean and it's just a really fantastic, really scary work environment. Someone keeps mugging me when I'm walking around the office!

(*She smiles.*)

I like your nails—are they from your hands?

SOFIA. Did you say someone keeps mugging you?

EVA. I don't think so! Did you say that?

SOFIA. *You* said that.

EVA. If you say so. Someone keeps mugging me, so it wouldn't be so crazy for me to say it out loud, but I'd certainly never dwell on it or claim that's what's happening, someone keeps mugging me.

(*Pause.*)

You seem lovely. Everyone here's going to hit on you.

SOFIA. Oh, well... thank you.

EVA. I'm trying to say that like it's a compliment, but really it's a warning. Everyone's going to hit on you, and you won't get anything done unless you shut it down. And even if you *do* shut it down, eventually they'll find a way around it and then they'll wear you down until you disappear.

SOFIA. Well, if people hit on me, I'll just tell them to stop.

EVA. What do you mean?

SOFIA. I'll say, "Please don't hit on me."

EVA. (*Laughing.*) No!

(*More frantic.*)

No, no—no. That doesn't seem like the best way to handle it. Maybe you should... are you dating anyone?

SOFIA. No, I'm not. Can I ask why that's relevant?

EVA. Okay, well...

(*Pause.*)

Maybe you want to *start* dating someone like, ASAP? I *just* broke up with my boyfriend—I was with him for ten years, even though I hated him the whole time. His name was—Marcus? Marco? Hold on—I could never pay attention to him when he was talking, so... I wrote it down. Okay... his name was...

(*Checking a piece of paper.*)

Jeffrey.

(*Pause.*)

Weird. Where did I get Marcus from?

(*Pause.*)

Anyways, Marcus—sorry, *blagh—Jeffrey* was a marine biologist, which sounds interesting, but it was *really* not...

(*Taking out a photo.*)

This is a photo from a trip we took upstate with a few friends... he's...

(*Looking at the photo.*)

Which one *is* he?
    (*Looking.*)
Oh—there he is. There, or there. One of those two guys was my Marcus. Shoot! My *Jeffrey*. It's so weird that I keep doing that. I don't even *know* any Marcuses, besides my dad.
SOFIA. Why did you guys break up?
EVA. Well—first, he started cheating on me—mostly getting hundreds of blowjobs from other women—and then eventually he ended up *murdering*. .
SOFIA. He ended up *murdering*?
EVA. Or, no—what's it called when you stab someone to death?
SOFIA. Murder.
EVA. Okay, so then yeah—he ended up murdering! And even then, I didn't really want to break up with him, because he was *so* helpful for the work dynamics, but I was like—he murdered more than one person, so... you know the saying.
SOFIA. I'm not sure I do.
EVA. No?
    (*As if it's a rhyme.*)
"If he murders one / It's all in good fun. / If he slaughters a whole crowd, and you realize you were sharing a bed with a stranger for ten years just to avoid a bad work environment..."
    (*She pauses.*)
Huh. *What* is the ending to that saying? "Just to avoid a bad work environment... something something something and serial killers' wives always finish last."
SOFIA. Well—good for you, that you got out of an unhealthy relationship.
EVA. Thanks, yeah, it's made my life so stressful, because now I'm scrambling to get a new boyfriend ASAP so that my work life can return to normal. Like—this date I went on last night?
    (*She shakes her head.*)
I mean, he wasn't terrible, but he said the phrase, "Egg is a man's best egg" a lot so, you know, just... not the perfect fit.
SOFIA. Can we go back to what you said before? About how someone's mugging you?
EVA. What? Oh no, that's okay, but thanks.
    (*She smiles.*)
Maybe we can just recap my advice instead: try to date someone like my dad Marcus—sorry, my *boyfriend*, Marcus—sorry, *my ex-boyfriend* Jeffrey, and then mention that person all the time, but do it really subtly, and then

never break up with him, even if he turns out to be a murderer, or—sorry—a "stabber to death."

    (*She laughs.*)

Because I wouldn't want you to end up in danger.

SOFIA. Danger how?

EVA. Like me—like how I'm in danger. And, I mean… I know that they keep saying Janie's just in the bathroom, but… it's been so many days!

    (*She laughs.* SOFIA *doesn't know why, but she laughs too.* JON *enters.*)

JON. Eva? Could I have a second with Sofia alone?

EVA. Of course!

    (*Playfully nodding to* JON *and* SOFIA.)

M'lady. M'sir.

    (*She giggles and then exits.*)

JON. So! All set for today?

SOFIA. Ah—yes! I was planning on checking out some of those calls, and then—can I just ask—Eva said something about being mugged in the office?

JON. Do you mean Janie?

SOFIA. I think—wasn't that Eva just now?

JON. Oh, Eva! Yes. She's spoken to me about that and I'm over it. Sorry—*all* over it. The safety of my employees is my *top* priority. Bottom line, over everything else, I really want to pretend that I'm a "good guy."

    (*He laughs, then pauses thoughtfully.*)

Isn't the situation with the homeless terrible? Just awful. They don't have much food but they have to eat to survive.

SOFIA. Right.

    (*She smiles.*)

And so did they explain how this works? Basically, I take your employees through the training, and once it's clear they understand the material, I sign the form they sent you, we pass it back up to head office, and we're done!

JON. Okay—so I imagine it won't take more than a day or two.

SOFIA. It usually takes closer to four or five weeks.

JON. Well, maybe in *other* offices. I know that you're used to intense clients—your office told me about the doctors you helped, who had forgotten that humans weren't objects—but I think you'll actually find that, so long as you quickly ingratiate yourself into the environment here, this is a fantastic place to work. For example—we have maternity leave now, where we let women leave when they're giving birth. To be honest, head office insisted on this, but I'm not even sure we *need* empathy lessons in the first place.

SOFIA. Except that—I see that you had another incident *just* last night. One of your employees was on the phone with someone and made up a new curse word and used it upwards of—forty-seven—

JON. (*Overlapping.*) Forty-seven times, yes. Although to be fair, it *was* an accurate description of what he wanted to do to her.

SOFIA. I think some empathy training could help you avoid a situation like that altogether. I'm going to turn this office into an empathy engine!

JON. (*Nodding, thinking.*) Okay...

    (*Pause.*)

And what *is* empathy, exactly? Is that... a type of... it's not a bird.

SOFIA. No, it's... empathy is the ability to understand other people's feelings.

JON. Like—hunger. And anger.

SOFIA. And sadness, or elation, or fear...

JON. And hunger, or anger—or horn.

SOFIA. Horn?

JON. When you want to have sex with someone.

SOFIA. Sure. The beauty about our feelings is that they're complicated, and they're hard to pin down, and each and every one of them is valid. And I'm excited to unpack it all with you.

    (*Off his look.*)

Look, Jon—I can see you're a little skeptical—

JON. Oh no! It's not that I have anything against *you* personally. I'm just protective over my employees! We've been together a long time, you know, and we're more than an office at this point—we're like a little family.

    (*He pauses and smiles.*)

Warts and all! Unresolved anger and all! Love and familial abuse and decades of bubbling resentment and ongoing power struggles and all!

SOFIA. Well—I'm not here to *mess* with your... family. I want to strengthen it.

JON. Yeah, sure. I've heard *that* before.

    (*Explaining.*)

I come from a pretty *dysfunctional* family myself.

SOFIA. I know *all about it.*

    (*He looks a little doubtful.*)

Really, Jon—I can relate.

    (*He shakes his head with shame.*)

JON. No, but I'm talking like—imagine... *a divorce.*

    (*Pause.*)

That's what it was—my parents got divorced. You could never understand.

SOFIA. (*She decides on something.*) You know what? Empathy in action!

(*Pause.*)

I do understand your feelings around a dysfunctional family, Jon, because—well, *just this week*, in fact, I found out my father has... a second family.

(*Pause.*)

Which he told me in an email.

JON. He told you... in an *email?*

SOFIA. To be fair, he's always been a little—you know—*thoughtless*, but—

JON. Can I see it?

SOFIA. No!

JON. Right. I'm sorry I asked. That was inappropriate.

(*Pause.*)

It's just that—I'm supposed to write my niece and explain why I'm not invited to Thanksgiving dinner anymore. But it's been kind of hard to...

(*He trails off as he pulls up an email and shows it to* SOFIA.)

SOFIA. (*Reading.*) "Dear Becca, Happy 9th birthday. I have something to tell you."

(*Pause.*)

"Justice Potter Stewart once said about hard-core pornography, 'I know it when I see it.'"

(*She continues reading to herself, then stops.*)

What's a Piss Chart?

JON. It's what I love. But see? I get stuck towards the end. And I want to get it right.

(*Pause.*)

Just because I don't only love Piss Charts, you know. I *also* love my niece.

(SOFIA *studies* JON.)

SOFIA. Well—fine, Jon. If you want to take a look at his email... it's not perfect, but it's self-reflective, so...

(SOFIA *shows* JON *an email and he begins to read it.*)

JON. "Dear Sofia, I'm sorry that you had to find out that I have a second family this way, in this letter, right now, sort of slipped in here as the direct object of this sentence. I'll be the first to admit that I messed up, but honestly, at some point your mother completely stopped meeting me halfway, and that was really hurtful. I only hope that *you'll* meet me halfway with all of this because, not to get too vulnerable on you, but that's what I want. And if you don't, I'll run off and get a second daughter! Just kidding, I already have one, but that doesn't mean that I don't love you with all my heart. Big hug, my little spider. I'm in pain. Love Daddy." Sofia—do you have a lot of rage? Towards your father?

SOFIA. No—*no!* I feel really sad for him.

JON. Even with this PS that he added here?

SOFIA. Oh—the—

JON. "PS—I also wandered away from your mother because she didn't like giving blowjobs without my ever reciprocating, and I love blowjobs without reciprocation. Oh, I'm sorry—there's no *way* I would have talked about how much I love blowjobs without reciprocation I love blowjobs without reciprocation I love blowjobs without reciprocation. What was I saying? I meant there's no way I would have talked about how much I love blowjobs without reciprocation—I *do* love blowjobs without reciprocation. I really love them a lot. Okay—see you later."

SOFIA. I think he just doesn't always know how to practice empathy, because no one ever *taught* him. Which I think is kind of heartbreaking! And it's funny, because—

JON. Oh—yes, it is! I love jokes! Well, it's good you're not angry, because this place really doesn't allow anger, except for in very specific circumstances. And also—

(*He smiles and studies her.*)

Hm.

SOFIA. What?

JON. Well—I want to say this delicately, so—

(*In a soft British accent.*)

You may excel more at your job if you wear a dress.

SOFIA. Did you just tell me to wear a dress?

JON. No. At least not in my normal voice!

SOFIA. I tend to be most comfortable in pants.

JON. Great then dress wear a dress.

SOFIA. Well, thanks for the tip. I appreciate this whole welcome.

JON. Don't mention it.

(*He studies her.*)

You know, you're not half bad. Although—that's also what they said about my cousin Ralph, until they found out what he does inside his shed, so…

(*Handing her some tapes.*)

But anyway, here are the tapes. Feel free to go over them, and then you can meet everyone later today!

(*He exits.*)

SCENE TWO

    SOFIA *is sitting in the conference room, waiting for the meeting to start.* JORDAN *and* HOWIE *enter together.*

HOWIE. You're in Janie's chair.

SOFIA. Oh—I'll move. There's mold growing in her coffee.

    (*She stands up.* JON *enters as* JORDAN *extends his hand to her.*)

JORDAN. I'm Jordan. It's a pleasure for you to meet me. *Au chawnj-jay.*

JON. Jordan—what did we learn about you recently, after you spoke with that client in Paris?

JORDAN. We learned I can't speak French.

    (*Pause.*)

We also learned that the way I was saying "medium rare steak," it actually meant, "big dog no friends." So yes, I'm Jordan. And *bu la du ma la plont*, but only on weeknights, okay?

    (*He laughs.*)

Au chawnj-jay.

HOWIE. I'm Howie. I have a terrible temper.

SOFIA. Hi, Howie.

    (*To* JON.)

I thought… didn't you say terrible tempers weren't allowed here?

JON. Well—like I said—only in particular circumstances, like if you're Howie.

    (EVA *enters.*)

SOFIA. Eva—do *you* have a terrible temper?

EVA. What? No! Why? Did someone say I did?

SOFIA. No.

EVA. Good—because I don't. Instead of anger, I choose to feel—what's the word for "nothing"?

SOFIA. Nothing.

EVA. Well, I feel whatever the word would be for "nothing," if it existed.

    (*She sits down in a chair.*)

Whew! I had an excellent first date last night. Or as my new boyfriend would say, an *egg*-celent first date.

JORDAN. What?

HOWIE. Who is he?

EVA. Well, his full name is actually Michaelangelo, but he just goes by Ra-*fal*-gore.

    (*Pause.*)

It was good, yeah. Sort of. Not perfect. He's mean and his hands are always sticky and he calls sugar "sweet pellets" and he has a floating kneecap that he talks about like it's a friend.

    (*Pause.*)

But at least I won't end up like Janie—single and getting punched in the face and in the bathroom for an eternity.
HOWIE. Well… you're not like *Janie*. Janie was crazy.
SOFIA. Janie was crazy?
EVA. Big time.
JORDAN. Yeah. I mean, I know that there's sort of a taboo against calling women crazy these days—and rightly so, because hargahla *mon*da bonder, but she was definitely a little… *batty*.
HOWIE. A *little batty?* We're talking about someone who once threatened to light the whole *office* on fire.
SOFIA. What? Why?
EVA. I have *no* idea. She just—snapped.
HOWIE. Yeah. One minute she was fine, and the next she was wielding this pack of matches like—how familiar are you with Dutch horror films?
JON. Janie was a little… challenging. Let's just leave it there.
HOWIE. Bitches be crazy!
JON. Howie.
JORDAN. I think you mean bitches be *batty*.
JON. Thank you, Jordan.
SOFIA. (*Turning to* EVA.) And—Eva? Before we begin? I was hoping—
EVA. Yes—I'm sorry.
SOFIA. What are you sorry about?
EVA. I didn't… wear…

    (*She looks down.*)

Shoes?
SOFIA. You didn't?

    (*Pointing to* EVA*'s feet.*)

Aren't those shoes, though?
EVA. Oh, sure. I meant I didn't… go to the… store?
SOFIA. You're not in trouble. I was just hoping to talk to you privately after the meeting.
EVA. Oh—sure.
HOWIE. Excuse me, "with all due respect" in quotes, why are you here? I could be making calls right now.

SOFIA. Well—my name is Sofia, and—

JON. Sofia? Pardon the interruption, but maybe you'd like to introduce yourself to the group?

SOFIA. Ah—yes. My name is Sofia, and I'm here to do some empathy exercises with all of you.

HOWIE. I don't mean to make you feel uncomfortable, but I'd love to have sex with you.

SOFIA. That actually does make me feel uncomfortable.

HOWIE. Well, I don't mean it to, so.

SOFIA. Well, it does.

HOWIE. *Okay...* now you've made *me* feel uncomfortable that you said I made you feel uncomfortable. I was just trying to tell you how I feel.

SOFIA. And I'm just trying to tell you how *I* feel.

JORDAN. If I can make this whole exchange more subtle for a second, I think what Howie *meant* is—the question "are you dating anyone."

SOFIA. Ah. No, I'm not—but please don't hit on me.

JORDAN. *What?*

HOWIE. *Excuse* me?

    (*The men fall silent.*)

EVA. Oh, you know what?

    (*Everyone turns to look at her.*)

I ate my sister in the uterus!

    (*Pause.*)

JON. Do you mean absorbed, Eva?

EVA. Oh—no, yeah, they use that word, "absorbed," for when one fetus absorbs the other, but no, I ate her. I ripped into her with my hands while my parents watched on the ultrasound machine, screaming, trying to stop me.

    (*Pause.*)

JON. Okay—well, great! I'll leave you to it, Sofia. And guys—be good, alright?

    (*He bows.*)

Aw chawnj-jay.

    (*He exits.* SOFIA *turns to the employees.*)

SOFIA. So—empathy.

    (*She writes "Empathy" on the board.*)

First off, what does "Empathy" *mean?*

    (HOWIE *raises his hand.*)

Howie.

HOWIE. When you're angry at someone.

SOFIA. I think you're describing anger. But I can...

(*She writes down "Anger."* JORDAN *raises his hand.*)

JORDAN. Empathy is a bird.

SOFIA. Empathy is the ability to *understand* someone else's feelings.

(*She writes this down. She continues to jot down notes on the board throughout the rest of the meeting.*)

HOWIE. Our job is to collect money from people. There's no time for feelings.

SOFIA. Actually, Howie! I understand why you'd think that, but what's so exciting about empathy is that it actually *increases* productivity! People are more cooperative when they feel like they're being heard.

(*Pause.*)

And I believe that one of the reasons for all of the lawsuits against this office is that people here are neglecting their *listening* skills.

EVA. Well—that and all of the threats of physical violence.

SOFIA. Yes. Thanks, Eva. So today I want to work on *compassionate listening*, which is a big part of empathy.

JORDAN. I don't have any problems with listening.

SOFIA. What did I just say, then?

JORDAN. You talked about how we're in this—room, you know, with walls, and there's a chair, and—well, people say I'm a poet, which, you know, whatever, I *have* been known to—

(*He breaks into poet voice.*)

"A *cow* a *man* a *boy* a *light!* A *song* a *rock* a *fish* a *star*—"

SOFIA. (*Overlapping.*) Jordan? Jordan?

JORDAN. Not right now?

SOFIA. How about this? I'm going to play a quick piece of a phone conversation from an employee here—and I won't identify who it is...

(*She presses play.*)

HOWIE (on recording). Hello, is this Donna Jacobs, from 16 Hampshire?

HOWIE. That's me!

WOMAN'S VOICE (on recording). Yes—this is Donna.

HOWIE (on recording). Donna, I am a debt collector with Cash Flow Accounts, CFA, and under federal law I must advise you that this is an attempt to collect a debt and any information given will be used for that purpose. We have a claim in our office from Wharton Industries in the amount of seven hundred and forty-four dollars and forty-eight cents. How are you today?

DONNA (on recording). Well, I'm not too good.
HOWIE (on recording). Um. Fine.
DONNA (on recording). My husband is very sick.
HOWIE. Oh, okay. I remember this one.
HOWIE (on recording). I said that's *fine*.
DONNA (on recording). And I take my debts really seriously, but he's in the hospital again, and... look, *please*—I spoke to someone at Wharton about this on *Monday*. Have you talked to them since Monday?
HOWIE (on recording). Well, shit. I wasn't asking for your whole life's story, bitch.

(SOFIA *pauses the recording.*)

HOWIE. You haven't gotten to the bad part yet.
SOFIA. Let's just talk about this part of the interaction for now. Does anyone see a problem right off the bat?
JORDAN. You're not wearing a dress.
HOWIE. Oh yeah.
SOFIA. I meant with the phone call.
EVA. He said, "Shit, I wasn't asking for your whole life's story, bitch."
SOFIA. Great. And why would that be a problem?

(EVA *looks at* HOWIE, *who glares at her. No one responds.*)

I want to try something. Inside your packets, you'll find a worksheet. I want everyone to think about what Donna Jacobs just told us, and fill out two or three things that she may be *feeling*. I'll do it too.

(*She writes, then waits.*)

Okay? Everyone finished? Jordan—what do you think Donna may be feeling right now?

(JORDAN *looks over at* EVA's *paper.*)

JORDAN. Scared and a shaved.
SOFIA. Scared and—a shaved?
JORDAN. Scared and—

(*Looking over at* EVA's *paper and trying to understand the second word.*)

Scared and... a-scorned? Or, what? No—*scarred* and *ashawned*.
SOFIA. Are you looking at Eva's paper?
JORDAN. No.
SOFIA. Eva, what did you write down?
EVA. I said, "scared and ashamed."
HOWIE. Ashamed isn't a word.

SOFIA. Yes it is.

JORDAN. Okay, so that's what I wrote down.

HOWIE. Same with me. Scared and *ashawmed*. Next!

SOFIA. So—let's stay on these adjectives for just a second.

(*She writes on the board: scared and ashamed.*)

Why might Donna be—let's start with scared.

(HOWIE *raises his hand.*)

HOWIE. Horn.

SOFIA. Horn. Oh—horny. You think this woman's horny?

HOWIE. What? No, *I'm* horny.

JORDAN. That's funny—I'm *also* horny, but I *just* had lunch.

SOFIA. So I don't want to talk about what *we're* feeling. I want to talk about what Donna Jacobs is feeling.

HOWIE. How are we supposed to do that? We don't know her.

SOFIA. Just based on what she said on the phone.

HOWIE. I don't understand why someone else's feelings should outweigh mine.

SOFIA. Well—they shouldn't *outweigh* yours, but they can be *in conversation* with yours.

HOWIE. But that's just giving me extra work.

(*He hits the table, annoyed.*)

I'm *so* hunger right now!

SOFIA. Well—Howie. Whether you realized it or not, you've actually just expressed a *feeling* to me, and I appreciate it. We're already on our way!

(*She looks at her sheet, and then writes on the board.*)

I wrote "worried," which is similar to "scared," and then…

(*She writes on the board.*)

Guilty. Now—I think this is interesting. Why might she feel *guilty?*

JORDAN. If she murdered

SOFIA. Specific to this situation.

HOWIE. Because she got into a lot of debt. But that's not *our* fault—she should have thought about that before she spent money that she didn't have.

SOFIA. So—thanks for bringing that up, Howie. I think that's really common. "She *should* have." I think we "should" others as a defense mechanism. We say what someone "should" have done to convince ourselves that we would *never* be in their position. But when we do that, we're also ignoring all of the specific things that complicate a person's life! Empathy asks you to *hold* your judgment, and accept…

(*As* SOFIA*'s talking,* HOWIE *has passed a paper to* JORDAN. *They're both laughing.*)

Accept... guys—what's funny?

HOWIE. It's about Eva.

(HOWIE *shows the joke to* EVA. *She looks, horrified. Pause. She scream-laughs.* SOFIA *approaches the men.*)

SOFIA. Can I see it, please?

(HOWIE *hands her the picture.*)

I don't understand what I'm looking at here. Who's this on the bottom?

EVA. That's Janie, right before she took out the pack of matches. And that's me next to her.

SOFIA. (*To the men.*) But why are Eva's legs bent up like that?

HOWIE. In order to make the joke *funny*—do you not understand jokes?

SOFIA. Got it.

(*Handing the picture back to* HOWIE.)

Okay—new rule! Jokes about Eva are not allowed here.

JORDAN. But—

SOFIA. End of story.

HOWIE. You're a bummer, you know that? Why am I even listening to you? I don't *know* you.

(*He stands up and begins to walk around.*)

SOFIA. Howie—please sit down.

HOWIE. (*Amused.*) Well, actually—*here*, in this office, I stand whenever I want.

JORDAN. And I say *this* poem whenever I want: "Life is an oblong."

SOFIA. Well, I'm running this meeting, so I would really appreciate it if we could all abide by *my* rules for now.

HOWIE. *Excuse me?*

EVA. You know what? I ate my other twin in the mitosis stage—

SOFIA. That's all right, Eva.

(*She turns to* HOWIE.)

I understand that my presence here may be disorienting. But I'm here to help, and I know what I'm doing. So I'm going to ask that you let me run these meetings the way I want to run them.

(*Pause.*)

Now that being said, Howie expressed that he was hungry, and I want to honor that, so—let's take a break.

HOWIE. (*Standing up.*) Yes. I think we *should* take a break.

JORDAN. I could eat. I'm super horn right now.

HOWIE. Same. Eva—

SOFIA. (*Gently to* EVA.) Eva—

JORDAN. Eva—

HOWIE. Eva—do you want to get lunch with me? In a sort of threatening way?

EVA. Oh—I'm eating with Rafalgore today.

(*Thinking.*)

Oh, darn. I bet he'll want eggs.

SOFIA. Actually, remember, Eva, I'd like for you to stay behind. And then— maybe *we* can eat together.

EVA. (*Relieved.*) Oh—great. Sofia and I are going to eat together.

HOWIE. Noice!

(HOWIE *exits.* JORDAN *begins to exit, but then hangs back for a second.*)

JORDAN. Hey, before I go, I just wanted to say that I'm really glad you're here, and I've totally got your back in private. Okay—see you later!

(*He exits.*)

EVA. Are we—do you actually eat lunch, or…?

SOFIA. Yes—I do! But first…

(*She guides* EVA *to a chair.*)

EVA. It's so cool that you're an empathy coach. How did you get into that job?

SOFIA. Oh, actually—my mom found out about it and really encouraged me to apply. Ever since I was little she made me feel like I had this special ability to communicate with—all different kinds of people.

EVA. That's great, that your mother knows you so well. Sometimes, by accident, *my* mother calls me Ear-va.

SOFIA. Well—I'd love to hear more about that. For now—I was listening to *your* calls too, as I was combing through the others. And…

(SOFIA *presses play on a recording.*)

EVA (on recording). Hello! I am a debt collector with Cash Flow Accounts, CFA, and under federal law I must advise you that this is an attempt to collect a debt and any information given will be used for that purpose. We have a claim in our office from Rye Tech, Inc., in the amount of forty-three dollars and sixty-eight cents.

EVA. Seems like that's all… by the book…

(SOFIA *fast-forwards a bit.*)

EVA (on recording). I feel like tigers only do that when they're provoked...

(SOFIA *fast-forwards more.*)

No, no, but I'm *stronger* on the flute...

(SOFIA *fast-forwards more.*)

[Hysterical laughter.]

(SOFIA *fast-forwards more.*)

Someone with a mask keeps coming up to me at work and mugging me, usually in the kitchen, and it makes me afraid to eat my lunch. And I'm usually too scared and ashamed to eat breakfast or dinner either.

MAN'S VOICE (on recording). I said that I'm *willing* to pay the money—

(SOFIA *stops the recording.*)

EVA. Okay, so—shorter conversations?

SOFIA. Well, yes. This call lasted for four hours and thirty-two minutes. But I'm more focused on...

(*She presses play again.*)

EVA (on recording). Sometimes, when it's happening, I try to shut my brain off. I pretend I'm someone who no one would ever want to mug—like sometimes I pretend I'm a mermaid...

MAN'S VOICE (on recording). Do you not *want* me to pay? Or is this some kind of a—

(SOFIA *stops the recording.*)

EVA. I know I broke the rule.

SOFIA. What rule?

EVA. (*Guessing.*) Don't... talk... about... mermaids?...

(*Pause.*)

During... times... when...

(*Pauses and sighs; she can't get it.*)

You go to the... *store*... and you....

SOFIA. You didn't break a rule. I want to help you with these muggings.

EVA. Oh! Thanks, but it's fine. I already sent everyone an email about it, a few months ago.

(*She pulls it up on her phone.*)

"Hi, all! So, so, *so* sorry to bother everyone and I know this is really silly, but I just wanted to drop a quick line to say that someone with a mask keeps mugging me in the kitchen and I would *love* it if they could stop." And then I put five pages of exclamation points so that no one would think I was mad at them.

SOFIA. But—with all due respect, the email didn't seem to work.

EVA. No, but Howie responded saying, "tooth" period, so I know he got it, which is great.
SOFIA. I want to help you.
EVA. Thanks, but—it's fine. I'm dating Rafalgore now, which will help. And we'll eat sweet pellets together and try to keep Mr. Knee Cap in place and that will be that.
SOFIA. Look. I know it feels *safer* to align yourself with Rafalgore. But if you start expressing yourself honestly, in this office—I promise you that I will have your back. Ditch Rafalgore, and stick with me!
EVA. I'll think about it.
SOFIA. That's all I ask! Now let's go to lunch.

SCENE THREE

> SOFIA *is setting up some papers in the conference room. She checks her voice messages.*

SOFIA'S MOTHER. Hi, my little spider. It's been a whole week. It's a little... *unusual* for me not to hear from you for this long. And I thought I'd try you, since—your father said that you called him yesterday, when you were on a lunch break? And... well, so, you must have heard from him that I kicked him out. And it's been good for me, because... more room in all the drawers!
> (*Pause.*)

He told me that—people at work are being a little difficult? Do you remember when you were ten, and you went up to our neighbor Timothy, who was such a *grump*, and within minutes you had him talking about his insecurities, and his family—
> (*She laughs, then pauses.*)

Just—those difficult people at work are lucky to have you.
> (*Pause.*)

And—okay, look. I *know* that your father told you about all of the lawyer stuff. And you don't need any of the gory details, but I just wanted to say that I really didn't *want* to bring in lawyers. Okay? I just—I felt I had to, and that's all you need to know.
> (*Trying to change the subject.*)

And I'm trying to get serious about that trip to Compass Point—but there are so many travel sites! Do you know which one you're supposed to use?
> (*Pause.*)

Anyways—call me back. I *love* you my little spider. Bye bye.
> (JON *enters and she closes her phone.*)

JON. Hey, Sofia!

SOFIA. Hi Jon! Ah—before I forget—there's no place to dispose of tampons in the women's room?

JON. Okay. And is that a riddle?

SOFIA. What do you mean?

JON. Is tampon a feeling? Or... the doctor's a woman or something?

SOFIA. No—tampons. For periods.

JON. Okay. And is *that* a riddle?

SOFIA. Is... ah... have you ever heard of periods before?

JON. You know what? Let me just call up this assistant from head office, and she can just—

(*He picks up the phone.*)

Missy? It's Jon. From the...

(*He looks to* SOFIA *and speaks more quietly.*)

From the night with all the hoses.

(*Pause.*)

Okay. Well...

(*Pause.*)

You know what, I'm going to politely abruptly interrupt you right now because I have a question for you. Would you mind looking up what periods are?

(*Pause.*)

That's great. Thanks so much.

(*He hangs up the phone.*)

I forgot I did that to her. But she's going to look into it!

(*He smiles.*)

In the meantime—how are things going?

SOFIA. Well—not great. Eva told me yesterday that she's still being mugged. She said someone keeps coming up to her and hitting her across the head?

JON. I know, yeah. I decided we should launch a formal investigation into the whole thing.

SOFIA. You did? That's—great.

JON. What about how *your* work's coming along? Are you ready to sign that form yet?

SOFIA. Am I...? No. It's only been a week.

JON. Right, but I already told head office that I'd get this taken care of in record time.

SOFIA. Well, you might want to let them know that things are actually moving kind of slowly. Yesterday instead of answering any of my questions, *both* Howie and Jordan just kept responding to me by saying they wanted to "set this burn on fire"...

JON. (*Laughing.*) Those guys, yeah. They're a pain in my neck, and Jordan's photography makes me really nauseous, but I love them to death.

(*Pause.*)

Has Howie said "Baby says No" yet?

SOFIA. Ah—no...

JON. Well, that's good. Because once that's happened, there's basically no getting through to him. It's three steps: he'll hit the wall, he'll go to sleep, and then... how familiar are you with Dutch horror films?

SOFIA. We just need a little more time.

JON. You have to be *strategic* about your approach. So do you want some strategy? From someone who knows this place pretty well, and has seen how you talk to my employees?

SOFIA. I'm not sure I need *strategy*...

JON. We're always using strategy with other people to *some* extent. Think about—well, say—your father. You use strategy with him, right?

SOFIA. I wouldn't call it *strategy*... I just—listen to him.

JON. Perfect, yeah. The only tip I have for you is simple: Lighten up! Families have customs, quirks—certain ways of doing things. Meanwhile, you're the new stepmom, just entering the home for the first time. And instead of... *ingratiating* yourself with the family, *you're* going—"New rules! Shoes *off* in the house. You're not allowed to hit on me." No one likes that kind of stepmom! I *hated* when *my* stepmom said those things to me.

(*Pause.*)

What *I'd* do, if I were you, is let these guys keep *some* of their customs. They'll be much more open to learning new ones that way. Like how I eventually let my stepmom teach me about forks. And I think you'll actually find that—

(*The phone rings.*)

Sorry—one second.

(*He picks up the phone.*)

Hello? Ah! Missy!

(*He listens.*)

Okay, wonderful. So—periods. What the heck are they?

(*Listens, still chipper.*)

Yeah...

    (*Listens, still chipper.*)

Okay...

    (*Listens, getting slightly more wary.*)

Okay... Missy—let me stop you. This... doesn't sound right. What's your source?

    (*Listens.*)

Personal experience. Well...

    (*Listens.*)

And WebMD. So... keep going, then...

    (*Listens—more worried.*)

Okay... keep going...

    (*Listens—more worried.*)

Ok*ay*, and then what?

    (*His face turns into panic.*)

And then—*what?*

    (*He listens.*)

Oh my God! No.

    (*He listens.*)

No, no, no! Please! No!

    (*He begins to cry.*)

Are you freaking *kidding* me right now. This is the worst day *ever.*

    (*Still sobbing.*)

I want to kill myself. I wish I were dead. I wish I were dead.

    (*He screams into the phone.*)

Just *tell me you made the whole thing up,* Missy!

    (*He listens, gets angry.*)

I don't *care* if you weren't lying, just—*tell me you were—*

    (*He listens.*)

Okay, fine, I'll give you back your chairs, and your dining room table, just... *say that you were lying!*

    (*He listens—gaining control of himself.*)

Yeah?

    (*He listens, starting to smile a little.*)

Really? Are you sure?

    (*He laughs a little.*)

Okay, yeah.

Okay. Okay.
> (*He's laughing and laughing now.*)

All right, Missy—I appreciate it. Thanks for looking into that for me.
> (*He hangs up the phone.*)

Okay, so now I know! Getting your period means extra pee.

SOFIA. …Extra… pee.

JON. (*He sees the others approaching.*) So—I'll leave you to it. And don't forget—customs, customs, customs! Because as I always say, in my classic, thoughtful way…
> (*He thinks long and hard.*)

"The wilderness? Oh boy, Mama. That's a big one."
> (*He bops her on the nose with his finger.*)

Boop!
> (*He exits as* EVA *enters.* SOFIA*'s phone rings. She silences it.*)

SOFIA. Hi, Eva.

EVA. Hey! Sorry! Am I interrupting?

SOFIA. Oh, no, it's just—my mom.

EVA. You can get it.

SOFIA. No, it's okay. She's just…
> (*She puts the phone away.*)

She's in a tough spot. But—
> (*Pause.*)

You know when you look at someone and you're just like, "Man. *Everything* you're doing, I'd do the opposite."
> (*She shakes her head.*)

Sorry. Overshare!

EVA. Don't worry! I used to overshare all the time because my ovaries were so big they had to manually enlarge my pelvic cavity, but I don't anymore.

SOFIA. Did you want to tell me something?

EVA. Oh, yes! I did what you said. I broke up with Rafalgore last night!

SOFIA. Great! How did it go?

EVA. It went well, at first, because he was asleep. Although when he woke up he started describing this awful thing that he likes to do with towels, but—anyways. It's a big weight off.

SOFIA. Well, that's great.
> (JORDAN *and* HOWIE *enter.*)

Hey guys.

(*They barely nod at her. They're busy looking at a drawing and laughing.*)

What's so funny?

HOWIE. It's nothing.

SOFIA. Okay, well—how's everyone doing today? Ready to learn about visual communication?

JORDAN. I want to set this—

SOFIA. Burn on fire, I know, Jordan. But maybe today you'll change your mind—because this exercise is usually pretty fun.

(*She smiles.*)

So I'm going to show everyone some pictures, and I want us all to name the feelings that are either visibly displayed, or *invisible but implied*, using this list of positive and negative feelings. Let's start off nice and easy.

(*She holds up a picture of two women laughing.*)

What do you think is happening here?

(JORDAN *and* HOWIE *begin laughing again.*)

Okay, guys, seriously—*what* is so funny?

EVA. It's about me.

SOFIA. But I already said—jokes about Eva—

HOWIE. It's not *just* about Eva, though.

JORDAN. It's also about you, Sofia, and other women, and a lot of other nouns.

HOWIE. And plus, it's a *joke*. Lighten up.

SOFIA. Can *I* see it?

(JORDAN *hands her the diagram.*)

Are those… our appendixes?

(*Handing the diagram back to the men.*)

No. I don't like this.

HOWIE. Wow.

JORDAN. Okay.

HOWIE. Eva? Do you *also* hate our funny joke?

EVA. I… ah… I'm going to go to the bathroom, really quickly.

(EVA *exits.*)

HOWIE. Do women sync up when they go to the bathroom?

SOFIA. Oh, well—

HOWIE. Jordan? Do women sync up when they go to the bathroom?

JORDAN. The thing they've realized, after doing lots of research, is that no one knows what syncing up actually *is*. Also, everyone's starting to say that the clitoris is a hoax.

HOWIE. I thought syncing up was when they all got a little extra pee at the same time. Or maybe it just means this…

(*He points to the diagram again and he and* JORDAN *start laughing.*)

Wait, no—we can't laugh about that, remember? Feelings only matter in this room when they come from people who have grossly mismanaged their finances.

SOFIA. Howie? Put the diagram away, please.

(*He puts the diagram away, frustrated.*)

Thanks.

HOWIE. Bad Mommy.

SOFIA. Okay. Let's keep going with this exercise, and Eva can jump in when she's back. So take a look at that list of feelings…

(*She starts handing out sheets.* HOWIE *is angry as he takes a sheet and she clocks it.*)

If you guys want to take a look…

HOWIE. (*Looking at the list.*) These aren't even real words. *Norvis?*

SOFIA. You mean—nervous?

HOWIE. No—I mean that I feel *angry* that I am being told what I can and cannot think is funny.

SOFIA. Howie—please. I'm not asking you to change your whole *worldview* here.

HOWIE. Baby says No.

(HOWIE *falls asleep.*)

JORDAN. Uh oh. Sound the alarm.

SOFIA. Wait!

(*Pause.*)

Wait for just—wait for *just* a second. Howie? Howie! I understand why you're *angry*, because I've just—swooped in here, and…

(*Pause.*)

You know what? I think I just didn't *understand* the joke.

(JORDAN *looks at her skeptically.*)

I'm serious. Can I see it again?

(HOWIE *wakes up to hand her the diagram.*)

Okay, so—I see the catfish, and there's Janie in the corner, with blood on her nose, and Eva is calling her crazy, and all of the other women are—

(*Realizing.*)

Oh. This is a Piss Chart.

(*She looks at it, disgusted.*)

I get it. That's really funny.

(*She scream-laughs.*)

HOWIE. You like the joke?

SOFIA. I like the joke.

HOWIE. (*Approaching her.*) That's very cool of you.

SOFIA. Also! I have a boyfriend. I have a boyfriend, Marcus.

JORDAN. Oh, no.

HOWIE. Oh *no*.

JORDAN. I *never* meant to disrespect Marcus.

HOWIE. Where does he work?

SOFIA. He works at… Jeffrey and…

(*She looks down at her shoes.*)

Shoes.

HOWIE. Oh—sure! I know him. Right? Jordan?

JORDAN. Of course! Marcus from Jeffrey and Shoes!

HOWIE. We were all on a team together, ages ago. Does he still eat lunch?

SOFIA. Yeah—he still eats lunch.

JORDAN. Is he still obsessed with ponds?

SOFIA. Is he still… yeah. He is.

JORDAN. (*Laughing like: Classic Marcus!*) *Yeah.* He's such a good guy.

SOFIA. Yeah, I'll tell him you say hi.

HOWIE. Great.

SOFIA. In the meantime… how would you feel about getting back into this exercise?

HOWIE. For Marcus's lover? Baby says *yes*. So…

(*He looks at the picture.*)

Well—when I look at this picture, I feel—that word you taught us before. Horn.

SOFIA. So I want to focus on what *these women* are feeling.

JORDAN. Maybe they're…

(*Looking at the picture.*)

When you don't feel safe.

SOFIA. Scared.

JORDAN. Right. These women are scared.

SOFIA. These women are—scared?

JORDAN. They have their danger-faces on.

HOWIE. Oh, duh! Which means one of them… has a gun? Or—a guy off to the *side* has a gun.

JORDAN. Is that what's invisible but implied?

HOWIE. Maybe there's a chainsaw event offstage?

SOFIA. But think about a scared person. Right?

(*She makes a scared face.*)

HOWIE. Oh, you look like my aunt, after I showed her how I brush my teeth.

SOFIA. How about—maybe you guys can think back to a time when *you* were laughing.

HOWIE. When we were—oh! Maybe these women just saw a Piss Chart.

JORDAN. So they're—happy?

(*Excited pause.*)

SOFIA. Yes, Jordan! These women are happy! Good—that's great! And so now—

(EVA *enters.*)

EVA. Guys? I have something to say.

(*She takes a deep breath.*)

I think that picture you showed us before… is *not* funny.

JORDAN. Wow.

HOWIE. *Okay.*

SOFIA. Eva—

EVA. I also wanted to say sorry, Sofia—I left you hanging, earlier, but I *agree with you*. I feel like—that picture's really mean.

HOWIE. Well—*I… feel…* like it's really *nice*, so.

(*Pause.*)

And she liked it too. Her was *just* laughing at it.

SOFIA. Oh, I—

EVA. You were laughing at the Piss Chart?

(*Pause.*)

When?

SOFIA. Well, when you were in the bathroom, I realized that—it *is* funny, actually.

EVA. Because I thought…

SOFIA. To some people, it's funny. And to others it's less funny.
> (*Pause.*)

And that's just—different feelings about this thing. And that's okay. Yeah?

EVA. (*Looking at* SOFIA, *not laughing.*) Oh. Okay.
> (*Pause.*)

SOFIA. How about… next picture!
> (*She holds up a picture of a woman crying.*)

So—what do you think is happening here?

HOWIE. (*Studying the picture.*) She's happy.

SOFIA. Is she, though? Really look at it, Howie. What expression is this woman making?

HOWIE. Ah… it looks like she's making…

EVA. Sorry, can we take a break?

SOFIA. Just—quickly, before that—
> (*Back to* HOWIE.)

You were saying—it looks like she's making…

EVA. I said *I want to take a break.*

SOFIA. Ah… okay. Let's just—let's take a break, but just—Howie. Remember what you were saying, okay? And then—we can regroup after lunch.

JORDAN. Great—I'm actually super horn right now.

HOWIE. Same with me! Sofia? Want to eat lunch with me? Or—no, duh. Marcus.

EVA. Marcus?

SOFIA. That's my boyfriend.

EVA. I didn't know you had a boyfriend, Sofia.
> (*Matter-of-fact.*)

Hot name.

HOWIE. Eva? Want to watch me eat somewhere?

EVA. I need to talk to Sofia for a second.

HOWIE. Okay. Tooth.
> (*Proud.*)

Or, watch this, Sofia—"I *feel* like a tooth." Eh?
> (*He exits.* EVA *looks at* SOFIA.)

SOFIA. Is everything okay?

EVA. It's fine, I just—
> (*Pause.*)

Why did you laugh at their joke?

SOFIA. Look, I wasn't laughing *at* the joke. I mean—sure, I laughed at the joke, but I didn't think the joke was *funny*. I just—I need things to start moving forward. Not just for the sake of my job—for *your* sake too.

EVA. You laughed at that horrible picture—for my sake?

SOFIA. Well—you saw what happened after I did that, right? They started participating! Jordan used the word "happy." We *finally* made *real progress* today! I'm telling you—in reality, I felt *nothing* about that joke.

EVA. Okay. Yes—okay, fine.

SOFIA. Also I asked Jon about the muggings again this morning, and he said he's on top of it. I promise you—I have your back.

EVA. Okay. Okay.

    (*Pause.*)

Do you ever wish that you knew yourself totally independent from everyone and everything that's ever touched you? Like, free of all context?

    (*Pause.*)

I had this picture of a mermaid in my room when I was little, and she always looked so happy. I mean, how cool is it to breathe underwater? And I used to think I was maybe kind of *like* her, in some way.

SOFIA. Sorry—one second. Howie emailed to say he's "meeting up with Marcus"—let me just…

EVA. (*Pause as* SOFIA *checks her phone.*) Anyways, one day this kid brought a Piss Chart into school and showed it to me during recess… and I went home feeling so sick to my stomach. And I looked up at the mermaid and I realized, like—duh—I could never be her! Because she *definitely* didn't know what a Piss Chart was, and I did. And I couldn't unlearn it.

SOFIA. (*She sends a response, looks up and focuses on* EVA.) Yes. A mermaid. Maybe one day you *will* be a mermaid.

    (*She smiles.*)

Now let's go get some lunch

SCENE FOUR

    SOFIA *is setting up a board and some papers in the conference room. She's wearing a dress. She checks her voice messages.*

SOFIA'S MOTHER. Hi, dear. I wanted to try you again. It's been three weeks now, and—well. Your father said he's spoken to you a few times. And he said people are still being a little tricky, at work. So I wanted to make sure you're okay.

(*Pause.*)

He also told me that he told *you* about, ah… just to be clear—I *don't* want you to pick sides! But I *did* want to remind you that there are always *two*. So just *trust* me that—yes, I did storm into his poker night and I screamed so loudly that I shattered all the mirrors in the house, but—I had my reasons. And so if you're not calling me back because—if you think that I'm—if you think I'm… what am I saying?

(*Trying to clear her head.*)

I'm just saying that it's still me over here. Your mother who loves you, and who worries about you. Your mother who cooks you Cheer-Me-Up burgers, who stole your bike back from Micky, and who once made a cardboard house with you that was so tall it hit the ceiling fan.

(*Pause. Affectionately.*)

So you call me back. Or I'll send a SWAT team after you. I love you, my little spider. Bye bye.

(SOFIA *looks at her phone.* JON *enters.*)

JON. You look nice today! I hear you went out to dinner with Jordan and Howie?

SOFIA. Yes! Jordan showed me how to order my big dog no friends in French. And yesterday, Howie identified *five* feelings for me. I mean, four of them were "hunger," but still.

JON. Yeah, I can see how much they've grown. It's all just—very…

(*He tries to find the right words.*)

Daddy says, "Good!"

(*He smiles.*)

So I guess you're ready to sign that paper?

SOFIA. Actually—not quite yet. Like, Jordan seems to *like* empathy now, which is great—but—

JON. But *what,* Sofia?

(*Exasperated.*)

Why are you always framing things in the negative? Think about where these guys *started*, and look at how far they've come!

SOFIA. But I think they may still think empathy's a bird. The other day at lunch they made a whole fuss over eating chicken…

JON. Who *cares? You* of all people should know that you can't blame someone for what they *feel*. If Jordan and Howie feel that empathy is a type of bird… if they feel it's a bird with sort-of…

(*He pictures a bird.*)

With strong, furry wings and big, detachable legs, then that's just not that big a deal. And if you're asking them to accommodate other people's feelings, I think it's only fair that you accommodate theirs as well. I guess here's what I'm getting at. I told head office this would be done by now, it *seems* done to me, and yet you keep finding ways to move the goalposts.

SOFIA. I'm not sure that's true.

JON. No? You think the two of us are getting somewhere? Or are *you* my cousin Rick, and *I'm* Auntie Eleanor, and we have these long and fruitful talks with one another but then at the end of the day, the *same* number of animals still end up inside the radiator with a note that says, "And once again, here be murdered babes"?

    (*Pause.*)

Some people are just... better at handling all different kinds of people. And if you're actually *as far* from finishing this job as you seem to think you are— then maybe you're just the wrong person to be handling these guys. You know? Maybe it would benefit *everyone* to bring someone else in instead.

SOFIA. But—no!

JON. It's not a *personal* thing! You're *objectively* really great, okay, but these guys are *tricky*, and it might just be better for them to—

SOFIA. Look. Let's set a goal of one more week. Okay?

    (JON *eyes* SOFIA.)

I promise that I can get them to where they need to be. And I think you're exactly right—I should be taking their feelings into account. You're usually right about these things.

JON. Thanks. Do you like my arms?

SOFIA. Yes, I do.

JON. Well... you're good company for *me*, so—one more week.

SOFIA. Thanks. And—sorry, Jon, but I spoke to Eva and she still seems really nervous about those muggings.

JON. I *also* noticed that she was norvis about it—

SOFIA. *Nervous* about it—

JON. Right, sorry—nor...

    (*He positions his mouth to get it right.*)

Nuer...veous about it...

SOFIA. So I'm wondering if you started that investigation yet?

JON. Yes! Of course I did. I said I would. Do you not trust me or something?

    (*Hanging his head.*)

Guess my good-guy persona has a longer way to go than I thought.

SOFIA. No—I *trust* you. I just—

JON. Great, so let's bring this thing home together! Okay? Because as I like to say…

(*He thinks.*)

A window is nothing but a square that they cut out and they put glass in it. Okay? That's for damn sure.

(*He burrows into her, gives her a quick hug and begins to exit. An* OLD MAN *enters.*)

Hey, buddy.

(*To* SOFIA.)

Is this Marcus?

SOFIA. What? No, it's…

JON. I'll give you two some privacy.

(SOFIA *looks at the* OLD MAN. *He stares back at her.*)

OLD MAN. I'm here to blow up this office.

SOFIA. You're here to—

OLD MAN. I don't mean to interrupt you, but I want to tell you a story first. Sit down!

(*He pauses.*)

When I was five years old, in kindergarten, our class would go out to the playground for recess. And I always dreaded the free period because, well, I had one friend, Joseph, who lived on my block, but he had a much easier time… *ingratiating* himself with the rest of the class, and so that meant I was usually alone during recess while everyone else played games.

(*Pause.*)

Anyways, one day I worked up the courage to just jump into the game and start running around! When all of a sudden a boy in my class, Sam, walked up to me, and told me that I couldn't play, because I was running in the wrong direction and I was messing up the game.

(*Pause.*)

So I turned to my friend Joseph, because I knew he would vouch for me. And Sam and the other kids turned to Joseph too. And Joseph looked up, and he locked eyes with me, then he turned away.

(*He shudders.*)

So I walked off the playground and I started to cry. And this teacher from the other class came over to me, and she asked me *why* I was crying. And I wanted to explain it to her, but the place that my tears were coming from—it felt so complex that I didn't even know where to *begin*. Was I crying because

I wasn't invited to play the game? Or because I had run the wrong direction? Or was it Sam, or Joseph, you know—all of my feelings were moving around so quickly inside of me that I couldn't get my finger onto any single one of them to keep it still and talk about it.

>   (*Pause.*)

So the teacher went over to Joseph to find out what happened. And as she walked away, I decided the most painless way to deal with all of these feelings was to push them outwards. I decided what I was feeling was anger, some complicated kind of *anger*, and I felt this incredible urge to express that anger onto everyone around me.

>   (*Pause.*)

Anyways, just as I was becoming increasingly trapped inside of my rage spiral, the teacher came back to me with all of the facts. And she knelt down to look at me, and she said, "So. You feel left out, huh?" When she said that—it pulled me right out of that hole and placed me down on earth, beside her. Because suddenly, what I was feeling was very precise. And so—it still hurt, but it was one single thing, and it had a name. I didn't feel some complicated kind of anger. I felt *left out*.

SOFIA. Do I… know you?

OLD MAN. I only realized the comfort in that clarity later, when I no longer had it. Because of course, soon after that, I learned that crying is actually shorthand for being really, really weak. And so I stopped crying. And the good news is—not crying made me really strong, according to a really specific set of standards. And Sam started inviting me to play during recess. The bad news is that by never crying, teachers stopped approaching me to find out what was wrong, and I never learned about any new feelings. So now the only feelings I know are: being left out, being angry, being hungry and… there's one more, I think…

>   (*He shakes it off.*)

Anyways, you've made me feel *left out*, I think, or pretty close to it—some complicated kind of being left out, so… I went and got these bombs… from my kitchen…

>   (*He takes some cans out of his walker.*)

And now I'm going to blow up your office! I'm going to—

>   (SOFIA *sharply inhales. He starts pressing the cans.*)

Where are the buttons on these things? Where are—

SOFIA. That's…

>   (*She looks.*)

Dog food.

OLD MAN. What?

(*The tension has left the room.*)

SOFIA. You're holding dog food.

OLD MAN. Oh. So I am, yes. Shoot—that was a little silly of me.

(*He shakes his head.*)

I *knew* I should have brought my lucky egg with me, to pull this off.

SOFIA. Your lucky... wait a second... are you—

(EVA *enters.*)

EVA. *Rafalgore!*

(*Going over to Rafalgore.*)

Rafalgore, what are you doing here? I'm sorry, Sofia, I—

(*Angrily whispering to Rafalgore.*)

I thought I was very clear the last time we spoke. I don't want to see you anymore.

OLD MAN. You're...

(*He turns to* SOFIA.)

Who are you?

SOFIA. I'm Sofia.

EVA. You're looking for me. *I'm* Eva.

OLD MAN. Oh, right. I have a story to tell you.

(*He takes a breath.*)

I was on the playground—

EVA. You're not supposed to be here.

OLD MAN. The bottom line is that I was going to come in here and shoot up your office, but the gun was too heavy for me. So I brought these small bombs instead.

(*He pushes the cans again.*)

Where the *heck* are the buttons—

SOFIA. It's dog food.

EVA. Rafalgore. Those aren't bombs.

OLD MAN. No? Oh—darn! I'm feeling a really complicated kind of hunger right now!

(*He slaps his knee angrily, then looks down at his knee.*)

Uh oh, little Mr. Knee Cap—where the heck did you go, my best friend?

EVA. You have to leave.

OLD MAN. I used to take baseball bats and beat people's faces into the sidewalk for fun.

EVA. You already told me that

OLD MAN. I once chugged gasoline to look tough and now the inside of my body looks like a bunch of Legos.

EVA. I *know*, and I'm serious, you've got to—

OLD MAN. Fine. I'll go.

(*She begins to escort him out of the office.*)

If I were forty years younger, I'd find a way to really hurt you. But I'm not ninety anymore.

(EVA *and* OLD MAN *exit*. HOWIE *and* JORDAN *enter.*)

HOWIE. Hey, Sofia. What's wrong?

SOFIA. How can you tell something's wrong?

HOWIE. Because you look—the face you taught us before.

(*He makes a scared face.*)

JORDAN. Yeah, you look scared right now.

SOFIA. I—*am* scared. Yes! Because someone just tried to blow up the office. And I'm so glad that you—

HOWIE. *What?* Who?

SOFIA. No—it's fine now. It was just Eva's ex-boyfriend.

HOWIE. Ugh.

JORDAN. Of course.

SOFIA. No, no—it's okay. Let's go back to—

JORDAN. (*He looks at her and thinks.*) You must feel *scared* right now.

SOFIA. I... right. You just said that. And I'm glad you can see it, because—

HOWIE. I'm sorry in quotes to interrupt you, but if you just said "Eva's *ex*-boyfriend"... does that mean Eva's single?

SOFIA. Ah... well, I'm not sure, Howie—

HOWIE. Because I would—watch this, Sofia—

(*He chooses his words carefully.*)

I would *be curious* to see how she would *feel* about giving me a blowjob without reciprocation.

JORDAN. Oh, yeah. I feel that I *love* blowjobs without reciprocation.

HOWIE. I *also* feel that I love blowjobs without reciprocation!

JORDAN. I also feel that *I* love—

(EVA *reenters, shaking her head.*)

EVA. Jeez. Rafalgore and his eggs! Sorry about that, Sofia.

HOWIE. I hear you're newly single?

JORDAN. More subtly, actually, we were wondering if you had a boyfriend...

SOFIA. Guys?

HOWIE. Sofia, if you don't mind…

(*There's incoherent screaming from offstage.*)

SOFIA. What's going on?

(*Everyone goes to the window to look down below at the parking lot.*)

EVA. Oh.

(*Explaining.*)

Right as we were breaking up, Rafalgore realized that if he removes his leg from his hip, he can swing it around like a baseball bat.

HOWIE. I'm going out there.

JORDAN. I'm going too.

HOWIE. (*Valiantly, to* EVA *and* SOFIA.) We're going to protect you.

JORDAN. I'm a poet.

EVA. I don't think you have to—

(HOWIE *runs offstage.* JORDAN *follows him.* SOFIA *and* EVA *watch from inside.*)

Yeah, see—he's already asleep. Aw. Although when he wakes up he's going to say some shocking stuff.

SOFIA. (*Turning to* EVA.) Eva—while we have a second together…

EVA. Yes. I know. I scream-cried on the phone for an hour and a half the other day. I didn't realize who I was talking to. *I* definitely wasn't answering phones when *I* was a little baby…

SOFIA. No, no. It's just—you were right before… it might be a good idea for you to pretend that you're dating someone.

EVA. Oh. Why?

SOFIA. Because—well, you know these guys. They're so easily distracted. But I think they're *right* on the brink of really understanding empathy!

EVA. So you want me to… pretend I have a boyfriend. But isn't that going back on what you said before? Because—you told me to break up with Rafalgore, remember—

SOFIA. I know, yeah, but—I actually don't *mind* being with Marcus, you know, we get lunch together, and go to different ponds—and so… I think we can acknowledge *their* feelings, or, more specifically, their *horn*, and look at how *strong* their horn is, and say, "Okay. They need to work on that. But in the meantime, since it's not that big a deal to shift my behavior around just a *tiny* bit, maybe I should…"

EVA. Maybe I *should*…

(SOFIA *sees the men reentering the office.*)

SOFIA. Look. We're up against a little bit of a clock, okay? So I think it's worth… being a little strategic here.

(JORDAN *and* HOWIE *enter the conference room.*)

JORDAN. Wow.

HOWIE. He *really* knows how to put together an upsetting sentence.

JORDAN. It never even *occurred* to me that you could use a towel that way.

HOWIE. Eva—

SOFIA. Thank you for protecting me, m'sir and m'sir. Let's jump right into today's exercise.

(*Going over to the board.*)

We're going to continue working on compassionate communication today.

(*She smiles.*)

So someone will describe a situation that elicits feelings in them. And then I want all of us to form sentences that follow this formula:

(*Pointing to the formula on the board.*)

"You feel blank because blank, is that right?" And then Person One will say, "Yes, that's right, I feel blank because blank," or, "No, that's not right, I do not feel blank because blank." Sound good? Who wants to start?

(*Pause. She looks around.*)

EVA. I can…

(HOWIE*'s hand shoots up.*)

HOWIE. Sofia? I can start.

SOFIA. Great. Go ahead.

HOWIE. So this morning, I stood in front of my mother's gravesite for like a half an hour, and I thought about how she was murdered—or, I guess not *murdered*, but, stabbed in the body until she died.

SOFIA. Okay. Thanks for sharing that with us. Who wants to respond to Howie?

EVA. (*Looking at the board.*) You feel *sad* because your mother was murdered, is that right?

SOFIA. Great! So, if that resonates—

HOWIE. (*Steamrolling her.*) No, that's not right, I do *not* feel sad because my mother was murdered.

SOFIA. Okay. Are you sure?

HOWIE. Yeah.

SOFIA. But—Howie. Have you ever been able to *really explore* how you *actually feel* about your mother's murder? Like—were you ever given permission to cry about it?

HOWIE. To *what* about it?

SOFIA. Cry.

(HOWIE *looks around.*)

HOWIE. Ah—I'm trying to understand what you're saying…

JORDAN. (*Gently and softly, to* HOWIE.) Howie, crying is when the top of a hose is connected to another hose, and so you can't figure out where the top one starts.

SOFIA. When—no. What I'm saying is—maybe you were taught that crying is a weakness. But it's not. It's a strength. And I want to give you permission to access your feelings.

HOWIE. Thank you, Sofia—but I really don't feel sad about my mother's murder. She died when I was *ten,* and the most I feel about it is…

EVA. Maybe you feel *powerless* because your mother was murdered.

HOWIE. *No,* I don't! I don't feel sad, and I don't feel powerless!

(*He throws a chair.*)

SOFIA. Now hold on a second—

JORDAN. Let me just—Howie!

(*Turning to* HOWIE.)

Maybe you feel… *nothing* about your mother's murder?

HOWIE. Maybe I feel… maybe I feel…

JORDAN. Maybe you feel *nothing.* Or, said differently—"You feel *nothing* because your mother was murdered. Is that right?"

HOWIE. I feel… oh my God. Of course.

(*He thinks, then gasps.*)

So many years replaying my mother's murder, and how I held her in my arms as she gasped for air and told me that she never really loved me, and I never understood how I felt about it. And now I know.

(*He takes a breath.*)

Yes. That's right. I feel *nothing* because my mother was murdered.

(*He is breathless.*)

Oh, wow. I feel *so seen.* Thank you, Sofia.

SOFIA. You're… welcome.

(*Pause.*)

JORDAN. I'd like to go.

SOFIA. Okay—great. Go ahead.

JORDAN. Well, so—yesterday, I asked a girl—I mean a woman—I mean an old woman—out on a date. I was sort of—ah—the word we learned the other day—vulner-ah-blay. And I guess—well, she said *no* to me, which is obviously her right, because keepee beepeep, but, yeah—she said no… and then all of these people around her—started laughing at me. And they were just laughing and laughing, as this enormous group and—so—yeah.

SOFIA. Wow. Okay—thanks. So who wants to go first?

HOWIE. I can.

(*Looking at the board.*)

Jordan.

(*Considering the sentence structure on the board*)

You feel like—like, you were putting yourself out there, right, and she laughed at you for it, and so you were like—like—you, like—like like like—

SOFIA. Embarrassed?

HOWIE. Right—you feel *embarrassed* because you put yourself out there and you were laughed at for it is that right?

JORDAN. Oh, I don't…

SOFIA. So—really think about that. Say it again.

HOWIE. You feel *embarrassed* because you *put yourself out there* and *you were laughed at for it*, is that right?

SOFIA. Jordan?

JORDAN. Well, I guess just a little.

SOFIA. Say it back as—

JORDAN. Yes, that's right—I feel embarrassed because I put myself out there and I was laughed at for it.

SOFIA. *Good.* Good job, guys

(*She turns to* EVA.)

Eva?

EVA. You feel ashamed because you were made to feel small, is that right?

JORDAN. Yes, that's right. I feel ashamed because I was made to feel small.

SOFIA. Great, Eva—*great*, Jordan.

HOWIE. You feel—

(*To* SOFIA.)

When you don't feel big?

SOFIA. Small.

HOWIE. You feel *small* because you were dismissed.

JORDAN. Yes. I feel small…

(*He begins to tear up.*)

Yes, I feel small because—I was dismissed.

(*Processing this.*)

I feel *small* because...

> (JORDAN *bursts into tears; he continues to cry throughout this next exchange.*)

Oh God! Yes, yes—that's right! She made me feel small! Oh no—now I'm hose on top of a hose so you can't see where the top one starts!

SOFIA. It's okay. That's *good*.

JORDAN. I was just using my normal line of saying, "Do you want to see a show-y?"

SOFIA. "Do you want to—" What's a show-y?

JORDAN. A show-y!

HOWIE. It's what you leave sort of open!

JORDAN. And she told me to stop talking to her... when I just wanted to do a little show-y...

SOFIA. So you can also *do* a show-y...

JORDAN. And the security guards started asking if I even had a *ticket* to this stupid charity dinner... and they began forcing me off the stage...

SOFIA. Off the—stage...

JORDAN. I bet she didn't even deserve that award! I don't even know what an oncologist *is!*

HOWIE. No one does!

JORDAN. (*Scream-crying.*) She was just so freaking hot—

HOWIE. I *understand*, Jordan—

JORDAN. (*Overlapping.*) And I just wanted to do a big show-y—

HOWIE and JORDAN. All over her tits!

HOWIE. Of course you did!

JORDAN. (*Overlapping.*) I'm a poet!

HOWIE. You're a poet!

JORDAN. Life is an oblong! *Nice guys always finish last!*

HOWIE. (*Like a monster.*) *We always finish last!*

> (JORDAN *lets out a scream-sob.*)

Do you see, Sofia? We're doing it! We're really doing it.

> (*A bird flies across the stage.*)

Oh wow—look!

> (*In awe.*)

Empathy.

> (*The men stare at the bird.* SOFIA *watches them warily.*)

JORDAN. (*Wiping his tears away.*) Wow.

(*Laughing.*)
We solved it. We solved empathy.
HOWIE and JORDAN. We. Solved. Empathy!
(*Pause.*)
EVA. I want to go.
SOFIA. Okay, great.
JORDAN. I'm shaking.
SOFIA. Okay, go ahead Eva.
EVA. The first time I got mugged in this office was two years ago.
SOFIA. Ah—hm. Eva? Let's just—
EVA. After it happened… The world was so normal when it was over. It was so exactly the same that the mugging started to feel like like this strange blip, to the point where I actually started wondering whether I had made the whole thing up, or drastically mis-remembered it or something. I thought, "Huh. That *felt* like such a big thing to *me*, but clearly it was *not* actually a big thing." Then it started happening more and more. This morning, I was mugged on my way into the kitchen to get some coffee. The person came up behind me and hit me across the side of my head… and I couldn't really feel it, but I touched my ear, and I noticed I was bleeding.

(*Pause.*)

Anyways, suddenly I was on the floor of the kitchen in a ball, and I wasn't being mugged anymore. So I went back to my desk without getting my coffee—and the world was still… the same.

(*Long pause. Everyone looks at her.*)

Is someone going to respond?
SOFIA. Yes. We're *all* going to respond, right guys? Can we respond to Eva, using the sentence structure?
JORDAN. Eva. You feel *tired* because *you didn't get your coffee*, is that right?
EVA. Yes, I guess so. But that's not really—
SOFIA. And so—we'll keep finding—but in the meantime, say the full sentence back to him: "Yes, that's right—I feel tired because…"
EVA. Yes, that's right—I feel tired because I didn't get my coffee.
JORDAN. You feel mugged because you got mugged.
SOFIA. Okay, Let's—Anyone else? Howie?
HOWIE. (*Looking at the list.*) You feel *content* because you got mugged… you feel *improbablay* because you got mugged… you feel *thrilled, inquisitive* and *hopeful* because you got mugged.
EVA. No. I *don't*. That is *so wrong*.

HOWIE. Whoa. Sorry.

SOFIA. Now—hold on, guys. Howie—Eva is sharing something sensitive with you—and Eva, Howie was patient with you when you assumed he felt sad about his mother's murder. It's really important that we stay *respectful* of one another.

>   (*Gently, to* HOWIE *and* JORDAN.)

Maybe you guys want to try some words from the bottom of the list?

JORDAN. Where?

>   (*Looking at the page down.*)

You feel distressed because you got mugged?

EVA. Yes! Yes, that's right, I feel distressed because I got mugged.

SOFIA. Good, Eva! Good, Jordan!

HOWIE. Where did you find that word? What does that mean?

JORDAN. Down under the "difficult slash unpleasant feelings" part.

>   (HOWIE *looks down.*)

HOWIE. These are all real words?

>   (*Reading from the list.*)

You feel *lost* because you got mugged, is that right?

EVA. Yes, that's right—I feel lost because I got mugged.

HOWIE. You feel in despair and disappointed because you got mugged, is that right? You feel alarmed, anxious, panic, doubtful—

JORDAN. You feel wary, afflicted, heartbroken and wronged because you got mugged, is that right?

EVA. Yes! That's right.

JORDAN. You feel *weak* because you got mugged.

EVA. I guess—that's also right, in a way...

HOWIE. You feel *inferior* because you got mugged.

SOFIA. As a question.

>   (HOWIE *speaks the next sentence fully like it's a command, but makes a question mark, up-sound after it.*)

HOWIE. You feel *inferior* because *you got mugged.* Eh?

EVA. I mean—I guess I...

SOFIA. Using the formula?

EVA. I don't—I'm having some trouble...

JORDAN. I can say it too, if that helps.

>   (JORDAN *moves closer to* EVA.)

You must feel very inferior because you got mugged. Very inferior, and very humiliated. Is that right?

EVA. (*Emotional.*) Yes. That's right.

HOWIE. This must be so difficult slash unpleasant.

EVA. It is. It really, really is.

(*She starts to cry.* HOWIE *moves closer to her.*)

HOWIE. Well, I'm glad that we're connecting, even though needless to say I wish it were under better circumstances…

(*He moves in for a kiss.*)

EVA. (*Snapping out of it.*) Wait—no.

SOFIA. Okay—hold on…

JORDAN. If I can make this exchange more subtle…

(HOWIE *and* JORDAN *move closer to* EVA. *She screams.*)

EVA. I don't want to kiss you. I don't want to kiss either of you.

SOFIA. Because aren't you dating someone, Eva? Aren't you dating… Marcus?

EVA. No, I'm *not*. I don't want to kiss either of you because you guys make me feel unsafe.

HOWIE. *What?*

JORDAN. Wow.

EVA. Sofia?

SOFIA. Well…

(*Pause as* SOFIA *looks at the men, and then turns to* EVA.)

I'm sure they don't *mean* to make you feel unsafe.

EVA. (*Frantically and angrily.*) Well, they *do*, Sofia—what do you *mean* they don't mean to? I'm telling you that they *do!*

SOFIA. Hey! I'm trying to *juggle* a lot of people right now, and empathize with everyone…

EVA. You're not *empathizing* with me!

SOFIA. I *am* empathizing with you! I *understand*, okay, you feel *unsafe*, and *norvis*, and it makes me sick to my *stomach*. But—

EVA. Nervous.

SOFIA. What did I say?

EVA. You said "norvis."

SOFIA. Okay, but—

EVA. I want to be left alone.

SOFIA. Fine. Why don't we just—take a breather. Eva, let's get some lunch—

EVA. (*A little unhinged.*) I said I want to be left alone! I want to be left alone! *I want to be left alone!*

(EVA *exits. Pause.*)

HOWIE. Geez.

JORDAN. Yeah.

HOWIE. So much for professionalism.

SCENE FIVE

SOFIA'S MOTHER. Hi, my little spider.

(*Pause.*)

I still haven't heard from you. And I don't know. I thought maybe you were just—not doing well or something, I was *worried* you weren't doing well, but—I hear you're doing well. I hear from *your father* that you're doing well. And I'm glad to hear it. I just… I'm not doing well.

(*Pause.*)

And I don't know. Your father's taken so much of my world from me. And now I'm standing here like—are you gone too?

(*Pause.*)

Whatever's happening, I feel like I'm bothering you. So I'm going to leave you alone. I love you. Okay—bye.

(SOFIA *is in the conference room, setting up.* JON, HOWIE *and* JORDAN *enter together, happily.*)

JON. Congratulations! The guys told me over lunch that they solved empathy.

SOFIA. That they…

JON. And so I thought we could celebrate as soon as you sign that paper!

SOFIA. Actually—we're not done quite yet. We have more exercises to go through.

HOWIE. Is this a joke?

SOFIA. It's *great* that you guys have gotten in touch with empathy. And now we have to apply that empathy to your work calls.

HOWIE. But—

JON. *Sofia.*

SOFIA. (*To* JON.) If you'd like to watch for a second, maybe you'll see what I mean.

(*Checking her watch.*)

Where's Eva?

JORDAN. She's in the bathroom.

SOFIA. Fine, then—let's just start. The phone call we listened to week one, with Donna. Here's a recap of her situation, on these sheets…

(SOFIA *begins to hand out sheets of paper to everyone.*)

So Donna's husband was sick, right, he was back in the hospital, and Donna owed money that she didn't have. So using the sentence structure, tell me how Donna must be feeling. Howie.

HOWIE. I don't know Donna. She's not even here.

SOFIA. Pretend I'm Donna.

HOWIE. "You feel like an idiot, Donna, because you spent money that you didn't have, is that right?"

SOFIA. Howie… try again please, without the judgment.

HOWIE. Okay. Without the judgment, I could say…

(*Looking directly at* SOFIA.)

Pay the money.

SOFIA. Using the sentence structure.

HOWIE. You feel scared because if you don't pay the money, I'm going to hurt you, is that right?

(SOFIA *inhales sharply and looks directly at him.*)

SOFIA. No, that's not right. Try again. And this time—

(HOWIE *stands up.*)

What are you doing?

HOWIE. I'm looking for my baseball bat.

SOFIA. What do you need your baseball bat for? You're talking to someone on the phone.

HOWIE. No, I'm not—you're right in front of me.

JORDAN. Sofia, you're being really hard on us. I noticed that you weren't sad for me *at all* about the traumatic situation I went through with the pediatric oncologist who was getting a Lifetime Achievement Award for creating a new technology to save terminally ill children.

SOFIA. *Excuse* me?

HOWIE. Where the *hell's* my bat?

SOFIA. Let's remember compassionate communication, Howie…

JORDAN. You feel like your bat is behind the bookshelf because Jon put it behind the bookshelf, is that right?

(HOWIE *grabs his bat. He holds it up, angrily.*)

JON. Oh darn. Howie! I'm with you, all right? Just put the bat down. I'm with you.

(HOWIE *puts the bat down.* SOFIA *turns to* JON.)

SOFIA. Thanks, Jon.
>   (*Smoothing out her dress.*)

Let's take a break.

JON. (*Disapprovingly.*) Take a *break?* Sofia…

SOFIA. "*Sofia*" what?

JON. I can't believe I didn't see it before. No *wonder* you haven't had success here! You're *provoking* my employees.

SOFIA. How am I *provoking* them?

JON. By telling them that other people's feelings should outweigh theirs! You're asking them to change their entire *worldview!*
>   (*Pause.*)

I have used so many different strategies with you. I've spoken your language, I've been the Auntie Eleanor to your Rick. But at some point, you know, I have to be the boss. I have to take care of my family.
>   (*He begins to sign the paper himself.*)

SOFIA. You can't just… sign it.

JON. I *did* just sign it. So I think we're done here.

SOFIA. Fine.
>   (*She starts to leave.*)

HOWIE. Hey—I heard you got fired. Want to talk about it over a drink?

JORDAN. Want to talk about it on top of a pond?

SOFIA. No, because—Marcus!

HOWIE. Marcus, right. Marcus is cheating on you.

JORDAN. We saw him in a grocery store last night, getting a blowjob without reciprocation from hundreds of women.

SOFIA. No you didn't.

HOWIE. And there was a catfish watching, just off to the side—

SOFIA. You didn't see that.
>   (*Turning to* JON.)

Jon?
>   (*Pause.*)

JON. (*Turning to* HOWIE *and* JORDAN.) Yeah—guys…
>   (*Pause. He sighs.*)

The Marcus thing. I saw it too. It's terrible, really—some men can be such pigs. Awful, awful.
>   (*He brightens.*)

So! How do you feel about blowjobs without reciprocation?

(*The men start to close in on her.*)

JORDAN. How do you feel about my poetry?

HOWIE. For me personally, I *love* blowjobs without reciprocation.

(*They all laugh.* SOFIA *tries to join in half-heartedly.*)

Why are *you* laughing?

SOFIA. Because it's a joke.

HOWIE. I don't think you get it.

SOFIA. Well all the same, maybe we can just—

(*Pause.*)

You wouldn't want to make me feel—remember scared?

JORDAN. Lighten up!

HOWIE. I love blowjobs without reciprocation.

JORDAN. I love them too.

JON. I do too. I think *they're* what I love the best.

SOFIA. Get *away from me.*

(*She picks up* HOWIE*'s baseball bat.*)

JORDAN. Calm down.

HOWIE. You're acting crazy.

JON. C'mon, Sofia—meet us halfway.

SOFIA. Meet you halfway?

(*Pause as she computes this.*)

I am meeting you *all the way!* You haven't moved *an inch.*

(*Getting increasingly angry.*)

I listen to you, I cater to you, I call you on the phone..

JON. Call us on the phone?

SOFIA. Well—not *you,* but—

(*She screams and smashes the bat onto the table.*)

SCENE SIX

Bathroom stalls appear onstage. Someone is in one stall with the door closed, and JANIE *sits in the other stall on the toilet with the door open, going through her purse. She's wearing her cardigan and holding her mug from the office.*

SOFIA *bursts into the room.*

JANIE. Hi.

(*Looking at her.*)

You must feel scared right now.

SOFIA. I do. I do feel scared.

JANIE. Do you want to sit down?

>   (SOFIA *sits.* JANIE *smiles at her and then turns to the closed bathroom stall.* EVA *speaks from the stall.*)

EVA. What were you saying? I'm still listening.

JANIE. Oh… I was saying that—I agree with you. Nothing happens in a split second. One tiny moment after one tiny moment turns into a *big* moment. So it's hard to blame *anyone* in one of those tiny moments—because it's hard to even recognize it as a moment in the first place! And what does that do to you?

>   (*She thinks.*)

I think when no one's reacting to it, you assume it must be normal. You put it onto yourself—you figure if you're the *only* person clocking this little *thing* as being some sort of *problem*, then *you* must be wrong. *You* must be the problem. And you sit alone with that and it seeps into your pores, and it morphs into… well, *that* becomes self-loathing. And meanwhile, all those little moments keep piling on top of one another.

>   (*Pause.*)

And then all of a sudden you look up, and you're setting the office on fire.

>   (EVA *comes out of the stall dressed like a mermaid. She begins to wash her hands.*)

And just to be really honest—I mean, at the end of the day, I *do* blame him. But more to the point, I'm mostly focused on not blaming myself.

EVA. Yes. That's a nice way of saying that.

JANIE. And I've decided that in the end, it's really not a *bad* thing to blame someone for wearing you down. Especially when you realize—they're only right because *they're* making up the rules.

EVA. (*She looks at* JANIE.) I understand—and Janie. I know I let you down.

SOFIA. Eva.

EVA. (*She sees* SOFIA.) Oh—hi.

SOFIA. You look beautiful.

EVA. Thanks.

JANIE. Are you here to sync up with us?

SOFIA. No, I—

JANIE. (*Entering the stall.*) Wait, wait. Or—no, keep going. But talk louder so that I can pee.

>   (*She closes the stall and begins to pee.*)

SOFIA. I came here to be alone. I'm not even on my period.

EVA. That's okay. Janie never gets hers.
JANIE. It's true.
SOFIA. Then how…?
EVA. Well, she can still *bleed.*
SOFIA. What about you?
EVA. Yes. I'm bleeding.
SOFIA. Mermaids still get their periods?
    (*Looking at her.*)
But where does it come from, when you have a tail?
EVA. No. I already told you.
SOFIA. You did?
EVA. Yes. Remember? I *told* you I was bleeding.
    (SOFIA *looks at* EVA. JANIE *exits the stall. She's bleeding from her nose.*)
SOFIA. Careful—your—your nose is…
    (*She goes over to* JANIE *and puts a paper towel under her nose. She then looks at* EVA, *who is bleeding from her ear.*)
Oh God—your ear!
    (*She runs over to* EVA *and starts trying to clean up the blood. There's a lot of it. The paper towels don't really help.*)
Why is it—it won't stop!
JANIE. No, it won't.
EVA. Oh—careful. Your hands.
SOFIA. My hands?
    (*She looks down at her hands and sees that they're covered in blood.* SOFIA *turns to* EVA.)
SOFIA. Eva.
EVA. I can't forgive you.
SOFIA. You can't?
EVA. I can't hear you! I've got blood in my ears.
SOFIA. Okay, but all the same. I should have—
EVA. I said I can't hear you, Sofia.
    (*The lights change. The bathroom is gone.* SOFIA *is alone onstage, still covered in blood. She stands in silence. Then she picks up her phone and calls someone. Across the stage,* SOFIA'S MOTHER *walks over to a ringing phone.*)
SOFIA'S MOTHER. Hello?

SOFIA. Mama? Mama!
SOFIA'S MOTHER. *Sofia.*
    (SOFIA *begins to cry.*)
SOFIA. I couldn't—I should have—
    (*Pause.*)
I'm *sorry.*
    (SOFIA'S MOTHER *basks in her daughter's voice.*)
SOFIA'S MOTHER. My little spider.
SOFIA. How are you feeling?

End of Play

EVOCATION TO VISIBLE APPEARANCE
by Mark Schultz

Copyright © 2018 by Mark Schultz. All rights reserved. CAUTION: Professionals and amateurs are hereby warned that *Evocation to Visible Appearance* is subject to a royalty. It is fully protected under the copyright laws of the United States of America and of all countries covered by the International Copyright Union (including the Dominion of Canada and the rest of the British Commonwealth), the Berne Convention, the Pan-American Copyright Convention and the Universal Copyright Convention, as well as all countries with which the United States has reciprocal copyright relations. All rights, including professional, amateur stage rights, motion picture, recitation, lecturing, public reading, radio broadcasting, television, video or sound recording, all other forms of mechanical or electronic reproduction, such as CD-ROM, CD-I, information storage and retrieval systems and photocopying, and the rights of translation into foreign languages, are strictly reserved. Particular emphasis is laid upon the matter of readings, permission for which must be secured from the Author's agent in writing.

Required royalties must be paid every time this play is performed before any audience, whether or not it is presented for profit and whether or not admission is charged.

All inquiries concerning rights, including amateur rights, should be addressed to: Creative Artists Agency, 405 Lexington Avenue, 19th Floor, New York, NY, 10174. ATTN: Olivier Sultan, olivier.sultan@caa.com.

ABOUT *EVOCATION TO VISIBLE APPEARANCE*

> *This article first ran in the* Limelight Guide to the 42nd Humana Festival of New American Plays, *published by Actors Theatre of Louisville, and is based on conversations with the playwright before rehearsals for the Humana Festival production began.*

You wanna know what the future looks like? For 17-year-old Samantha, who thinks she's pregnant, the world seems built upon hollow promises—and always on the verge of slipping away. She yearns for solid ground, but everywhere she looks, there's evidence that her fears are well-founded. Trevor, her college-bound boyfriend, wants to become a star on *America's Got Talent*. Her unemployed dad is falling apart when he's not asleep on the couch, and her troubled older sister is in treatment. Plus, Sam's job at Bear Burger Barn smells like sodium-induced extinction. So when she meets Hudson, a tattooed musician and devotee of a band called Häxan 13, she hopes she's found someone with whom she can share her sense of impending doom…and a Slurpee. With black humor and black metal, Mark Schultz's *Evocation to Visible Appearance* gives form to a gathering darkness.

For the playwright, this teenager confronting a fallen world embodies a constellation of ideas that came together in his imagination. "I thought it would be fascinating for someone to write a black metal musical," Schultz explains, "because it seems so unwieldy and counterintuitive, and that felt like something to lean into." This subgenre of heavy metal has attracted serious philosophical analysis—and the "black metal psyche" piqued Schultz's curiosity because of its extreme vision, pitched at the outer limits of human experience and expression. "There's a really desperate longing in black metal," he says, "not for anything recognizably good, but for an end, for something that will never come. It's been described as reliving an epic battle that has already been lost, but you're bound to fight it anyway."

While contemplating the dark impulses in this music, Schultz—who's also an Episcopal priest—was pondering what it might mean to write about the Devil. "I was thinking about the various depictions of the Devil in literature. He's often a very charming figure, seductive and witty, but I don't think that gets it quite right," argues Schultz. "Perhaps that image speaks to the way evil can be incredibly familiar to us. But I think there's another part that has to do with absence, a void—not in the sense of something that's beyond our comprehension, but just nothingness." Considering how this absence might manifest in live performance led Schultz to an even more compelling challenge: "Could I stage an encounter with that void?" he wondered. "I began to think, what would it be to write a play that wasn't *about* the Devil, but somehow *was* the Devil? How to make this void visible, so that we can recognize it?"

To Schultz's surprise, these vast questions coalesced in the journey of one young woman apprehending the emptiness stretching before her. With a favorite Sex Pistols song, "No Future," also kicking around in his consciousness, Schultz admits that Samantha "just showed up in the play, and I loved her." "Suddenly," he recalls, "I was writing about a possibly pregnant teenager, for whom the future appears foreclosed. Those things people often say—'This is the best time of your life,' or 'The future is wide open!'—well, Samantha suspects that it's not, and the only navigational tools she has are for a world that died a long time ago. And this is a situation in which I think a lot of young folks find themselves. The trend of children doing better than their parents? That's done."

The older generation—especially Samantha's crumbling dad, Russell—has nothing to offer in the face of these limitations. "She blames her father for being part of the problem," Schultz notes. Also unhelpful is Martin, Sam.'s well-meaning but clueless boss at Bear Burger Barn, whose tendency to give pep talks makes him the antithesis of Russell's despair. This inverted image is no accident, and Schultz uses mirrors throughout the play, both to humorous and unsettling effect. "I was taken by the idea of mirroring as a way to reveal various facets of the thing that's being reflected," observes Schultz. "And I was thinking of the old image of the Devil as the ape of God—'ape' as in someone who mimics. There's something about the endlessness of reflections when you put two mirrors together, the emptiness of that."

Mirrors are also used to contact spirits in magic traditions, and in another sense, the play arranges these reflections to conjure, to open a door to the ineffable. "The title, *Evocation to Visible Appearance*, comes from old magical texts," Schultz reveals. "The point is to evoke a spirit into the triangle of art, so that you can either command or exorcise it. So maybe the play is a kind of exorcism—creating a space in which an encounter can be staged, so we can then decide what to do with it." As Samantha tries to find someone who can help fathom her future, it's with increasingly clear eyes that she learns to perceive and to mourn all that seems out of reach. "Mourning is a way of recovering love for a world that is passing away," Schultz contends. "In acknowledging the thing that will not be, you're acknowledging your relationship to what actually is. I think it's the first step towards moving to action."

—Amy Wegener

BIOGRAPHY

Mark Schultz is a playwright and Episcopal priest. A resident playwright at New Dramatists and a member of Rising Phoenix Repertory, his plays include *Evocation to Visible Appearance, The Blackest Shore, The Gingerbread House, Ceremony, Deathbed, Gift* and *Everything Will Be Different: A Brief History of Helen of Troy*. His work has been performed or developed by Actors Theatre of Louisville, Soho Rep, Playwrights Horizons, Rising Phoenix Repertory, MCC Theater, The Catastrophic Theatre, Birmingham Repertory Theatre (U.K.), Actors Touring Company (U.K.) and Tiyatro Yan Etki (Turkey). He has received the Oppenheimer Award and the Kesselring Prize, commissions from Manhattan Theatre Club/Sloan, Playwrights Horizons, Actors Theatre of Louisville and The Exchange, and was selected for a Royal Court Residency. Schultz holds an MDiv from Yale Divinity School, a diploma from Berkeley Divinity School, a certificate from the Yale Institute of Sacred Music and an MFA in playwriting from Columbia University.

ACKNOWLEDGMENTS

Evocation to Visible Appearance premiered at the Humana Festival of New American Plays in March 2018. It was directed by Les Waters with the following cast:

> RUSSELL .... Bruce McKenzie
> HUDSON .... Luke F. LaMontagne
> SAMANTHA .... Suzy Weller
> TREVOR .... Lincoln Clauss
> NATALIE .... Ronete Levenson
> MARTIN .... Daniel Arthur Johnson
> DEMONS .... Nayib Felix, Sergio Caetano

and the following production staff:

> Scenic Designer .... Andrew Boyce
> Costume Designer .... Kathleen Geldard
> Lighting Designer .... Paul Toben
> Sound Designer .... Stowe Nelson
> Media Designer .... Philip Allgeier
> Fight Director .... Ryan Bourque
> Stage Manager .... Paul Mills Holmes
> Assistant Stage Manager .... Jessica Kay Potter
> Dramaturg .... Amy Wegener
> Casting .... Kate Lumpkin
> Properties Director .... Mark Walston
> Music Coordinator .... Bruce McKenzie
> Directing Assistant .... Jelani Cornick
> Assistant Dramaturg .... Vivian Barnes

Evocation to Visible Appearance was commissioned by Actors Theatre of Louisville.

CHARACTERS

SAMANTHA, 17.
TREVOR, Sam's ex. 18.
RUSSELL, Sam's father. Early 40s.
NATALIE, Sam's sister. Early 20s.
HUDSON, Sam's friend. 18 or 19 or so.
MARTIN, Sam's boss. 30s or thereabouts.

PLACE

Various blighted suburban locales.

TIME

Present. Relatively.

NOTES ON THE TEXT

Punctuation does not represent de facto beats or pauses. It's to do with indicating how a thought is constructed and with the tone of how those thoughts are expressed: with how shifts in emphasis or the drift of a thought sound, but not how quickly or slowly those shifts occur. For the most part, a question mark (?) is an upward inflection, while a full stop (.) is not an upward inflection. That's not dogma, though. That's just how I heard it. You may hear it differently

If you're thinking that observing all or most of the punctuation as punctuation is important or meaningful, chances are it's going to sound a bit portentous. In which case (and maybe in any case), it's probably best to pretend they're not there.

Text in brackets [ ] is not spoken. Text in parentheses ( ) is spoken.

Please note that the conjuration in the last scene is a quotation from the beginning and the end of the Second Conjuration of a spirit (with a couple words added from the First) found in the old *The Lesser Key of Solomon* (both the Mathers/Crowley [1904] and the Peterson [2001] editions were consulted).

I don't remember where I heard that joke about the cobblestones.

For the curious, it should also be noted that *Pure Fucking Armageddon* is the name of a 1986 Mayhem demo album.

And, finally, as the epigraphs attest, the last surtitled line is from Kenneth Anger's film *Invocation of My Demon Brother*.

We are on the edge of disaster without being able to situate it in the future: it is always already past, and yet we are on the edge or under the threat, all formulations which would imply the future—that which is yet to come—if the disaster were not that which does not come, that which has put a stop to every arrival. To think the disaster (if this is possible, and it is not possible inasmuch as we suspect that disaster is thought) is to have no longer any future in which to think it.

—Maurice Blanchot
The Writing of the Disaster

The book of the cosmos is … the ultimate expression of the most horrible heresy: the fact that anything is happening at all.
—Nicola Masciandro
"Anti-Cosmosis: Black Mahapralaya" in
Hideous Gnosis: Black Metal Theory Symposium I

Zap
You're pregnant
That's witchcraft
—Kenneth Anger
Invocation of My Demon Brother

Suzy Weller
in *Evocation to Visible Appearance*

42nd Humana Festival of New American Plays
Actors Theatre of Louisville, 2018
Photo by Bill Brymer

EVOCATION TO VISIBLE APPEARANCE

Scene 1.

>*Above the stage, a surtitle display. Unless otherwise explicitly indicated, surtitled text is double indented.*
>*A clearing in a sparse, suburban-adjacent, largely defoliated forest.*
>*A circle of sad trees.*
>*Litter everywhere.*
>*Sound of cars / a highway of some sort nearby.*
>*Nothing at all happens.*
>>Shhh.
>
>*Nothing happens.*
>>Shhh.
>>It's okay.
>>Everything's gonna be okay.
>
>*Nothing happens.*
>>There's no need to be afraid.
>>Everything's actually very fine.
>
>*Nothing happens for a very long time.*
>>It's coming.
>
>*Nothing.*
>>It's coming.
>
>*Nothing.*
>>Rise. Rise. Rise
>
>*Nothing.*
>*The lights flicker.*

Scene 2.

>*Silence.*

RUSSELL. You're looking at me. You're looking at me with this look. I think I know this look.

You're wondering if you should risk it. Right? Am I right? You're wondering if. If hiring someone like me. Someone older. Someone a little older? If that's a good investment.

Well. Let me tell you. Let me put you at ease: It is. It really is. A good investment. I have experience. I am an experienced worker. And. You know. Excellent.

I've done a lot of stuff in my day. I have patience? I'm a patient guy? I'm good with younger people? I have a daughter. Two daughters. Really. We get along. Real great. I can identify with younger employees. Co-workers. Really well. It's no problem. With me. Is what I'm saying. I'm good with kids.

And I don't mind having younger. Younger. Managers. Over me. Either. I think that's fine. I think that's really okay. I know my place. I can find my place? If I don't know it? And I can I can go there. And. Deal with that. *From* that. That place. And and be a productive. A really productive. A member of the team. You know. With direction. From anyone. Including someone younger. I don't mind. Teenagers.

I am a standout. Team. Team player.

I have. With me. Right here. You may be interested. It's a. It's a collection. Of recommendations. From previous employers. And family members. Some of them. You'll see the. The diversity. Of positions? Of jobs? Some of them are. Some of them. You know. I have pictures. I had pictures taken. With some of them. So you'd know: I'm not lying. I'm the real deal. (I'm sorry I'm not as photogenic. As I'd like to be. That's not. I can't. Really. Change that. But.) Anyway. There's a copy. Also. Of my resume. In there. Too. In case you. Lose the other one.

You can see: I'm very well organized.

So.

Thanks for this opportunity. To be with you. To show you. Um. My um. To show you. How valuable. To show you I'm valuable. To show you. My value.

    Silence.

    You should hold my hand.

Scene 3.

    Suddenly:

    A stage. A banner that reads HÄXAN 13.

    HUDSON *plays and sings. Poorly. His guitar may not be plugged in. He may not know how to play.*

    Lyrics are surtitled.

HUDSON. *Aaaaaaaaaaaaaaaaaaaaaa!*
Thou with hate I worship
Spite of Nordic winter frost
Bitter albatross thee!!!!!!
Aaaaaaaaaaaaaaaaaaaaaa!
Satan's hammer blazing
Torment of four horsemen riding
Accursed art thee!!!!!!

HUDSON. Okay at this point? In the song? Imagine like a fuck ton of blast beats. Like a fucking explosive fucking drum like aaaaaaah-oh-my-god like mindblowing fucking— Like—

    Silence. HUDSON *imagines. We imagine.* HUDSON *resumes.*

Aaaaaaaaaaaaaaaaaaaaaa!
Ignorance of blind betrayal
Stone black wyrding of the eldritch welkin
Rise rise rise!!!!!!
Aaaaaaaaaaaaaaaaaaaaaa!

    It's barely intelligible. And it ends abruptly.

    Silence.

    HUDSON *takes a drink of water.*

    Silence.

That was "Satan's Hammer"? I wrote it myself? I hope you liked it.
I have a new guitar. You may have noticed. So.
Thanks. I love you guys.
Hail Häxan!

                    Things just started going black.

Scene 4.

SAMANTHA. Pregnant.
TREVOR. --
SAMANTHA. Yeah. Pregnant.
TREVOR. Um.
    Beat.
SAMANTHA. Weird right?
    Beat.
TREVOR. Is it—

SAMANTHA. Definitely.
TREVOR. It is?
SAMANTHA. I mean. Lately? It's just been you. So.
TREVOR. Right.
Okay.
Huh. Great.
    Pause.
SAMANTHA. You keep picking at that blanket you'll unravel it.
TREVOR. Right. Sorry.
    Beat.
SAMANTHA. I thought we could get an apartment. Or a house. I haven't told anyone yet.
You look worried. Don't look worried.
TREVOR. --
SAMANTHA. Do you think we should paint it blue? Our apartment? I like blue.
Have I surprised you? Like really surprised you? I didn't mean to. What's that like?
TREVOR. No. It's fine.
SAMANTHA. [It was a] surprise to me. Right? I was really. Surprised. But.
It grows on you. You get used to it.
Then you get happy.
TREVOR. Okay.
    Beat.
SAMANTHA. We should think of names. Right? We could name it. Together. Now. I mean: him or her. It's so weird saying "it." Right? But.
TREVOR. --
SAMANTHA. You will be happy. Trust me.
    Pause.
TREVOR. Maybe. Sarah? Maybe? For a name? If it's a girl?
SAMANTHA. Right. Good. Sarah. That's thinking. Nice.
Only. I don't like Sarah. It's too old.
Will you write a song about her? Sarah? Your daughter? Do you think? That'd be really nice. You should do that.
I really don't like Sarah though.
Natalie. No. Silly.
Gita.

TREVOR. Gita?

SAMANTHA. Why not.

TREVOR. Tabatha.

SAMANTHA. I really doubt Tabatha is a very good choice.

Do you like blue? For an apartment color?

TREVOR. Um.

Silence.

SAMANTHA. This is a lot.

TREVOR. Yeah. It is.

I have a scholarship. Sammy.

SAMANTHA. Right.

No right. Yes. I know. Which is. Very nice.

TREVOR. Yeah.

SAMANTHA. Definitely.

Do you like blue though?

TREVOR. --

SAMANTHA. I think you'll make a really wonderful dad. I do. I think you don't know what sort of dad you'll make. I think you doubt yourself. Don't you. I think you *really* doubt yourself. And you shouldn't. You'll be terrific. She'll like you. Sarah. I could live with Sarah. It's growing on me I think. See? [It] grows on you.

TREVOR looks out the window.

And anyway. I don't think you'd like it: School. College. Whatever. I don't think you'd like it at all. I think you'd find yourself being probably being. The *worst* student. The worst one. In the class. I know you have a scholarship. And that's great. But it's not like high school. It really isn't. It's *very* easy to fail. And you'd hate it. A lot. Once you got there. And people would hate *you*. Too. I imagine. They're bound to. That's how they are. I know. I've seen it happen. My sister? She never had a chance. Obviously. I mean. And she was way smarter than you. Just saying.

I'm not being mean. I'm being honest.

We could have a house.

TREVOR. I liked your sister.

SAMANTHA. Yeah. Of course. Me too. She was a coward.

You're not a coward.

TREVOR. --

SAMANTHA. We could have a house.

Beat.

TREVOR. I actually. I think. Sammy?

SAMANTHA. You should hold my hand.

TREVOR. Okay. Um.

SAMANTHA. --

TREVOR. I think. I need to break up with you.

> *Beat.*

SAMANTHA. You should hold my hand.

TREVOR. Yeah I need to break up with you.

SAMANTHA. Huh.

Um.

That's. Really weird. That you say that. Trevor.

TREVOR. Is it?

SAMANTHA. Don't you think? Don't you think that's really weird? That you say that *now?* Isn't that a little weird? Because. You know. I'm pregnant. I think I mentioned that. And that puts me. What you said puts me. In a really. In a very. Awkward. Position.

TREVOR. I know.

SAMANTHA. Vis a vis the baby. And parenthood. And everything.

TREVOR. I know.

SAMANTHA. Do you.

Nothing ever changes for the best. Trevor.

You're gonna wish. You never went. You will. I can tell.

I don't want you to be sad. Or a loser.

Hold my hand.

> *Beat.*

TREVOR. You're not actually. Pregnant. Though. Are you.

SAMANTHA. Um.

TREVOR. You're not though.

SAMANTHA. Yes. Yes. Of course. I'm pregnant. Yes. I told you. I'm pregnant.

TREVOR. I don't think I believe you.

SAMANTHA. That is so stupid.

TREVOR. I mean. You're such a liar, Sammy. Usually. I mean. *All* the time. Everybody knows.

And anyway. We didn't even I didn't even put it—We did anal.

SAMANTHA. Accidents happen.

TREVOR. I was responsible. I used protection.

SAMANTHA. Protection? What is what is that. I don't even. What.

Accidents. Fucking. Happen. Trevor.

TREVOR. Yeah. But not miracles.

SAMANTHA. Of course they do.

Sometimes.

TREVOR. Come on.

I mean. Here's the thing. Right? This wasn't. This wasn't actually. I mean. Us? Sammy? Really?

I mean I *like* you. For what it's worth. But I don't actually *like* you. Right? Not very much. I mean. Not in a meaningful like: I'm-gonna-move-in-with-you sort of way.

You're actually sort of basically shitty. I mean: in general. As a person.

And my mom. I mean. The way she talks about you.

SAMANTHA. --

TREVOR. Anyway. If you're pregnant. *If* you're pregnant If you *really* are pregnant—

SAMANTHA. Yeah. Which I am.

TREVOR. Then: I'm sorry. I'm really sorry. I fucked up. *We* fucked up. Somehow. But.

I'm actually not *that* sorry. Because A: I don't really think you're pregnant? And B: You have options. It's not like you don't have options.

You'd be stupid to keep it. You really would.

SAMANTHA. I'm not stupid.

TREVOR. Okay. Then.

    Beat.

SAMANTHA. Maybe I've just been really sick lately.

TREVOR. Yeah maybe.

SAMANTHA. Wouldn't that be funny? I thought I was pregnant but I've just been really sick?

TREVOR. Huh.

SAMANTHA. I *have* been feeling really nauseated, though. I mean I can barely think. It's crippling. It's stupid. It's useless.

Ha. Right.

TREVOR. I really tried To like you. Sam.

SAMANTHA. --

TREVOR. But I have a career. A potential career. I'm gonna have a double major. I'm gonna be on *America's Got Talent*. Or *The Voice*. *The Voice?* I mean. Or whatever. I will. Or an engineer? Or both. I don't know. Who knows what I'll be.

Only I can't be with you.
SAMANTHA. Right.
Okay. It was a joke.
TREVOR. I know.
SAMANTHA. No. I mean. That I liked your music. I never really liked your music. I mean I told you I did. That was the joke: I was joking. *You're* the shitty one. Right? Right? I mean it's not that you don't have talent? It's just that it's not what you think it is.

Also the pregnancy. That was a joke too. I guess. Ha.

It's not gonna last, you know. All of it. This. Stuff. Us. Give it a few more years, they say. Ten, twenty years. The planet hates us. It really does. You can't blame it. I don't. We're all really shitty. I mean. As a people? We're gonna be wiped out. Rising oceans? Hurricanes? Killer bees? They're still out there. Who knows what else.

Ten, twenty years. That's not long. I mean. For a career. If that's what you're looking for. And what is that? Big waste.

You have no idea what you're doing.

Who cares.

We could make a baby. Us. Now. If you want.

                I'll hold.

Scene 5.

> *A duck pond.*
> NATALIE *smoking.*
> *Silence.*

SAMANTHA. There's one.
There's one.
Look.
NATALIE. Yeah alright.
So: feed it.
> *Silence. She does.*

SAMANTHA. [I] like this.
Gorgeous day. Sun big and bright and beautiful. The water. The ducks.
NATALIE. It's alright.
> *Beat.*

SAMANTHA. Do they treat you well? Do they feed you? What do they feed you?
NATALIE. Course they feed me.
SAMANTHA. What though.
NATALIE. Food.
SAMANTHA. Good food?
NATALIE. No. It's not fucking. Gourmet. It's just. Food.
SAMANTHA. But they're nice to you.
NATALIE. Sometimes.
SAMANTHA. And you like them? The people?
NATALIE. Sometimes Yeah. They're alright.
They're mostly old, though. So. I mean none of them are attractive. I don't *like* them like them.
SAMANTHA. Right.
NATALIE. If that's what you mean. And anyway, you're not supposed to Like them like them. They're like furniture.
SAMANTHA. Right.
NATALIE. The other patients are nice, though. One or two of them.
And they've seen things. Yeah? Some of them? You look into their eyes and you're like: Holy fuck. You've *seen* things.
SAMANTHA. Like what. Have they told you?
NATALIE. No. Don't wanna know. Have my own shit.
You have another cigarette?
SAMANTHA. Yeah. Here.
NATALIE. Thanks. I live for this. Now.
Dad okay?
SAMANTHA. He's fine. Yeah.
NATALIE. He have a job yet?
SAMANTHA. Almost.
   Beat.
NATALIE. Hate those fucking ducks.
SAMANTHA. I like them.
NATALIE. Don't let it come too close.
   Beat.
SAMANTHA. Can you tell me? I don't know if you can tell me. Like if it's a bad thing for you to tell me or like if you shouldn't. But I'm really curious. What it was like.

NATALIE. What do you mean.

SAMANTHA. When you broke.

Beat.

NATALIE. [I] don't wanna talk about it.

Beat.

SAMANTHA. Okay.

Silence.

NATALIE. How old're you anyway?

Graduating soon, right? Shouldn't you be graduating?

SAMANTHA. --

NATALIE. Right.

You don't get to be the troubled one. Just so you know.

Pause. Smoking.

Okay.

Things just started going black. Yeah? Not like blackouts. They just started—going black. And it was really heavy. Everything felt heavy. And it was hard to breathe.

Sometimes voices.

SAMANTHA. Is it very hard for you to talk about?

What did they say? The voices.

NATALIE. Nothing. Mostly. Nothing important. Sometimes they were helpful. They knew where the pills were. I had no idea.

One of them had a Russian accent.

SAMANTHA. Really?

NATALIE. Yeah. I miss him. He was funny. He told jokes. "Two nuns in a taxi. One of them says, 'I've not come this way before.' Other one says, 'I know. I think it's the cobblestones.'"

Funny. Like that.

SAMANTHA. I don't get it.

NATALIE. Ha.

SAMANTHA. Oh right.

NATALIE. See?

Beat.

SAMANTHA. Do you think you're actually *very* crazy? I mean I think you seem really fine to me.

NATALIE. I'm on drugs.

SAMANTHA. Yeah. But.

NATALIE. I'm on drugs.

> *Beat.*

SAMANTHA. Will you be coming home? Soon? Do you think?

NATALIE. Maybe.

I actually like it here, though. That's the problem. I don't really feel—I'm not really interested in coming home. Not right now.

> *Beat.*

SAMANTHA. Do you think you're crazy because you're a weak person?

NATALIE. --

SAMANTHA. I mean. Do you imagine it's the weaker sorts of people who get crazy?

Sometimes I think I must be very weak. But then. I surprise myself.

I mean I don't see black. I don't hear voices. I don't take pills. Not a lot. At any rate. I don't tell jokes.

But there's less air to breathe. I think. I really feel that. A lot less air. And the walls don't seem as reliable as they should be? And things seem to be moving very fast. I feel like I only just got here. Right? And I'm being moved along. By invisible hands. To something someplace else. And I don't like it. I like it *here*. I just got here.

I mean not *here* here. Obviously. I'm not crazy. Now.

I think I could probably take just about anything. And not crack. Not really. And I hate that. That's the thing I hate most. About me.

I feel I'm just waiting for it to come. It'd be a relief. If it did. But it doesn't.

I used to really look up to you.

NATALIE. Ha. Stupid.

SAMANTHA. I used to love how distant you were. When you were smoking. It seemed like the right distance. To things. It's not stupid

It's nice they let you wear your own clothes.

NATALIE. What other clothes would I wear?

SAMANTHA. I don't know.

Sometimes I wear your clothes. Sometimes I sneak in your room and wear your clothes. Is that weird? I like how they smell. I don't wear them out. Like outside. I put them back. When I'm done. It's not often. I like your clothes.

Do you think I could live here? With you? For a bit?

NATALIE. Why.

SAMANTHA. Just to try it out.

NATALIE. No. That's stupid.

SAMANTHA. I like the blue. On the walls. It seems very soothing. I'm not stupid. That's not stupid.

NATALIE. Actually. It is. Sort of.

>   *Pause.*

Sam I wish I could be your sister. I was really getting to like you.

And it's not that I don't like you now. You're not boring or anything. I mean you kind of are. But. Everything's a bit boring right now. So.

It's not you.

Sorry.

I mean I say that. But.

Anyway.

>   *Silence.*

SAMANTHA. I've run out of bread.

NATALIE. Good. Let 'em starve.

SAMANTHA. Ha.

>   *Silence.*

NATALIE. It's not a relief. Nothing is. Whatever it is you're waiting for: it's not coming. Not the way you want it to.

>   *Silence.*

You should give me another cigarette.

>   *Pause.*
>
>   *She punches* SAM *in the arm.*

SAMANTHA. Ow.

>   *Pause.*

NATALIE. Stop wearing my fucking clothes.

You wanna know what the future looks like?

Scene 6.

RUSSELL. No. No no. Yeah. No. The reason I called. Right. The reason I called. Is.

No I'd love to set up a plan. A payment plan. I'd really. I'd love that. Only. You know. I don't think I could really. I don't think I could—Actually: it's tricky. Because. I can't pay it. Which is why I called.

No yeah of course. No. I I got it. Definitely. I open my mail. I probably just. I missed this. By accident. On accident.

I mean. Look. Okay. Look. Don't. Berate me. I mean are you berating me? Are you scolding me? For being for not having for—? Because don't. Because just. Because. Don't. Because I don't need it.

Look. Okay. Look. Could you get someone. Could you get someone. Else. Please. Could I talk to someone else. Please. Please. Please. I'm asking very nicely. Please.

Well because I don't think you can help me. No. I don't think you can help me. Because I'm trying. No because I'm *trying* to explain. Right? I'm *trying* to explain. And you're not *listening* to me. And you don't *want* to listen to me. And no of course no. I don't. Want it cancelled. I want to talk to someone else. Please let me. Talk. To someone else. Can you do that? Can you please do that? Can you put someone else on?

Do you get off on this? Do you enjoy this? Do you actually enjoy this? Are you enjoying this?

I know I'm fucking useless. I know I'm fucking useless. I know I'm fucking useless. You don't need. You don't. Need. To tell me. That. I know that. Already. That's not. That's nothing.

It's not new.

Yeah. No. Yeah.

No. Of course.

I'll hold.

I'll hold.

I'll hold.

Silence.

What does Satan think?

Scene 7.

SAMANTHA *and* MARTIN.

SAMANTHA. Is that all?

MARTIN. Um.

Yeah. Pretty much.

SAMANTHA. Okay.

Pause.

MARTIN. I mean we're disappointed. To be honest. Someone with your potential.

SAMANTHA. Ha.

MARTIN. Someone with your potential. Don't laugh. Someone with your potential: it's disappointing. You have potential. You could do things. Good things. Better things. It's nothing to laugh about.

SAMANTHA. Right. Sorry. Yes. Very serious.

MARTIN. Good.

It would be terrific if we thought you were actually invested. If you showed any investment.

SAMANTHA. Sorry. In what.

MARTIN. Your work maybe? The quality? Your betterment? As a person?

SAMANTHA. Right right. Yes.

MARTIN. There's a general feeling that. You know. Your co-workers. That. You'd rather be elsewhere.

SAMANTHA. Elsewhere like where.

MARTIN. Anywhere. Elsewhere.

SAMANTHA. Huh.

I mean. Yes. In many ways. I would rather be elsewhere. Like in this moment? I'd rather be elsewhere.

MARTIN. Of course. But. Generally though. Right? Generally? There's a *general* feeling. That. You know: Elsewhere.

SAMANTHA. Right. Yeah. I get that.

Silence.

MARTIN. Are things okay? At home?

SAMANTHA. What? No. Yeah. Perfect.

MARTIN. Okay.

Good.

Silence.

Are you invested? *Can* you be invested?

SAMANTHA. In what. In food service?

MARTIN. In food service. Yes.

SAMANTHA. In mopping floors maybe? In cleaning sick off bathroom sinks? Shit off toilets? In wiping down countertops? In playing nice to fucking. Dead people?

MARTIN. Dead people. Who's dead. Who're the dead people.

SAMANTHA. Doomed people.

MARTIN. Right.

SAMANTHA. Have you seen the amount of sodium we're pushing? Let alone. You know.

She makes a vague gesture.

I mean. Invested? What is that. What does that even. What is that.
MARTIN. Your life? Howabout your life invested in your life?
SAMANTHA. Huh.
MARTIN. Nod if you understand the question.
SAMANTHA. No one wants to be on a sinking ship.
MARTIN. I'm sorry?
SAMANTHA. No one wants to be on a sinking ship.
MARTIN. Um.
SAMANTHA. Do you have kids? Are you the sort of person who has kids?
MARTIN. Um. Yes. Yeah. You can see. On the desk.
SAMANTHA. Right.
MARTIN. The pictures.
SAMANTHA. Yeah. Sorry.
MARTIN. Two of them.
SAMANTHA. They're cute.
They're doomed.
You know that right? That they're doomed?
MARTIN. Um. No. Actually. I didn't know that.
SAMANTHA. Yeah. Ten, twenty years? Doomed. So. I mean. Invested?
You wanna know what the future looks like? It doesn't look like your kids. I'm just saying. The future's a google search away. If you know what you're looking for. It's horrible. It's tasteless.
Speaking of which: I've always admired your taste in ties. I think you match colors and patterns really very well. Though there was the odd occasion? I thought maybe you were colorblind. Are you colorblind?
MARTIN. Yes. Actually.
SAMANTHA. See? I'm very perceptive.
I don't mean to startle you. When I think about the future. I don't generally think of kids. Of the future being the sort of place where kids would be very happy. So I don't generally tend to think the future has too many of them, yeah? I'm not much of a sadist. Truth be told. Not where kids are involved.
Are you a sadist?
MARTIN. No.
SAMANTHA. Right.
Well maybe not consciously. Wink wink.
Anyway. I'm joking. I'm pregnant. Honestly. No joke. Totally pregnant. I believe the children are our future.
So we have that in common. Apparently.

Pause.
What do you feed them? They look so happy.
Seriously.

    SAMANTHA *looks as if she might vomit.*

MARTIN. [Are] you okay?
SAMANTHA. No. Yeah. Sorry. Wow.
I just got nauseated all of a sudden. I felt very very nauseated.
I don't know if it's you or.
I just got—
I'm fine.
My kids'll eat your kids for breakfast. I have that feeling.

    You look like you're gonna cry.

Scene 8.

    SAMANTHA *and* HUDSON.
    Bus stop.

SAMANTHA. You have a lot of tattoos.
I say that. Because. It's true. Obviously. And because I've thought. I've often thought. I might get one. A tattoo. Maybe more than one.
Does it hurt?
HUDSON. Are you talking to me?
SAMANTHA. Clearly. Yes. Silly.
HUDSON. Right.
    Silence.
SAMANTHA. I said I've been thinking about tattoos. And you seem to be something of an expert and I was wondering if they hurt. Do they hurt?
HUDSON. Yes. Yeah. Yes. They hurt.
SAMANTHA. Okay.
Should I not get a tattoo then. Do you think. Because of the pain?
I was thinking of getting the word Thuglife. You know the word Thuglife? I was thinking of getting the word Thuglife. Here. On my stomach. Right here. I don't know what it means. But it seems true. Somehow.
You can look at me. I don't mind you looking at me. I look young maybe. But I'm not.
    He looks at her.
    Beat.

HUDSON. Do what you want.
SAMANTHA. That's very refreshing. Your attitude.
I said I think your attitude is very refreshing.
HUDSON. --
SAMANTHA. What're you listening to.
HUDSON. Satan.
SAMANTHA. Oh.
I was gonna say that's a bit extreme. But then I thought. No. That's actually a bit silly.
HUDSON. It's not silly. It's Häxan 13 it's not silly. Okay?
SAMANTHA. Okay.
Do you think you'll suffer from early hearing loss? I'm afraid I'll go blind. Or be in a coma. One day. You never know what can happen. But looking at you: Hearing loss. Or maybe just heart disease. And a stroke.
What does Satan tell you?
HUDSON. Are you a little fucked up?
SAMANTHA. Sorry?
HUDSON. Are you a little fucked up? Like on drugs or whatever?
SAMANTHA. No. Would that be better for you? What would you recommend? I mean I took these. From my sister. She's crazy. You want some?
You know: you *look* very tough. You have this very tough image thing going on. It's very attractive. But I don't think it's real. I don't think it has anything to do with reality.
It's sort of disappointing. Because I was looking for someone to have sex with. And maybe do something fun with. I have a head full of plans. Bridges to burn. Lives to ruin. I'm joking. I'm not joking.
I thought you might be the sort of person I was looking for. And then you mentioned Satan. Which is a dead giveaway, really: you're a joke. Are you a joke?
HUDSON. I'm just waiting for the bus. Okay?
SAMANTHA. Right. Do you think you'll actually be going anywhere?
I ask that. Because. Everyone thinks they're going somewhere. No one is. That's the problem. It's everything else that's going places. We're just along for the ride.
Do you think that's true? What does Satan think?
    Beat.
HUDSON. He thinks you're a bored little girl.
SAMANTHA. Really? Do you have to be Satan to figure that out?

HUDSON. Look. Leave me alone. Right? I don't know you. I don't like you. I don't wanna argue with you. Just leave me. The fuck. Alone.

SAMANTHA. Is that your girlfriend? On your arm? Or your mom. Or your daughter. I can't really tell. Maybe it's a lion? Or a cat? Or a mongoose? It's very confusing.

Does getting a tattoo make you more prone to skin cancer? Or stupidity.

> HUDSON *walks away.*
>
> SAMANTHA *alone. For a very significant amount of time.*
>
> *It starts to rain.*
>
> HUDSON *returns.*

HUDSON. It's raining.

SAMANTHA. It is.

HUDSON. Just fuck off.

> *Pause.*

SAMANTHA. Do you think you may have fallen in love with me? Just a little bit?

> *He looks at her.*

>> I am the star of every show.

Scene 9.

> SAMANTHA *and* HUDSON.
>
> RUSSELL *on the couch.*
>
> *TV is on.*

SAMANTHA. Daddy. This is Hudson.

HUDSON. Hey.

SAMANTHA. Hudson's a Satanist.

HUDSON. Not really.

SAMANTHA. He listens to Satan.

HUDSON. Häxan 13. They're a band. They're *my* band. Actually. *Were* my band. I mean: I auditioned for them.

SAMANTHA. He listens to the sort of music Satan listens to.

HUDSON. Stop.

Hey. Your dad? Is totally out cold.

SAMANTHA. No he's not.

HUDSON. Yeah. Definitely.

> *Beat.*

SAMANTHA. Right.

>*She searches her dad's pockets.* HUDSON *looks on*

He said he'd give me some money. He keeps saying he'll give me some money and then he never does. I'm not stealing.

HUDSON. I'm not judging.

>*Beat.*

SAMANTHA. There's food in the kitchen. If you want it. If you're hungry.

HUDSON. Nice.

>*He exits to the kitchen.*
>
>SAMANTHA *stands over her father.*
>
>*Silence.*
>
>HUDSON *reenters with a bowl of cereal.*

HUDSON. You have a really nice house.

SAMANTHA. Maybe.

HUDSON. No. You do. Honestly.

SAMANTHA. There's another one just like it next door.

HUDSON. Yeah but you have all this stuff. All this kitschy stuff. It's houselike. It's nice.

You really wanna make some money? You should sell all this shit. Everyone collects something. Someone'll want it. Doesn't matter what it is.

You okay?

SAMANTHA. No. Yeah.

Looking for something.

>*Beat.*

HUDSON. You could start with that TV. Someone'll pay a fortune for that.

You look like you're gonna cry.

>*Beat.*

SAMANTHA. I'm not.

I always look like this.

Next door it's all blue. Everything. Inside. Exact same house. But blue. Nicer. I always wanted to live *there*. Though if I did. Maybe I'd just want to live here. Which would be: really. Really. Shitty.

Nevermind.

There's nothing here.

Let's go.

HUDSON. Oh wait. Hold on. [I'm] really into this commercial.

It has bears.

>*They watch the commercial.*

COMMERCIAL. You're a hungry bear.
And what're you gonna do to satisfy that hunger: eat a salad? Not a chance.
You're gonna have a Bear Burger.
And now, for a limited time, feed the whole hungry family
with the Bear Burger Picnic Party Basket Meal Deal Deluxe
Four Bear Burgers,
Extra Mayo,
Four large soft drinks,
And an avalanche of fries all for nine ninety nine.
You got a bear-sized hunger? Well there's a bear in your future:
A Bear Burger at Bear Burger Barn.

> *Hypnotic stillness.*
>
> *It ends. They leave.*
>
> *Door closes.* RUSSELL *opens his eyes. Checks his pockets. Straightens up. Looks around.*
>
> *Continues watching TV. For a very long time.*
>
> *Closes his eyes.*
>
> *A light from the grid above the stage falls very loudly.*

Am I as hollow as I feel?

Scene 10.

TREVOR. You want me. You definitely want me. On like a whole number of levels. You want me. Sexually. Personally. I mean. I have a smile? And a sense of humor that is fucking— Also: I'm wearing some really very incredibly fucking tight. Jeans. That are massively suggestive to you. The things going on in your mind: they are. I mean. Obscene. Really. If you're honest. And you can be: honest. With me. I'll let you. You feel that. What a relief that is. You have my permission. To love me. You can love me. Any way you like. I am the star of your show. I am the star of every show.

So it goes without saying right? You want me to win. You definitely want me to win. Because. Because I'm I'm not just really incredibly like very very cute. And intensely like flexibly fuckable. To you. And. Nice. And everything. I'm definitely. That. All that. But I'm also really really like incredibly amazingly talented. And you feel that. Too. From the minute I walk out on stage. You're fucking. Gob-smacked. Completely silent. Because. Because. It's like. Heat. Heat waves. And everything. From my skin. From me. From *me*. I don't need to do anything. And you *know*. You *know* that.

And when I sing. When I start to sing. There is no way your life will ever be the same. Completely. I'm singing directly and especially right to you. Directly. Because as much as you love me? I love you. I do. You feel that. Completely. And it breaks your heart. As the music swells and the lights do their stage light routine thing that is really fucking: awesome and amazing. It breaks your heart to think: I mean, there could have been a world. There could've been. A world. In which we didn't exist. Like this. You and me. Together. Because. Somehow. I save you. Somehow I make it all worthwhile. Somehow I wipe every tear from every eye. Somehow it's gonna be okay. Somehow. There's a future. A world. For us. Finally. Again.

And you vote for me. You vote for me as many times as you can. I'm the best thing ever. And you want everyone to know that. In case they don't already know that. Multiple votes. An ocean of votes. For me.

And if I *don't* win. If I *don't* win if *we*. Don't. Win. You. Will be angry. That's right. You won't just be hurt. You *will* be hurt. Definitely. But also: angry. You'll make phone calls for me. You'll write op-eds and tweets and blog posts and updates. For me. You'll sign petitions. You'll threaten people. Random people stupid people. People who just don't fucking get it. You'll refuse to recycle. You'll renege on your generous pledge to the ASPCA. You'll eat red meat again. You'll cut yourself. You'll drink bleach and set yourself on fire. You'll sell yourself for bitcoins to fund secret death squads run by child soldiers in central Montana. You'll join a cult and massacre your friends on a live-feed red-room from the dark web. You'll blow up cars, buildings, city blocks. You'll kill and you'll kill and you'll slaughter: men women children animals and everything you think you love and anything you know you don't. All. For. Me.

But.

Thank God it doesn't have to come to that, though. Right? Thank God. Because. Because when the votes are tallied? When the celebrity judges meet in their well-appointed back room. With the booze and the drugs and the hookers and the amazing. Fucking. Exotic. Fucking. Animals? From every corner of the world and televisions and bon-bons and and fucking and and. Donuts. And M&Ms of every color millions of colors. The consensus. Is clear. I've won.

I. Have fucking. Won.

And there's no need for another season. There's no need. For it to go on any more. The whole thing. Suddenly. Cancelled. *This* is the finale. *This* is it. And it all just. Ends. Perfectly. Ends. There. Then. For all of us. In love. Together. Blissful. Over. Blackout. Heaven. Done.

You can't hear me.

Scene 11.

      MARTIN *and* RUSSELL.

MARTIN. I'm a little concerned about your daughter.
RUSSELL. My daughter.
MARTIN. Yeah.
RUSSELL. Which one.
MARTIN. Um.
RUSSELL. 'Cause they're both a little concerning.
MARTIN. Ha. Okay.
RUSSELL. Seriously though.
MARTIN. Right. Well. I only know. The one. So. It's. It's Sam. Samantha.
RUSSELL. Got it. Okay.
You want a drink or anything? We have cereal. Too. If you want like. If you want a snack or something.
MARTIN. No.
RUSSELL. Okay.
I'm sorry I'm not dressed.
MARTIN. That's fine.
RUSSELL. Only it's embarrassing. Right? I'm sorry. If I'd've known. I would've. I would've. Um. I would've. Made an effort. More of an effort.
MARTIN. It's fine.
RUSSELL. Good. That's kind. You have kind eyes.
MARTIN. Ha.
RUSSELL. Have I met you?
MARTIN. No.
RUSSELL. Before?
MARTIN. No.
RUSSELL. Right.
So my daughter. My Sam. Yeah?
MARTIN. Yes.
RUSSELL. What's wrong.
MARTIN. Um. She just seems. Lately. You know.
Distracted's not the word. It's. It's something else.
And I. I care for people. You know. Who work for me. Deeply care. And.
And I have two daughters. Too. So. I get it. I get. What it means. To be a dad. And if there were something wrong. With *my* daughter. And if maybe. I

could *fix* it. I think. Maybe. You know: I think I'd want someone to tell me. To talk to me.

RUSSELL. Right. Yeah. Definitely. Thank you.

So what's wrong.

MARTIN. Good question. Right?

RUSSELL. Yeah. Yeah. It is.

Pause.

MARTIN. Um. Well. You know. When I. When my wife and I. When we Separated. Right? My daughters. It was hard on them. And. There were behavior issues. And. You know. Acting out. And everything. In new ways Which was sort of. Surprising. And. Um.

You know sometimes. Things like that. Big changes—

I kinda wanna make sure. Everything's. Okay.

RUSSELL. Right. Is it?

MARTIN. I don't know.

RUSSELL. Me neither.

Pause.

MARTIN. Is her mom around?

RUSSELL. No.

MARTIN. Where is she?

RUSSELL. You sound like you're a really good dad.

MARTIN. Ha. I don't know about that.

RUSSELL. Sure. But. You sound like you're a really good dad. And. Person. Really. Like. It's hard to believe. You exist. Right? That you're real. Are you real?

MARTIN. Um

RUSSELL. Like. I think I saw you in a commercial once.

MARTIN. Ha.

RUSSELL. Right? I mean. Are you? Don't answer. Seriously. That's a weird question. That's really. I don't wanna. Know.

Anyway. If you could give me advice. On dad stuff? Or. Maybe. Um. I could watch you. Sometime. You know Parent. Your girls. I could be I could stand. Just a little bit. In the background. And I could learn. From you. How to be. How to become. A good. Um. Dad. Right? So.

I'd be really. Quiet.

Beat.

MARTIN. Um.

RUSSELL. Hey you know what? It's fine. It's. Forget it.

It's done anyway.

MARTIN. What's done.

>   *Beat.* RUSSELL *smiles.*

RUSSELL. Are you hiring?

MARTIN. What?

RUSSELL. Because. I'm looking for a job right now. And. I think. I might like. To work with you. To have a job. With you. Are you hiring?

MARTIN. No.

RUSSELL. Oh.

I don't make the best first impression.

MARTIN. No. You don't.

RUSSELL. Thank you. For that. For being honest. That's kind. In its way.

We didn't get separated. She left. Poof.

MARTIN. I'm sorry.

RUSSELL. Yeah. Thank you. Me too.

And then Natalie. The other one. Sam's sister: it was like. I don't know. Bad things happen.

>   *He smiles.*
>
>   *Beat.*

MARTIN. Can I just. Put something. On the table. Here. For a second.

RUSSELL. Sure. Yeah. Go ahead.

MARTIN. More of a question really. Have you talked. With Sam. About what you're going through?

RUSSELL. Yeah. I mean. No. Only: what am I going through?

MARTIN. You're grieving. Right? Aren't you grieving?

RUSSELL. --

MARTIN. Are you getting help?

RUSSELL. You're helping me. Aren't you? Now?

MARTIN. No. Real help.

RUSSELL. This is real. Right? Don't answer.

Can I say something? Something. Sort of. Difficult? To you?

It's really. Really. Hard. To become. A new person.

How d'you do it?

MARTIN. You decide.

One day. You wake up. And you decide. To be the sort of person. You know you can be.

And you stop fucking around. And wallowing. In your misery. And you realize people depend on you. Some people. Depend on you. And you remember you're building a future. For those people. Those other people. That you remember you love. Very much. And you make a choice. A conscious choice. Every day. To remember. That you fucking love those people. Very much. And you make everything you do. About them. About making them smile. Making them. Happy. Happi*er*.

And it doesn't matter what you do. Or how you do it. You start. To do. Something. To make a difference. Something positive. You make a change. In your life. Slowly. And you begin. To imagine. That there's a future worth living for. Right? Worth living into. With the people you love. With the newness. You're discovering. In yourself. And you do what it takes. Whatever it takes. To live into it.

You decide. And you do not give up. You fucking decide.

And make no mistake. It is the hardest. Thing. In the world. To get. Your. Life. Back.

Silence.

RUSSELL. And then what?

MARTIN. I don't [understand the question].

RUSSELL. Then what?

Pause.

Hey do you think this room needs more light? I don't know.

Do you think I should shave? What brand of tie. Should I wear. I like that: what you have. Should I buy poly-cotton shirts or just plain cotton? What are you wearing? Do I look good in colors? Patterns? You look good in patterns. It's clear you should never wear white socks with black shoes, but what if that's all you have?

Am I as hollow as I feel? You can tell me. You're kind.

Would you hold my hand? If I asked you?

This is our music.

Scene 12.

SAMANTHA *and* NATALIE.

Cigarette.

SAMANTHA. I think I might've found someone.

NATALIE. Yeah?

SAMANTHA. Yeah. Is that okay?

NATALIE. Why wouldn't that be okay.

SAMANTHA. I don't know.

Is it stupid? Like really stupid?

NATALIE. I mean.

SAMANTHA. It is. It is. I knew it. It probably is. Nevermind.

>   *Pause.*

NATALIE. Sammy? This is gonna sound weird? Maybe? Coming from me? I need you to hear it.

SAMANTHA. Okay.

NATALIE. You're not gonna like it.

It's okay to be stupid. Seriously. Like really stupid. It's okay to like things. Love them. Really. It's okay to be really. Really. Really. Passionate. About things. About. Really really. Fucking stupid things. It's okay. To forget. For a little bit. That you're gonna die. It's okay to give yourself permission. To live. In the meantime. And to be happy.

And I say all that. But.

I mean. I know. I know. It sounds. Really. Like. Stupid. And it is. And I don't even believe it. Myself. But. I want to believe it. I can't believe it. But you should.

And I need you to hear it. From me:

I don't have. The right distance to things. Sam.

SAMANTHA. I don't. Um.

NATALIE. I don't have. The right distance. To things. You can't think. I have. The right distance. To anything. I am too. Fucking close. To most things. I'm—it is just. A matter. Of frequencies. Right? I am. Just. A few wavelengths. Away. From everything. And. It is terrifying. And somebody else. Is changing the channels. It's happened before. And I don't know. Who. Or what. Or how. Or.

I'm saying something important.

I don't know how to say it.

>   *Pause.*

You can't hear me.

>   *Pause.*

No. Sam. It's not stupid.

Don't look so confused.

SAMANTHA. Um.

>   *Silence.*

I brought you a cookie. I thought maybe you didn't get cookies here. Or snacks. I can bring you things. Besides cigarettes. If you want.

NATALIE. Did you make it?

SAMANTHA. No?

NATALIE. That is the shittiest looking cookie ever.

That is the stupidest fucking cookie I have ever seen in my life. You definitely made that.

>   *Smiles. Briefly.*

I can't have it.

I can't have cookies: Drugs. Diet. You should have it.

>   SAM *holds the cookie.*

SAMANTHA. I'll give it to the ducks.

NATALIE. Right. You like the ducks.

Which is so fucking stupid I can't even—

But.

Good.

It'll probably kill 'em.

SAMANTHA. Ha.

>   *Pause.*

NATALIE. Don't listen to me. Please. Don't listen to me. Don't ever listen to me.

>   *Silence.*

SAMANTHA. Natalie?

NATALIE. Yeah.

SAMANTHA. Who else should I listen to?

>   *Silence.*

>   Light is fading.

Scene 13.

>   SAM *and* HUDSON.
>   *A parking lot.*
>   *They sit or stand on the curb. And drink Slurpees.*
>   *Silence.*

HUDSON. [I] like your hair.

SAMANTHA. Yeah?

HUDSON. Yeah. [It's] nice.
SAMANTHA. Thanks.
HUDSON. No problem.
    Pause.
SAMANTHA. You have good hair. Too.
HUDSON. Yeah?
SAMANTHA. Mmmm.
Actually no. It's a little. I mean. I honestly think: you should shave it. All of it. Off. You'd look better. You really would. No joke. I could do it for you. If you like.
HUDSON. Alright.
SAMANTHA. Okay. We'll do that.
    Silence. Slurpees.
HUDSON. I don't know what to say to you.
SAMANTHA. What?
HUDSON. I mean. I don't know. What to say. To you.
SAMANTHA. You just. You literally just said the same thing twice.
HUDSON. Yeah. I mean. I wish there was something. I could say. That would be. Like. That would *mean* something. To you. That you'd think was important. I don't know what that is. I mean what do you like? Do you like anything?
SAMANTHA. Yeah. Of course. Yes. I like. Things. Plenty of things.
It's just. What's the point though. Right? Who cares what I like.
HUDSON. I care. I think.
SAMANTHA. Okay. Well. That's nice.
I like this Slurpee.
    Silence.
Everybody says. When you're growing up. Everybody says: life's an adventure. And: life is an adventure. And: enjoy life. Right? Because this is the best part of your life. High school. And then it's college. And then your first job. And then making a home. Maybe. If you're lucky.
But in the end.
    Loud long Slurpee slurp.
    Pause.
Nobody has a clue. What's coming. Nobody.
HUDSON. What's coming.
SAMANTHA. I don't know.
Nothing. Probably. More of the same. Which is worse.
    Silence.

I'm pregnant. That's coming.

HUDSON. Yeah?

SAMANTHA. Maybe. I mean. Who knows.

There's something. In me. I can feel it. With hands. And teeth.

So yeah maybe. Or maybe not I don't know. Probably.

I'd really really like. To be pregnant.

Shut up.

HUDSON. Didn't say anything

SAMANTHA. No but. Still. Just. Shut up.

This is hard. For me.

    Pause.

I feel like I wanna hold your hand. Or something. Is that stupid? That feels sort of stupid.

HUDSON. No.

SAMANTHA. Like. I sort of feel like. I don't know. I really wanna wear your clothes. Is that weird? Tell me if that's weird.

Would you let me? If I asked you?

HUDSON. Maybe.

SAMANTHA. Would you wear mine?

HUDSON. No.

SAMANTHA. Not even. Like. Not even like a really great jacket I have? That would probably fit you? Like really well?

HUDSON. No. Maybe.

    Beat.

SAMANTHA. It's hard being only yourself I think. I think it'd be better to be other people. Sometimes.

HUDSON. You can hold my hand. If you want.

SAMANTHA. Okay.

Only it's weird now. Maybe later.

    Silence. Slurpees.

HUDSON. I could mean a lot. To you. If you'd let me.

I'll cut my hair. I'll wear your clothes. You can take pictures. Post them everywhere. You can humiliate me. I don't care.

I could mean a lot. To you.

    Silence.

SAMANTHA. Um.

    Puts out her hand.

> *Pause.*
> *He takes it.*
> *Silence.*

This can't change. This can't ever change.
> *Silence. Slurpees.*

You ever seen him before?

HUDSON. Who.

SAMANTHA. I don't know. The devil.

HUDSON. No. Why. You want to?
> *Pause.*

SAMANTHA. I imagine he's really boring. I imagine he's just the most boring and awful and just. Predictable. Insufferable. Person. You could ever meet. Just. Really sad. And boring.

HUDSON. Maybe. I don't know.

SAMANTHA. What does your music say?
> *A video of a close-up of a record playing.*
> *Light playing off unknown peaks and valleys of black vinyl.*
> *We hear the following backwards. It's also surtitled.*

>> **BEHEMOTH.** People like to say we're Satanists.

>> **LEVIATHAN.** I don't give a fuck about Satan. What is Satan.

>> **BEHEMOTH.** Or. Better. What isn't Satan?

>> **LEVIATHAN.** What isn't in exile? What isn't outside its original nothingness? Wanting to go back?

>> **BEHEMOTH.** This is our music. To evoke the Outside. To invocate, conjure and command the Outside. To be the voice of the Outside. How do you hear it? You undo hearing. You hear it from the ashes.

>> **LEVIATHAN.** It destroys you. It destroys everything. You hate it. You want it. Your life is over.

>> **BEHEMOTH.** Your life has always been over.

>> **LEVIATHAN.** This is the sound of your life being over.

HUDSON. There is no Satan. Not really.

Just. You know. This.

Which is worse. Probably. Or better. Or not. Or I don't know.

But who cares though. Right? I mean.

Who cares.

When it's all over. Who'll be around to notice.

I mean there's a weird kind of beauty to it, right? A kind of. Pointless sort of.
Beauty. How lost it all is. Maybe that's the devil. Right? The lostness to things?
Maybe everything's the devil.
Maybe it's all pure fucking Armageddon. Everything at war with itself.
I don't know. No use being sad about it, though.
I mean. Fuck it. Literally. Just: fuck it.
If that's the way it is. I mean.
Where else can you belong? What else is yours?
Hail Häxan.
> *Pause.*

SAMANTHA. I wanna shave your head really bad right now.

> The sound of you.

Scene 14.

> *Häxan 13 plays very loudly.*

Black ice dead skies
The swirling dark
That tears apart
Everything
And you.

> SAM *and* HUDSON *stand looking at each other.*

An open void
The master's call
All shadows fall
On everything
And you.

> *They strip quickly and put on each other's clothes.*
> *They stare at each other out of breath.*
> *They kiss each other. Violent. Desperate.*
> *One by one, five or so lights fall around them from the grid.*

Light is fading
Dark unending
Dead-life dawning
And everything
Is you.

> *Häxan 13 plays very loudly.*

> You would see a miracle.

Scene 15.

TREVOR. Hi. Welcome to Bear Burger— Oh.
SAMANTHA. Hey.
TREVOR. You actually want anything. Or.
SAMANTHA. We can't talk?
TREVOR. I'm at work?
SAMANTHA. Yeah.
TREVOR. So I'm at work? I'm working? I'm not socializing? Hey. Yeah. And I meant to say this? The other day? It's fine if you still want to go out and everything? But it's just not an option. So.
SAMANTHA. Oh. Right.
TREVOR. Yeah. For the best.
SAMANTHA. Probably.
TREVOR. You still pregnant?
SAMANTHA. Yes.
TREVOR. Right. Good for you. Whatever. What's wrong with your face?
SAMANTHA. Nothing.
TREVOR. Are you sure? It's fucked up.
SAMANTHA. You're so fucking stupid.
TREVOR. Okay. Wait. What's wrong.
SAMANTHA. What.
TREVOR. You seem. Like. I don't know if I've ever seen you. Actually. I mean. Are you happy? Is this you happy?
SAMANTHA. --
TREVOR. It looks weird. What happened.
SAMANTHA. I'm dating someone.
TREVOR. Oh. Right. Good. What's he like?
SAMANTHA. Strong. Stronger. Than you. Definitely.
TREVOR. Got it. Okay. So this is. What. This is. Like. Am I supposed to be jealous? He's a fucking idiot. Whoever he is.

SAMANTHA. He's not an idiot.

TREVOR. He's definitely an idiot. He's fucking stupid.

SAMANTHA. I told him all about you.

TREVOR. Yeah?

SAMANTHA. The way you treated me?

TREVOR. How did I treat you.

SAMANTHA. Doesn't matter.

TREVOR. *Well.* That's how. I treated you *well.*

SAMANTHA. Fuck *well.* Doesn't matter.

You afraid? You feeling a little afraid? Nervous?

TREVOR. No.

This is like. So childish, right? This is way childish. What're you doing. What do you think you're doing.

SAMANTHA. Nothing. Just. I've come for my last check. I quit. A bit ago. Yeah. I mean. Between you. And the job. And the fucking. Boring. Fucking. Job. I was like. Nauseated. All the time. Every day. The stench of this place. And the sound of you. Going on and on. Singing or whatever. Did you know: most tone deaf people don't know they're tone deaf? Yeah. It's true. Fact. Scientific. Everything. You should look into it. How're the auditions?

TREVOR. I'm working on them.

SAMANTHA. Right. Good. You work hard. Work real hard. You don't wanna let that opportunity pass you by. You don't wanna watch that dream fade away. Right?

TREVOR. It's not bad to have dreams, Sam.

SAMANTHA. Dreams. Delusions. Whatever. It doesn't matter.

But you don't care, right? You're happy. Look at you. You're at work. You're working. At Bear Burger Barn. You've got a bear in your future. Good for you.

You know what I miss most? Here? It's really weird. Don't laugh: the bleach smell. Of the bathroom. I always thought. It was. Comforting. Somehow. Standing there. Knowing. I was literally. The only living thing. In that room. Is that weird?

If the future smells like anything. It smells like bleach.

You're right: I'm so happy. I can't even say. Something's finally happening. I feel like I can breathe.

I'm your friend.

Scene 16.

RUSSELL. I feel like. It's just. Sort of. Falling apart. Yeah? I mean. There's the normal stuff. Right? There's the hair. It's. Um. It's. Thinning. Um. Which is weird. Because. No one. In my family. No one. Really. The men. No one loses hair. Ever. Not that I noticed. Growing up. But. Still. Thinning. That's normal. Eyesight. Fading. Um. The fading. Vision. That's all. That's. You know that's fine. It's. I expected that. And the hearing. Slowly. I mean. I listen. To sounds. Right? I can hear things. But. I've noticed. The TV. Is up. A lot louder. These days. Recently. Lately.
But all of that. All of that is. Um. Is fine. That's just. That's. Aging. Right?
I was drinking coffee. Yeah? And I looked. And. It was wrong. The coffee. Was. Tasting. Awful. Because my nose. Just. Pouring. Blood. Right? Into my coffee. And that.
I lost a tooth. The other day. A few. Teeth. The other day. And it wasn't. I mean. I was just brushing regularly. Soft bristle toothbrush. And. And.
My bones. Feel more brittle. I can't explain that. But. They do. And my. Um. I can't. There are no. Erections. Anymore. Which is. But I bleed. Also. I mean the urine. Is. Just: colors you don't expect. Or want. Millions of colors. And that's. So that's. What I'm dealing with. Right now. I feel. Just.
Apart.
If you ran some tests. If you could run some tests. If you could see me. Examine me. If you took my pulse. If you could. Listen. To my heart. It would be. You would know. You would know. You would see. That there is something. Wrong. I really feel you'd see.
And when you did. And when you did? I think you would you would. You'd put your arm around me. Is what you'd do. My shoulders. That are getting. So thin. I'm losing weight. And you'd comfort me. You would comfort me. And you would hold me. And you would warm me. And you'd whisper to me. It's okay. It's okay. Shhh. Shhh. It's okay. Everything's gonna be okay. There's no need to be afraid. Everything's actually very. Fine.
And I guarantee you. You would see a miracle. You would see. In me. A miracle. I could be your miracle.

      I can't taste it.

Scene 17.

    HUDSON *and* TREVOR.
    At Bear Burger Barn.
    HUDSON *is hiding something like a billy club or nightstick.*

TREVOR. Hi, welcome to Bear Burger Barn.
HUDSON. Bear Burger Barn. Yeah.
TREVOR. Can I help you?
HUDSON. Oh. Yeah. I hope so. Definitely.
I fucking love your commercials by the way. With the bears? Dancing? The picnic? The disco picnic?
TREVOR. Yeah. It's really cute.
HUDSON. No not cute. Not cute. Skilled. Amazing. How do they do it?
TREVOR. I'm sorry?
HUDSON. The bears Who trains them. Does someone train them?
TREVOR. No. No. It's. It's a commercial.
HUDSON. Right.
TREVOR. No one trains the bears. They're people. In bear suits.
HUDSON. Right. Right.
TREVOR. It's kinda clear.
HUDSON. Makes sense.
Do you think I'm fucking stupid?
TREVOR. I'm sorry?
HUDSON. Of course they're fucking people in fucking bear suits. It's fucking obvious. Do I look stupid?
TREVOR. No.
HUDSON. Then why'd you fucking call me stupid.
TREVOR. I'm I'm sorry. I didn't.
HUDSON. So now I'm a liar.
TREVOR. Um.
HUDSON. Why the fuck would you think that.
TREVOR. I'm sorry. I'm really. It's really late. And. You know.
HUDSON. Right. It is. Late.
   Beat.
Ha. Ha ha.
I'm totally just messing with you.
TREVOR. Right.
HUDSON. It's okay. I'm your friend.
TREVOR. Good.
HUDSON. Yeah.
I definitely wanna order something from you.
TREVOR. Okay.

HUDSON. Like your soul.

Ha. Kidding.

Hey you ever worn the suit? The bear suit?

TREVOR. No.

HUDSON. Come on. I'll bet it's lots of fun.

TREVOR. Maybe.

HUDSON. You wear it out? Like for a night on the town?

TREVOR. Ha.

HUDSON. Tooling around in your bear suit. Scaring the kids. Right? "Look there's a bear! Aaack!" But it's. No. It's only. It's just. It's: you.

Is it here? You have it here? Could you put it on.

TREVOR. There's no bear suit here.

HUDSON. You're joking.

TREVOR. No.

HUDSON. Does it have claws? The suit? Like working claws? Like: Rawr. That'd be amazing.

You don't have much upper body strength though. Do you.

TREVOR. Um.

HUDSON. Bears. Have lots. Of upper body strength. For the: swiping.

You'd make a pretty shitty bear.

TREVOR. Probably.

HUDSON. Right? I *will* order something. I'm very hungry. Hungry for a Bear Burger. Right?

TREVOR. Can I tell you about our specials?

HUDSON. No. I mean. Sure. Only: why? Right?

Don't be nervous.

Relax. Smile. Nice.

Why don't you find the bear suit.

TREVOR. Maybe actually, you know, maybe I should get the manager.

HUDSON. Oh yeah definitely. Definitely get the manager. I mean: does he have the suit? If he does, come on: that's a no brainer: get the manager.

I'll wait.

TREVOR. Do I know you?

HUDSON. Know you. I fucking *am* you.

TREVOR. What?

   MARTIN *enters.*

MARTIN. Everything all right?

HUDSON. Definitely definitely. Yeah. You the manager?

MARTIN. Yes. Can I help you.

HUDSON. I hope so. I really do hope so. I was hoping for a Bear Burger. A Bear Burger Deluxe. No mayo. Extra pickles. But your friend here. Is really reluctant to get it for me.

TREVOR. That is not.

HUDSON. Called me stupid. He called me stupid.

TREVOR. I did not.

HUDSON. (*To* TREVOR.) I am not. Fucking. Stupid. Alright? Get that crystal *fucking* clear. Alright?

(*To* MARTIN.) And then he went off on these weird fantasies of his. Where he's dressed in a bear suit (a fucking bear suit right!) and scaring the kiddies. Now you wouldn't happen to have a bear suit here would you? Because if you do. Keep an eye out. A *watchful* eye. Out. On this one.

MARTIN. Sir, I'm gonna have to ask you to leave.

HUDSON. I'm gonna have to ask you to fuck off. Right? Like. Deliberately. Fuck off. This one's mine. I take him. You give him to me. Don't get involved.

TREVOR. What?

HUDSON. Seriously.

MARTIN. I'm calling the police.

HUDSON. You are so fucking boring.

> HUDSON *reveals his weapon. Quickly hits* MARTIN *with it. Then* TREVOR. *Jumps behind the counter and beats the shit out of them both.*
> *Silence.*
> *Häxan 13 plays very loudly. Stops suddenly. Stutters. Stops.*
> *Silence.*

Learn to suffer.

Scene 18.

> HUDSON *and* SAMANTHA.
> *In a car. Parking lot.*
> HUDSON *enters with a bag of burgers.*

HUDSON. Got some burgers.

SAMANTHA. Thanks

You're bloody.

HUDSON. Right. Yeah. Um.

None of them have mayo, by the way. I don't like mayo.

SAMANTHA. No. Me neither.

> *She stares at him.*
>
> *Pause.*

HUDSON. Yeah I feel. Really weird. Right now. Um. I shouldn't eat.

> *Suddenly starts eating.*

I'm probably gonna be really sick. Soon. So.

I'm probably gonna vomit. Like immense amounts. Of vomit.

> *Continues eating.*
>
> *Silence. Eating.*
>
> *He cries.*

I can't taste it. I can't taste it. I can't even—

> *He cries.*
>
> *Continues to eat.*
>
> *Eat and cry.*
>
> SAMANTHA *stares.*
>
> HUDSON *cries.*
>
> *Hits his head on the steering wheel. Honks the horn as he does. He does this for a long time.*
>
> *Stops.*
>
> *Wipes his face.*
>
> *Eats.*
>
> *Turns to* SAMANTHA.

HUDSON. You okay?

SAMANTHA. Yes. Thank you.

I don't know why. But.

I'm really very happy. Right now. Just right now. And. Completely. Terrified. And I'm afraid it might not last very long. But right now—

Thank you. Thank you.

HUDSON. I think I'm dying.

Ha.

> *He opens the car door and vomits.*

Morning sickness.

> *Smiles.*

A very sad dance.

Scene 19.

> SAMANTHA *and* NATALIE.
> *Duck pond.*
> NATALIE *smoking.*
> *Pause.*

SAMANTHA. I'm pregnant.

NATALIE. Oh yeah?

SAMANTHA. Yeah.

> NATALIE *blows smoke away from her.*

NATALIE. Congratulations. What's that like.

SAMANTHA. Solid. It feels solid. For once.

NATALIE. Really. That's a neat trick.

SAMANTHA. I'm naming her Natalie. After you.

> *Pause.*

NATALIE. I'd say that's nice. But. It's kinda stupid.

SAMANTHA. It's not stupid. I'm not stupid.

NATALIE. Kinda though.

> *Pause.*

You should get rid of it.

SAMANTHA. --

NATALIE. Seriously.

You will be. The worst. Mother. Ever. Trust me. [You'd] be doing it a favor.

> *Silence.*

But you're not really pregnant though. Are you.

> *Pause.*

I mean look at you. You're so fucking hollow.

Just because you're aching to be full doesn't mean you are, Sam. Just because you *want* to be solid doesn't mean you're not still a ghost.

SAMANTHA. I'm not a ghost.

NATALIE. No right. Sure.

> *Pause.*

SAMANTHA. Will you ever. Say something nice. To me?

NATALIE. If I have to.

> *Silence.*

SAMANTHA. I think I might've done something. Something probably awful.

NATALIE. Okay.

SAMANTHA. I think some people may be hurt. Or maybe even— I don't know. Worse. Because of me.

I think if people talk to you? About it? I think you should probably just. Pretend. You don't know me.

Which shouldn't be hard. I mean. You don't. Know me. Not really.

I wish you did.

I mean: kind of.

I wish you knew the me I feel like I'm becoming.

NATALIE. Fair.

I'm your sister, though. I can't pretend I don't know you. Or some version of you. This version of you.

Cigarette.

Whatever you're becoming. What's it like.

SAMANTHA. Strong. Stronger. Less afraid.

NATALIE. Hmm. Not really you, then, is it.

SAMANTHA. --

NATALIE. You sad about it? This awful thing?

SAMANTHA. No.

Somehow: everything's brighter. Now. More vivid. Millions of colors.

I feel like I could do anything.

NATALIE. You can't.

You know that, though. Right?

SAMANTHA. --

NATALIE. Right.

And that brightness. Sam: there is nothing bright about that brightness. Believe me.

I mean. Or not. You don't have to. You're a big girl. You'll find out.

It doesn't make me happy. Sam. To constantly shit on you. I'm doing my best. This is the most. Loving. I can be. To you. I'm really sorry.

And I know: it's not what you want. It's not what I want. And you're gonna find this hard to hear. But. You know what? I don't care.

I'm trying to get healthy. *Stay* healthy. Sam, I don't need the world more vivid. I don't want more brightness in my life. I've had it. It's amazing. It's horrible. I don't want it.

I know what's out there. I know what's coming. Insofar as it can. Come. And I know how badly you want it. But you don't get to choose the disaster. And it's best not to want to.

It doesn't get better.

You need to go home. And never come back.

Cigarette.

SAMANTHA. Natalie?

NATALIE. Hmm.

SAMANTHA. I hope one day you get out of here. I hope one day they let you go. And I hope. On that day. I hope. You're terrified. And afraid. And alone. And don't know what to do. And I hope you come looking for me. Because you think I might want to help you. Or be nice to you. Or love you. Or something. And I hope you find me. And I hope I see you, walking up the walkway to my house. To my door. And I hope. The moment you ring that doorbell. I hope I can murder. I hope I can drown or suffocate or decimate or completely destroy. Whatever it is in me. That might want to let you in. And give you shelter. And let you be loved.

Pause.

NATALIE. Huh.

If we live that long.

Anyway, it's been nice knowing you.

I mean I say that. But.

Learn to suffer, Sam. You'll be a lot happier when you do.

Hail Häxan.

Scene 20.

A circle of sad trees.
TREVOR and MARTIN in bear costumes dance a very sad dance.
There's a rumbling sound that fades away.

The world has to end sometime.

Scene 21.

SAM *and* HUDSON.
A parking lot. They sit on the curb. Drinking Slurpees.
Loud long Slurpee slurps.
Nothing at all happens
Slurp.
Nothing happens for a very long time.

Slurp.

SAM *looks at* HUDSON.

SAMANTHA. She'd've been called Natalie. Definitely.

She'd've been beautiful. Like actually beautiful.

She'd've grown up. Loving rainbows. And princesses. And ballerinas. And glitter. And cookies. And sunshine. And Saturday morning cartoons. And flowers. And baby animals. And all the stupid shit that doesn't matter. And it would've mattered. It actually would've. For a little bit. At any rate. Because she loved it.

She'd've believed in magic.

She'd've had a future. Not because I said so or anyone else said so. But because. For her. It'd actually be there. It'd be waiting. For her. Especially for her.

And she would never die. She would never ever die. Ever.

She'd've been the perfect disaster.

She'd've been completely impossible.

She'd've been me. Only more real. The real me.

SAM *cries. Softly at first. Drops her Slurpee. Head in her hands.*

HUDSON *stares at her.*

It's never coming. Is it. It's never actually coming.

HUDSON *shrugs.*

HUDSON. I don't know.

Maybe the police'll come. That'd be fucked up.

That'd be great. Actually.

Maybe bad things just happen. And maybe one day you figure out: you're the bad thing. That keeps happening.

Who knows.

Hail Häxan.

Slurp.

It's coming.

Scene 22.

RUSSELL *and* SAMANTHA.

RUSSELL *on the couch, watching TV.*

Silence.

SAMANTHA *slowly sits on the couch with* RUSSELL.

Silence.

RUSSELL *turns to look at her.*

> *Pause.*
>
> SAMANTHA *slowly takes out of a pocket a bloody Bear Burger. Tentatively offers it to her father.*
>
> RUSSELL *takes it. Looks at it. Begins to devour it.*
>
> SAMANTHA *watches him for a time. Then.*

SAMANTHA. I wish I could love you. I wish somewhere there were room. For that.

But.

How do you love something. That insists. On dying. Endlessly. Dying. That keeps. Dying. But never. Actually. Ends. It's infuriating.

There's nothing I can be that won't feature you. Falling apart in the background. No future without the stale smell of you.

It's impossible to be young with you. And your world. And your illness. And your plague. And your miasma of filth.

There's no life, no living at the edge of the cliff. But maybe, in the falling, in the falling at last. There's something, some spark of something. Some precious doom to blaze towards. Some Outside. Some reversal. That may finally look. Like life.

I have been pregnant with disaster for as long as I can remember. With miscarriage after miscarriage. It can't just go on. The world has to end sometime.

I invoke, conjure and command.

I invoke, conjure and command.

I invoke, conjure and command you, unborn unliving impossible daughter of disaster, to appear and show yourself visibly to me before this circle in fair and comely shape without any deformity or tortuosity. I conjure you that forthwith you come visibly, peaceable and affable, now without delay to manifest what I desire, speaking with a clear and perfect voice, intelligible to my understanding. Come. Come. Come.

> *Pause. Then:*
>
> *All the lights in the grid fall loudly. The doors of the theater are somehow blown open, and light (again, somehow) explosively floods the space from everywhere.*
>
> *For a time.*
>
> *Until: the light fades. Perhaps the houselights flicker on/off in the wake of the fade. Something in the space is profoundly broken.*
>
> *Pause.*
>
> RUSSELL *changes the channel.*
>
> *The other cast members assemble.*
>
> *Pick up instruments.*

They are Häxan 13.

They play a devastatingly loud song. It feels desperate. Broken.

RUSSELL *slowly dances the sad bear dance by himself as the lights fade to nothing and the houselights flicker dark or stabilize, who can tell.*

Unwelcome
The swarming abyss
The dilated dark
    Coming to be
    Coming to be
Unhomed
Shattered horizons
Where light is dying
    Coming to be
    Coming to be
Unloved
The glistening void
Between the stars
    Coming to be
    Coming to be
    See it rising

    Break
    Fall
    Burn
    Bliss
    Break
    Fall
    Burn
    Bliss
    Break
    Fall
    Burn
    Bliss
    Breathe
    At last
    At last
    Again

Zap. You're pregnant. That's witchcraft.

End

we, the invisibles
by Susan Soon He Stanton

Copyright © 2018 by Susan Soon He Stanton. All rights reserved. CAUTION: Professionals and amateurs are hereby warned that *we, the invisibles* is subject to a royalty. It is fully protected under the copyright laws of the United States of America and of all countries covered by the International Copyright Union (including the Dominion of Canada and the rest of the British Commonwealth), the Berne Convention, the Pan-American Copyright Convention and the Universal Copyright Convention, as well as all countries with which the United States has reciprocal copyright relations. All rights, including professional, amateur stage rights, motion picture, recitation, lecturing, public reading, radio broadcasting, television, video or sound recording, all other forms of mechanical or electronic reproduction, such as CD-ROM, CD-I, information storage and retrieval systems and photocopying, and the rights of translation into foreign languages, are strictly reserved. Particular emphasis is laid upon the matter of readings, permission for which must be secured from the Author's agent in writing.

Required royalties must be paid every time this play is performed before any audience, whether or not it is presented for profit and whether or not admission is charged.

All inquiries concerning rights, including amateur rights, should be addressed to: The Gersh Agency, 41 Madison Avenue, 33rd Floor, New York, NY 10010. ATTN: Leah Hamos, 212-634-8153, lhamos@gersh.com.

ABOUT *we, the invisibles*

> *This article first ran in the* Limelight Guide to the 42nd Humana Festival of New American Plays, *published by Actors Theatre of Louisville, and is based on conversations with the playwright before rehearsals for the Humana Festival production began.*

A young woman steps out onto an empty stage and shyly introduces herself. *"Hi everyone. My name is Susan. I'm a playwright?"* Susan proceeds to tell us how she stumbled into a survival job at a swanky boutique hotel called The Lux, and that she was working there when news broke that the leading candidate for the French presidency, Dominique Strauss-Kahn, was accused of sexual assault by an immigrant hotel maid named Nafissatou Diallo. The scandal deeply troubled Susan, and she was sickened by the thought of similar abuse happening to her fellow employees at The Lux. And so, Susan tells us, she resolved to write a play—not about Strauss-Kahn, but about the fascinating, complex people working alongside her in unseen service positions.

Susan Soon He Stanton's funny, poignant, and brutally honest new play, *we, the invisibles*, is a celebration of her real-life coworkers, whom she got to know over the course of ten years working in a New York City hotel. "It feels really cathartic to share that part of my life," says Stanton. "To amplify the stories of these people who I think are amazing and funny and interesting—it's been like a weight has been lifted. I feel a lot of joy in sharing this world with people." The play begins with Susan introducing us to some of her colleagues through a series of interviews. A small ensemble of actors (who collectively portray upwards of 60 characters) re-enact conversations that Stanton had with her fellow employees as part of her research process for writing the play. We meet dishwashers and room attendants, security guards and cocktail servers, many of them having newly arrived in the United States. "I've been thinking a lot about what it means to be an immigrant in the United States and work really hard at a job that's *designed* for you to never be seen," reflects the playwright. "No one thinks about the back of the hotel, or the back of the restaurant. When you do your job well, nobody notices you at all." In a sharp rebuttal of that reality, *we, the invisibles* illuminates who these people are beyond their occupations—the kinds of food they love, their quirky personality traits, their desires for the future, and what they have overcome to relocate to this country.

As the play gives voice to these rarely heard stories, Susan's documentary project transforms into a deeply personal journey—after all, Stanton has written herself into her own play. According to Stanton, this artistic gesture happened somewhat organically: "I started by interviewing coworkers with a tape recorder or my iPhone, and then transcribing them into scenes. And at some point I started to take myself out of the scenes," she recalls. But when a fellow writer encouraged her to reconsider, she thought, "Well, this is going to be a much more personal approach So I leaned into that discomfort and said: okay, I'm going to name my character Susan and that's that." What emerges from that choice is a remarkably honest look at a playwright grappling with her role as the storyteller. Much of *we, the invisibles* is built from verbatim transcripts or from Stanton's memory—but as Susan candidly tells us in the play, sometimes they are pure invention. Why? Her notes are spotty. Or people declined to be interviewed, and she can only make assumptions about why. Or sometimes, she doesn't speak the language of the person she'd like to know better. Has she captured these people authentically? How much does she truly understand about their struggles and successes? How much does she understand about her own?

The breadth of Stanton's inquiry expands as the play moves forward, exploring an ever-accumulating pile of questions with startling theatricality. As we watch the small group of actors slip in and out of multiple roles, the space, too, transforms—whisking us from The Lux's glossy, opulent lounges and lobbies to its intimate, even claustrophobic back-of-house areas. "What's exciting about it to me is that there are so many characters, there are so many stories—it's an ambitious play for me in terms of its expanse," enthuses Stanton. "It's larger in scope and more deeply personal than anything I've ever written."

—Jenni Page-White

BIOGRAPHY

Susan Soon He Stanton's plays include *Today Is My Birthday* (Page 73), *Takarazuka!!!* (Clubbed Thumb and East West Players), *Cygnus* (WP Theater Lab), *Solstice Party!* (Live Source Theatre Group), and *The Things Are Against Us* (Washington Ensemble Theatre). She is a two-time Sundance Theatre Lab Resident Playwright, and she was awarded the inaugural Venturous Playwright Fellowship at The Lark, as well as the Leah Ryan Prize. Her work has been included on The Kilroys List from 2015–2017, and she is currently under commission at Yale Repertory Theatre, South Coast Repertory, and Ensemble Studio Theatre. Writing groups past and present include Page 73's Interstate 73, The Public Theater's Emerging Writers Group, and Soho Rep Writer/Director Lab, among others. She writes for *Succession* (HBO). She received an MFA in playwriting from Yale School of Drama and a BFA from New York University.

ACKNOWLEDGMENTS

we, the invisibles premiered at the Humana Festival of New American Plays in March 2018. It was directed by Dámaso Rodríguez with the following cast:

AIDA, AND OTHERS	Tricia Alexandro
JANY, AND OTHERS	William DeMeritt
NAFISSATOU DIALLO, AND OTHERS	Rebecca S'Manga Frank
NAMGAL, AND OTHERS	Emily Kuroda
JANSEN, AND OTHERS	Kurt Kwan
RICH, AND OTHERS	Luis Moreno
SUSAN	Rinabeth Apostol

and the following production staff:

Scenic Designer	William Boles
Costume Designer	Kara Harmon
Lighting Designer	Gina Scherr
Sound Designer	Jake Rodriguez
Media created by	Philip Allgeier
Stage Manager	Janette L. Hubert
Dramaturg	Jenni Page-White
Casting	Erica Jensen, Calleri Casting
Dialect Coach	D'Arcy Smith
Properties Master	Katelin Ashcraft
Production Assistant	Codey Leroy Butler
Directing Assistant	Joan Sergay
Assistant Dramaturg	Meghan McLeroy

DEVELOPMENT

This play was developed with The Civilians' R&D Group 2016, and workshopped at American Conservatory Theater in San Francisco and the Studio Tisch New Play Initiative at New York University Graduate Acting in 2016. *we, the invisibles* was part of the PlayLabs Festival at the Playwrights' Center. *we, the invisibles* was the 2017 winner of the Leah Ryans Fund for Emerging Women Writers Prize and was named to the 2017 Kilroys List.

DRAMATIS PERSONAE

The play can be performed by as few as six actors. Below are possible doublings for a cast of seven. When a character appears, their [number] will appear next to their name. Although some roles are not specified by race, ideally, this cast should be as diverse as possible.

1

Jansen – Catering Server from Hawai'i
Dennis – Chinese Housekeeping Manager
Assistant
Sofitel Security Guard
Jason – Chinese Sous Chef
DSK Defense Lawyer 1
Rizal – Drag Queen/Food Runner
DCPI
Diwata – Housekeeper

2

Aida – Uniform Room Attendant from Kosovo
Prostitute
Kara – Cocktail Waitress and Model from Vermont
Sofitel Front Desk
Sasha
Allison – Front Desk
Novagen Rep
Trish – Works at Merrill Lynch
Tristane Banon
Nadine – Housekeeper
Kate – British Reporter

3

Angry Diner
Rich – Catering Server
DSK – Dominque Strauss-Kahn
Tipsy Douche
Dog Food Man
Jewish Mystic
Fernando – Colombian Ex-Lawyer
Spencer – Wealthy White Man
Peter – Famous Playwright/Director
28/38-Year-Old Man – British

4

Balfour – Dishwasher from Ghana
Jany [pronounced Hanee] – Dominican Security Guard
D-List Celebrity
Muhammad – Bengali Busser
Sofitel Head of Security
Dairy Delivery Guy
DSK Defense Lawyer 2
Adjo – Norwegian-Liberian Bartender
Detective Halk
District Attorney
Reporter

5

Nafissatou Diallo
Hotel Guest
Dog Food Man's Woman
Patty – Puerto Rican Chef
Vinny – Engineer from the Bronx
Sofitel Housekeeper 2
Joan
Dreshawn – Bellman
Package Man
April – Works at Merrill Lynch
Abdur – Bengali Busser
FOIL – Freedom of Information Law

6

Evelyn – Manager at the Hotel
Namgal – Nepalese Uniform Attendant
Mark – Executive Chef
Tenzin – Nepalese Security Guard
Sofitel Housekeeper 1
Alvin – Catering Dude from Hawai'i
Jen – Vietnamese, Works in HR
Mystic's Wife
Tiffany – Works at Merrill Lynch
Shati – Tibetan Housekeeping Prospective Hire
Piroska Nagy
Tanya – Housekeeper

7

Susan

SYNOPSIS

In 2011, the director of the International Monetary Fund was accused of sexual assault by a hotel maid, Nafissatou Diallo, but all charges were dismissed. *we, the invisibles* introduces hotel workers like Diallo who have come to New York from all over the globe. This play is an investigation of the complicated relationship between the movers and shakers and the people who change their sheets.

When elephants fight, it is the grass that suffers.
—Kikuyu Proverb, Kenya.

I think I must have a form of sexuality which is rougher than the average. I am beginning to realize that and I deplore it. But I had no idea at the time that these experiences were so unpleasant as the women now say.
—Dominique Strauss-Kahn, 2015.

Kurt Kwan, William DeMeritt, and Rinabeth Apostol
in *we, the invisibles*

42nd Humana Festival of New American Plays
Actors Theatre of Louisville, 2018
Photo by Bill Brymer

we, the invisibles

ACT I

1. The Beginning

SUSAN *enters*.

SUSAN [7]. Hi everyone. My name is Susan. I'm a playwright?

It's kinda too early to be getting into all of this with you but in August 2004, my mother was in a catastrophic car accident. I went home to care for her, but because I took so much time off work, I got fired from my publishing job.

In the same month, I temporarily went blind in one eye, my grandfather died, and I ended a seven-year relationship with my childhood sweetheart.

The accumulation of all of these traumas triggered an incurable autoimmune disease, although it took several years of medical testing to figure that out. I was broke and uh…broken.

Then my most beautiful and glamorous friend told me about a hostess position opening up at a restaurant-club inside The Hotel Lux, a high-end boutique hotel.

My friend set up a trail for me with the manager, Evelyn. A trail is where you work an eight-hour shift, unpaid, to see if you can cut it.

It's an extended job interview, on your feet.

EVELYN [6]. You didn't get the job. You don't have the right look—

SUSAN. —By that, she meant figure—

EVELYN. —And, you're not fashionable—

SUSAN. —By that, she meant—

EVELYN. Hon. You're wearing flats and a dress from The Gap. But it's more than how you look. This is the Service Industry.

You must be personable, assertive, and likable.

SUSAN. I'm not…any of those things?

(EVELYN *shrugs*.)

I really need the work. I'll do anything.

—Evelyn said I could answer the phones. I was 22. Then one day the beautiful-stylish-personable-assertive-likable hostess didn't show up.

EVELYN. Carla's no call, no show. You're on the floor.

SUSAN. Oh shit.

—Evelyn taught me—

EVELYN. When someone asks for directions, never, ever point. It's vulgar and aggressive. You gesture. Like this. With your whole arm.

    (EVELYN *gracefully gestures with her arm.*)

SUSAN. I can't point anymore. I haven't pointed in over a decade. Welcome to the (*Name of Theatre*).

In case of fire, the Emergency Exit is that way.

    (SUSAN *gracefully gestures with her arm.*)

EVELYN. There are only two things that make restaurants successful. Music and light.

SUSAN. Not food?

EVELYN. Meh. The profit's in the beverages. You got to get them to stay and drink.

SUSAN. Then I got promoted to maître d', which was controversial at the time because all of the past maître d's had been tall, socialite models or gay, extroverted European men. Then I became a manager.

ANGRY DINER [3]. I want to speak with the manager.

SUSAN. Crap. That's me—Solving problems in the hotel is called "Service Recovery." Usually, it involves sending over free drinks or some apps.

Then I got into grad school, so I left. They threw me a big party. Everyone was so happy for me. It felt like the end of *Pretty Woman* or maybe *Casablanca,* where only the good can leave.

There was a pervading sense of—

AIDA [2]. You got out.

BALFOUR [4]. Good for you.

RICH [3]. Thank god, you got out. You're out of F&B.

SUSAN. F&B means Food and Beverage.

JANSEN [1]. Send us a postcard.

EVELYN. Congrats, kid. Always knew you had it in you.

    (*A shift.*)

SUSAN. Evelyn died three years ago. One day, I saw her crying at the podium.

EVELYN. Sorry, kid. Got some bad news about my health.

SUSAN. That's all she ever said. It was her heart.

She worked her usual six-day week and died on her day off.

A few years later, when I returned to the city, degree in hand, no job, and defaulting student loans, I—

AIDA. Hey! You're back.

BALFOUR. *Mon Sou.* Nice to see you, again.
JANSEN. There she is!
RICH. Didn't you go away for awhile?
SUSAN. I'm not 22. I'm in my mid 30s. Every time I go to work, I feel like a failure. An old failure. In my employee ID photo, I can see the baby fat in my cheeks and never in my wildest imagination did I think I'd be stuck working here for longer than six months.

(NAFISSATOU DIALLO [5] *appears.*)

I first read about it on the subway ride to work. You probably heard the story, or at least remember seeing the photos in the *New York Post* about Dominique Strauss-Kahn in handcuffs, doing the "perp walk."

Here's the gist.

[1]. Dominique Strauss-Kahn, the head of the International Monetary Fund, and the leading candidate for the French Presidency was charged with sexual assault and attempted rape by a hotel maid, Nafissatou Diallo, in a six-minute encounter.

[2]. The seven charges of attempted rape, sexual abuse, and unlawful imprisonment were dismissed.

SUSAN. What? What about all of the physical evidence?

The DNA—

[6]. Although a DNA test of the semen on Diallo's shirt matched Strauss-Kahn's, the physical evidence was deemed inconclusive.

SUSAN. What the hell could be inconclusive about it?

[4]. The charges against DSK were dropped due to Diallo's questionable credibility.

[2]. But he stepped down from the IMF, his wife divorced him, and his chances of a French presidency are in tatters.

SUSAN. This is such bullshit.

He needs to be held accountable for his actions.

(DSK [3] *appears. He speaks to a male CNN reporter.*)

DSK [3]. You wish to talk about accountability? I was—

SUSAN. No. Nope.

We're here to talk about what happened to Nafissatou Diallo.

Her accounts about her immigration to America are inconsistent,

but does that make her any less of a victim?

[6]. After Diallo sued DSK in a civil suit, he counter-sued, and they eventually reached a settlement, where he paid an undisclosed sum for her silence.

(SUSAN *approaches* NAFISSATOU.)

SUSAN. How much money is enough for her to look at herself in the mirror and feel okay?

[4]. Is this self-professed *"libertine"* a rapist who walked free?

[2]. We will never know what really happened at the Sofitel in Room 2806.

ENSEMBLE. (*Staggered.*) We will never know what happened.

DSK. (*To* SUSAN.) You'll never know.

SUSAN. I try to track down Nafissatou Diallo.

But after all that's happened to her, all she wants is to be out of the spotlight. And after all of my attempts, she's nowhere to be found.

(NAFISSATOU *exits.*)

Meanwhile, back at The Lux, I can't stop thinking about the women in the housekeeping department. The thought of anything that despicable happening to them makes me feel ill.

So I begin interviewing coworkers at the hotel and learning their stories. People whose journeys remind me of Nafissatou's.

I start crafting scenes.

Some from interviews, some from memories, some inventions.

DSK is so offensive, I don't want to see him, think about him, or hear him.

So, I decide this play I'm writing about DSK?

He's not in it.

DSK. Yes, but actually I came here to the (*Name of Theatre*), to say one thing.

SUSAN. So this play I'm writing about Dominique Strauss-Kahn?

He is not in it.

He's not in it.

(*A standoff with* DSK.)

DSK. Pff. You think I like to be here?

SUSAN. We don't need to hear from men like you, anymore.

(SUSAN *sends* DSK *away.*)

And so…I discover, rather than focus on DSK's fall from grace, or rather, fall from power, I want to give a voice to the people I've worked alongside.

People who aren't powerful.

People who, if they do their jobs correctly, are never seen at all.

(*The* ENSEMBLE, *the members of The Lux, stand with* SUSAN.)

I'm not sure I've done that.

But here's what I've got so far.

2. Uniform Room

SUSAN. Hi Namgal. You still okay to do this?
NAMGAL [6]. This is for school?
SUSAN. A play.
NAMGAL. Oh, okay.
SUSAN. Namgal is a uniform attendant in the Housekeeping Department. She's in her late 60s. She's so tiny that when she hugs me, she doesn't hug my waist but just kind of hugs my butt.

>(NAMGAL, *a Tibetan housekeeper, late 60s, irons uniforms in the Uniform Room.* SUSAN *records with her cell phone.*)

NAMGAL. My name is Namgal. I am uniform attendant. You are recording me?
SUSAN. Is that okay, Namgal? I'm a slow writer.

>(DENNIS [1] *appears.* SUSAN *hides the phone and notepad.* NAMGAL *stiffens.*)

DENNIS [1]. Namgal. Fernando is still looking for his pants.
NAMGAL. Big one right? Okay. I find. Thank you, Dennis
DENNIS. Oh. Hi. Did you need help?

>(SUSAN *shakes her head. A moment.* DENNIS *leaves.*)

SUSAN. —That was Dennis, the Head of Housekeeping. It's best to avoid him completely.
NAMGAL. Okey. We do this quick, okey? Originally, I from Tibet. But then I living in Nepal. Lots of mountains. Is very cold. When snow comes, sometimes two months we don't get out from house. It's very cold. We don't have any shovels.
SUSAN. Why don't you have shovels?
NAMGAL. We don't have it. We don't have shovels. We don't have. Tibet so poor. We don't have any shovel or snow salts. We don't have it. We stay home for months and my mama cooks. Mostly we eat some kind of Tibetan flour. It's called Tsampa. And old milk.
SUSAN. Old milk??
NAMGAL. We have yak.
SUSAN. Do you miss yak meat?
NAMGAL. Oh yeah. It good. No can get in New York. Cannot find it. When I was seven, I walking from Tibet to Nepal. I don't know how long we walked. Was very cold. We left in 1959 and now, I not allowed to go to Tibet anymore. I probably never go back again.

SUSAN. When did you come to the U.S.?

NAMGAL. Took a long time for sort out. I came here first, then few years later, my husband and children come. No English. Was very hard. But now. I been here 24 years. Worked nineteen years here at The Lux. I working at The Lux when first open.

    (*The phone rings.*)

Yes, Dennis.

    (*To* SUSAN.)

I have to go back work.

3. Balfour

SUSAN. Balfour is a dishwasher from Ghana. He is the son of a chief. He has *donkor,* deep tribal scarring on both sides of his face.

Balfour always greets me in the same way

BALFOUR. *Ey! Mon Sou. Eti sen?* [Hey, Mademoiselle Susan, how are you?]

SUSAN. *Atta Balfour. Boko. Aye?* [Mr. Balfour, Good. And you?]

In Twi, he calls me Miss Susan, and I call him Mister Balfour. —Are you ready?

BALFOUR. I ready. Bring it, *Mon Sou.*

I've been in New York, America almost thirteen years. And I work in The Lux as a full-time employee dishwasher. I'm from Ghana, West Africa. From Koforidua. It's a beautiful place. There are mountains. It's a place where all white people should visit. It's a quiet place. I love it there. I love—Ah. *Mon Sou.* Turn it off. Turn it off.

SUSAN. You're doing so well, keep going.

BALFOUR. I'm trying to, you know. Raise my kids here, lead a better life in America. I have three kids. One is here, two in Ghana with my wife. It's very, very hard living like a single parent, but I'm trying. Maybe they will come next year? I hope so.

You cannot compare Ghana to America. America is far, far better than Ghana. But I miss Ghana. *Mefi Ghana.* [I miss Ghana.] When I retire, I will go back to Ghana. I want to bring America to Ghana. There are no jobs in Ghana. If I could get a job doing work back home, I never come here.

SUSAN. Tell me, why do you only eat apples here?

BALFOUR. Ah Girl! You notice what I eat? Ha ha ha! I work in the kitchen but sometimes they cook things with the alcohol. And I don't want to taste that. Then I go home and I eat my country food. I cook for my son. My favorite food is fufu. It's the plantain and the cassava. In the kitchen, sometimes I make peanut soup. Ghana peanut soup, chef calls it. And everyone try it and says, "Oh wow. Balfour. This so good. Give recipe." But I cannot, because I only have recipe in my head. Not on the paper.

SUSAN. You have to let me know next time you make this soup.

4. Housekeeping

SUSAN. The sweetest member of housekeeping is Aida. Sometimes I sneak her cookies from the kitchen, and she brings them home to her girls.

(AIDA, *housekeeping, early 30s, Albanian, organizes her cart.* SUSAN *records* AIDA *with a cell phone.*)

AIDA. My name is Aida, I'm—Oh my gosh. Susan, I can't do this.

(AIDA *retreats.*)

SUSAN. Aida, it's okay! Am I making you nervous?

AIDA. A little. You are recording?

SUSAN. Is that okay?

AIDA. Em. Yes. I'm sorry. I'm only doing this because it's you, Susan.

SUSAN. Thank you Aida…Tell me about where you are from?

AIDA. I'm from Pristina, Kosovo. I attended college there for couple of months until war started. We had to leave, cuz the war was going on and the Serbs were raping and all kinds of bad things, so my mother was afraid for me and my sisters, you know.

(DENNIS *enters.* AIDA *tenses.* SUSAN *hides phone and notebook.*)

DENNIS. 713 is late checkout.

AIDA. Yes, Dennis.

(DENNIS *scrutinizes* SUSAN.)

DENNIS. You need help?

(SUSAN *shakes her head.* DENNIS *exits.* AIDA *relaxes.*)

AIDA. I'm mixing everything. I'm very, very shy, Susan.

SUSAN. You're doing great. Maybe…could you tell me more about the war?

AIDA. We had to leave in a hurry. We left everything in the house. We never live there again. We were sent to a camp in Macedonia near the border. On the transport bus, they were separating men, women, children. It was very scary. Some buses were going to Montenegro, some back to Albania. We all end up on the same bus because my brothers were still children. We were so lucky, Susan, oh my God, you have no idea.

When I first got here, people spoke English so quickly. It's amazing to see all the Albanians in New York. What do they do, where do they work? So many Albanians in America. When I first started working here, I thought, what kind of job is this? But they train me. Now I like it here. I wanted to go back to university but I got married and had babies here. Next year, maybe my daughter and I start up university at the same time.

SUSAN. What was the most—

AIDA. Oh shoot. Sorry Susan, I have to keep moving.

5. How to Make a Bed

NAFISSATOU *makes a bed.*

NAFISSATOU. Okay, if you really want to know, here is how to make a bed, professionally.

First, take away the old bedding.

Ignore the blood. The stains.

On top of the bare mattress, make a bed sandwich.

Put the clean starched fitted sheet on the bed.

The seam of fitted sheet should be in middle of the mattress corner.

Then lay down the flat sheet on top of that. Then thin blanket on top of that.

Then you tuck, tuck, tuck.

Not just corners of bed, but even edge of pillowcase.

Everything folded, square, and neat.

Then the duvet. Lay on gently so it stay fluffy.

Two standard pillows.

Four decorative.

Accent pillow.

Smooth with your hand. Smooth. Smooth.

Place the runner six inches from foot of bed. Congratulations.

Now you have made a bed.

Clean the room. Take away the trash and dirty things.

Vacuum. Scrub the bathroom. Fold the toilet paper into a point.

Replace all of the toiletries and towels.

Repeat fourteen times.

SUSAN. Nafissatou Diallo was alone on floor 28, the day she was attacked by Strauss-Kahn. Her efficiency led to promotions, and eventually she was assigned to clean an entire floor of hotel rooms by herself. Which also meant when she cried for help, there was no one to come running.

6. Security Base

SUSAN. A familiar cliché is that many of the servers are aspiring actors. What you might not know, is that many of the security guards want to be cops. But no one wants to join "the force" more than—

(JANY [4] *stands very stiffly, with a walkie-talkie, wearing an eyepatch.*)

JANY [4]. (*Speaks in very deep cop voice. Stands in parade rest.*) My name is Jany Santos Figueroa. I am a Security Officer at the Hotel Lux. Born and raised in the Bronx but *yo soy* 100% *Dominicano.*

SUSAN. Jany, oh my God, why are you wearing an eye patch?

JANY. (*Relaxes, higher-pitched normal voice.*) Okay Susie, so, like, Me, Angel, Vinny were at the Tavern.

SUSAN. Vinny?

JANY. Vinny from Engineering.

SUSAN. Does he prefer to be called Vinny? Shit. I've been calling him Vincent for like six years.

JANY. We was at the tavern. And this dude wants to fight. So Angel breaks it up but then they jump us down the street. It was like the four of us against ten guys. Vinny who basically escalated the entire situation, gets knocked out cold on the first punch and lays out, spread out like a (*Mimes a crucifix.*), you know. Angel gets it bad and I got hit, double *cocatazo*, right in my eye and my cornea is all jacked. And it's scarred. Wanna see?

SUSAN. Oh man. That looks bad.

JANY. They're going to do some laser treatments on it? Hold on.

(JANY *talks into a walkie-talkie. Deep voice.*)

Security. Room 802? Copy.

SUSAN. Hey, will you take me through your day?

JANY. Yeah. Sure, Susie.

(JANY *walks with* SUSAN *through the hotel.*)

Mostly, I'm at the base watching the security cameras. Sometimes, you'll see the most beautiful, classy shortie you've ever seen in your life, then she'll scratch her butt in the elevator or something, and it's a real bummer.

SUSAN. —Every employee knows exactly where the cameras are. On camera.

(ENSEMBLE *stands up stiffly. They shift five inches over.*)

Off-camera.

(ENSEMBLE *does something silly "off-camera."*)

I have a huge crush on Jany. I'm pretty sure he's still dating the beautiful housekeeper from Haiti named Mano-chee-ca…? *Manoucheca?* Hmm.

JANY. And then about once an hour, I do a round of all the public spaces.

> (*At the bar. High-end* PROSTITUTE [2] *and* DSK *sit at the bar.* SUSAN *and* JANY *watch them.*)

See that lady at the bar? She's a prostitute.

SUSAN. How do you know?

JANY. You can spot 'em.

DSK. You know the first thing I did while I was in the holding?

PROSTITUTE [2]. You'd think, "call a lawyer." **DSK.** Called a lawyer?

> (*They laugh together.*)

DSK. I called Angela Merkel to postpone our meeting the next day.

Angela Merkel? The Chancellor of Germany.

SUSAN. Aren't you going to kick her out?

JANY. Nah. Not unless she's bothering somebody.

> (*The walkie crackles.*)

Copy. The GM is making rounds.

> (SUSAN *hides her phone.*)

See you, Susie.

> (JANY *walks away.*)

7. How to Succeed/Laws of the Podium

> SUSAN *stands at the podium in the restaurant.*

SUSAN. The new General Manager of the hotel is a former hostess. I trained her. She hates me now.

She's been making sure nearly everyone who knew her as a hostess is treated badly until they get fired or quit.

I passed on everything I learned from Evelyn.

Never point.

> (SUSAN *gestures with her whole arm.*)

You must wear heels over an inch and a half on Friday and Saturday nights. No exception.

Once a hostess had foot surgery, and she had a boot on one foot and a high-heeled shoe on the other.

At the podium, you are God. You control everything and everyone.

These are the laws of seating. The attractive people, VIPs, fashionistas, they all go in the front, or in the prestige section.

VIPs are coded into groups. VIP1s are famous or important. They can be identified by one name. VIP2s are B- to D-list celebrities, fashion people. The less famous they are, the more entitled they act.

D-LIST CELEBRITY [4]. Un-be-lievable. Do you even know who I am? I could have you fired.

SUSAN. Also terrible are personal assistants.

ASSISTANT [1]. Hi—I need a Diet Ginger Ale for Mr. Sutherland.

SUSAN. We have regular Ginger Ale. Or Diet Coke.

ASSISTANT. This is for Donald. Sutherland.

SUSAN. I'm sorry, we don't carry it. There's a bodega across the street.

ASSISTANT. You are fucking useless.

SUSAN. Sometimes celebrities get downgraded from VIP1 to 2. That's always a little sad. VIP3 are business people who spend big money but aren't famous. Tourists are seated out of sight, in the dining area. They will complain—

HOTEL GUEST [5]. Excuse me, Ma'am? We paid a lot of money to stay here. Why can't we sit in the lounge? There's empty tables everywhere.

SUSAN. I place reserved signs on empty tables, for the sole purpose of preventing hotel guests from sitting in the lounge. I hate doing this. But if the owner of the hotel saw someone wearing sandals and a fanny pack in the lounge on a Saturday night, I would immediately lose my job.

If a group of men want to come in on the weekend and get a table, they can only reserve it by ordering bottle service. We call this upselling. Bottle service bumps a check that might have been 200 into 2,000. It also turns men into entitled monsters, who must be handled.

The phrase "Lux Life" was coined as a way of luring guests into staying at this Grand Hotel. And we are told over and over again, that we are extensions of this luxurious way of living. The overall look of the hotel, includes not only décor but also the people inside. The bellmen all look like Calvin Klein models. And the specialty dresses for the cocktail waitresses only come in size 00 to 4.

> (KARA [2], *a cocktail waitress delivers drinks and pushes through men.*)

This is Kara. She's from a small town in Vermont. She's a cocktail waitress in the club and a model and a former ballerina. We're friends but just standing next to her makes me feel like a human potato.

KARA [2]. I've been invited to The Hamptons. Vegas. St. Barts. All sorts of places. These guys are desperate for a release from their jobs. They promise everything. One particularly memorable line was:

TIPSY DOUCHE [3]. Sweetness, I'm gonna treat you so good. I'm gonna pay off your student loans.

KARA. I've seen marriages end here. I've seen former movie stars waste themselves into oblivion. Here, at night, the women go to the bathrooms two by two. Sometimes they invite me to partake in a "microbump" of coke with them.

(KARA *storms into the kitchen with a plate.*)

SUSAN. What's that?

KARA. The GM sent the food back *again*. This time the branzino was *too* flakey.

(MARK [6], *the chef, throws up his hands.*)

MARK [6]. That fish is fucking perfect. Look. She didn't even try it. Balfour, you want it?

(BALFOUR, *the dishwasher, eats the fish.*)

SUSAN. Balfour! I just told everyone you only eat apples.

BALFOUR. Eh.

SUSAN. It should be inspiring that the GM of the hotel is a young woman who worked herself up from hostess. But at the same time—

BALFOUR. *Mon Sou!* She's the worst. They fire Ed to hire her.

JANSEN. Oh shit. You guys talking about Ed?

BALFOUR. Ed work so hard. Fix problems.

JANSEN. Ed knew everyone's name.

BALFOUR. Yes. Ed was good man. Good GM.

What's her training?

JANSEN. When she's not partying in Europe, I hear she does drugs in the unoccupied hotel rooms.

BALFOUR. Every time I see her, she gets blonder. Like, more blonder more evil, right? There's this expression.

You know it, right. A fish rots from the head?

That's how it is here.

You think they care about us?

No. They do not.

KARA. *Psst. Psst. Susan. Come here.* The dog food man is back. Over there.

SUSAN. Excuse me?

KARA. An elegant couple walks in, and the woman comes up to me.

DOG FOOD MAN'S WOMAN [5]. Do you see that man over there? Well, he would just LOVE it if you would spit in his drink for him.

SUSAN. What???

KARA. I don't think I can do that.

DOG FOOD MAN'S WOMAN. Oh. He'll tip you REALLY well.

KARA. So, I spat in his drink and—

SUSAN. You did?

KARA. Do you know how many TIMES I have wanted to spit in customers' drinks and refrained? This was my chance. So I spit in his drink and bring it over.

DOG FOOD MAN'S WOMAN. Did you do what he asked?

KARA. She gives me a hundred bucks. Meanwhile, this guy never speaks, he just smiles.

(THE DOG FOOD MAN [3] *smiles.*)

But you just know he speaks English perfectly.

SUSAN. He's kind of. Handsome. I hate to say that. He has kind eyes. How is that possible?

DOG FOOD MAN'S WOMAN. You know, he would REALLY enjoy it if you would step on his hamburger.

KARA. I'll get fired.

DOG FOOD MAN'S WOMAN. Then he wants to lick the meat juices off your stilettos.

(THE DOG FOOD MAN *smiles.*)

SUSAN. Gross. I can't handle this story anymore. Is this what the 1% is really like?

(THE DOG FOOD MAN *smiles.*)

The night continues. Kara steps on various courses and spits in drinks, until the man, still hungry, orders another meal, through his interpreter.

DOG FOOD MAN'S WOMAN. He would just LOVE it, if you would serve him dog food in a silver bowl. And he wants you to spit in that too.

KARA. I rang in the dog food as "Open food $50." That night I made over a grand.

(KARA *walks away.*)

SUSAN. And what I want to tell her is: You're worth more than that, Kara.

DSK. I have made but one mistake.

SUSAN. Really?

DSK. I don't have any problem with women. All I have done is made a mistake with thinking that men in a higher office can have a private life. No one expects this heterodox behavior from a public figure. Besides. I had diplomatic immunity. A laissez-passer. Special travel document from the United Nations.

SUSAN. Diplomatic immunity does not mean you get to—

8. Kitchen Protocol

PATTY [5]. Yo Susan—Whatchu call a lesbian with fat fingers? Well hung.
>(DSK *exits chuckling at* PATTY's *joke.* MUHAMMAD [4] *grabs food from the window.*)

Yo, Muhammad, you get it?
>(PATTY *laughs and makes an obscene gesture.* MUHAMMAD *exits.*)

SUSAN. Patty is the only girl in the kitchen who works the line. She's a hard-as-nails Puerto Rican lesbian.

PATTY. Soy una tortillera.[1] A tortilla-maker.
>(PATTY *winks.*)

SUSAN. She holds her own and talks about hot women more crudely than any of them.

Her solid arms are covered with tattoos and burns. None of the cooks have any hair on their forearms. Their hair gets singed off by the heat. And every cook can show you a scar from
>(PATTY *shows a series of scars and burns. Shows one up close.*)

PATTY. —a Japanese mandolin. Four stitches. Deli slicer. Nine stitches.
>(TENZIN [6] *walks into the kitchen.*)

TENZIN [6]. Hey! Patty! Are those...crabs? They're alive?
>(PATTY *chases* TENZIN *with a crab.*)

PATTY. Hu-hu-hah! Soft-shell crabs!

SUSAN. Tenzin is a security guard from Kathmandu. We watch Patty work in the kitchen. With a small pair of scissors, Patty snips the eyes off of living crabs, then digs out their intestines and tosses them, still living, writhing, into a pot.

TENZIN. It's terrible. It's terrible what she's doing to those crabs.

PATTY. You gotta cook them this way. Can't be helped.
>(TENZIN *walks back to the security base,* SUSAN *follows.*)

TENZIN. I don't eat meat or fish. I don't do that.

SUSAN. Good for you.

---

1. Tortillera, tortilla-maker, is Spanish slang for lesbian.

TENZIN. On Saturdays, I go to the fish market, and I buy live fish and return them to the water. The fishermen get so upset. They start screaming at me. "Why are you throwing away this? Give to me." And I say, "No. I bring back to ocean."

SUSAN. That's lovely, Tenzin. But are you sure you are dumping the fish back in the right place?

TENZIN. What?

SUSAN. There's been problems with people dumping pet fish into water streams and it throws off the ecosystem.

TENZIN. Oh. I dunno. I don't know about that, Susan.

SUSAN. It's. It's okay. Probably a few fish a week doesn't make a difference

TENZIN. I think, I think what I do is good, and fish happy that I do it.

SUSAN. Well, that's for sure.

—Later I learn that Tenzin's uncle is one of the most famous monks in Nepal and Tenzin has met the Dalai Lama several times

I ask—Tenzin, why didn't you want to become a monk?

TENZIN. I don't want to be monk. Who wants to be monk?

(JANY *relieves* TENZIN. TENZIN *gives him the walkie and keys.*)

SUSAN. Hey Jany! How did the laser treatments go?

JANY. It's helping.

(JANY *shows her his eye.*)

SUSAN. It. It looks better. That ring is gone.

JANY. Yeah.

VINNY [5]. Still ugly though

JANY. *Cállate tu boca, cabrón.* [Shut yer trap, dumbass.] Vinny, you went down like a bitch.

VINNY. *Si, pero tu sigues Feo.* [Yeah, but yer still ugly.]

SUSAN. So what did the doc say?

JANY. I think it's always going to be cloudy, like when I look down and to the right.

SUSAN. That sucks. Well. If there's anything I can do...

—Why did I say that? What could I do?

JANY. Thanks Susie.

Hey Susie. I just put in my notice. I'm going to be called into the Academy. For real this time.

SUSAN. Wow! Finally. Can I have a photo of you in uniform? Then if I get in trouble with the popo, I can pull out the photo and say you're my friend.

JANY. Haha. Sure. I'll even sign it.

SUSAN. Am I going to see you after you leave? We still never got that lunch. Jany. We've never hung out outside of here in six years.

JANY. Is that true? Wow. Sad. Yeah, Susie, let's do it before I leave.

SUSAN. You're going to make a great cop, Jany.

It gives me faith knowing there are good people like you on the job.

JANY. Thanks. Oh yo, we got some new stuff from Lost and Found.

(*Everyone cheers. They dig through Lost and Found.*)

SUSAN. Every six months, all of the unclaimed items get donated. But if they're feeling generous, security lets us go through it first. It's Sketchy Christmas.

JANSEN. Check out this coat.

KARA. God. That's hideous—Oo. These are fucking Prada shoes.

SUSAN. But do they fit?

KARA. If I cut off my toes.

JANY. Oh hey, Susie. I set aside books for you.

SUSAN. Thank you.

VINNY. Nobody else wants 'em.

NAMGAL. How can people leave these things behind?

SUSAN. Namgal, you should take something.

(NAMGAL *shakes her head and moves away. People shrug and continue to go through the contents of the bags.*

SUSAN *looks at her phone. She celebrates.*)

RICH. Hey. You look weirdly chipper.

SUSAN. This is Rich. He's from San Jose. He's a server in the restaurant.

—Oh. Well. DSK just got accused of aggravated pimping.

RICH. As opposed to nice pimping?

SUSAN. He and 13 of his friends organized lavish sex parties in a hotel in Lille that were so extreme it could be considered a prostitution ring. He could get 10 years.

RICH. That's a bit harsh. I heard prostitution is legal in France.

SUSAN. Are you serious? He's appalling.

—Things that came out during the trial.

In his text messages, he refers to women as

(SUSAN *is startled when* RICH *becomes* DSK.)

DSK. "Gifts," "equipment," and "material."

SUSAN. He wrote:

DSK. "Do you want to discover a magnificent naughty club in Madrid with me and some equipment?"

SUSAN. In court, he said:

DSK. "During Libertine afternoons, things happen pretty quickly."

SUSAN. His former mistress said:

[2]. If you had become president, you would have transformed the Élysée into a giant swingers' club. You claimed that you were ready to give your blood for your country when in fact you would have used this country to spill your inexhaustible sperm

SUSAN. DSK also said:

DSK. "I think I must have a form of sexuality which is rougher than the average...But I had no idea at the time that these experiences were so unpleasant as the women now say."

SUSAN. DSK's lawyers argue that he only took part in four orgies a year.

RICH. Yeah but. Isn't he just being punished for his lifestyle? Should a moral indictment also be a legal one? He's a modern-day satyr.

(SUSAN *looks daggers at him.*)

Well, whatever. I don't know all the deets.

You should make a movie about it, or something.

SUSAN. I'm writing a play about it.

RICH. Yeah but. Wouldn't a movie be better?

9. Welcome to New York

SUSAN. Okay. So. Abel Ferrara made a film called *Welcome to New York*. Here are all of Nafissatou Diallo's lines in the two-hour-and-five-minute film.

NAFISSATOU. (*Flat.*) Housekeeping. Hello?

Hello? Housekeeping?

Housekeeping? Hello? Hello? House—I'm so sorry sir. No. Please. No. Please. Sir no. No Please. No no. No. No please. No. Don't. Stop. Stop I beg you please. No. No. Please. Stop it please. Please don't.

SUSAN. The encounter occurs off-screen, as if the filmmaker can't even commit to showing if it was rape or consensual.

Her final words in the film are to a police officer, where she recounts a much tamer version of what was actually reported.

NAFISSATOU. I started to clean the room. I go into the living room area. And a naked man, he—

SUSAN. Actually. Let's stop here. We don't have to do this version.

10. A Failed Search

    SUSAN *on her phone in the hallway.*

SUSAN. How do you find a person that doesn't want to be found?
Nafissatou Diallo has a Facebook page. It has 37 friends.
Friend request sent.

NAFISSATOU. Friend request accepted.

SUSAN. Wow. Okay.

—Hi. My name is Susan.—

NAFISSATOU. Greetings Susan.

SUSAN. Hi. Could I just ask you a few—

NAFISSATOU. http://pure-chiba.info/powerful.php?please=n2ngf

SUSAN. I guess I'm not surprised.

NAFISSATOU. My colleague sometime past solicited for your transaction in regard to getting some funds transferred—

SUSAN. Unfriend. Block.

JANY. Susie, you shouldn't be on your phone out here. The GM almost fired Vinny for checking his voicemail.

SUSAN. Thanks.
Hey Jany, do you know how to track down a person who doesn't want to be found?

JANY. Cell phone triangulation. Credit cards.

SUSAN. I don't have her phone number. And this person isn't a criminal.
She hasn't done anything wrong.

JANY. You could hire a private investigator who has access to the database. It'll cost though. At least a grand.

SUSAN. I can't afford that. Do you think…Would you be willing to ask one of your cop friends to check?

JANY. …This is for one of your stories or real life?

SUSAN. It's for a play but I'm looking for a real person.

JANY. If this was you trying to track down your sister or something, maybe, maybe.
But Susan. This is a really big ask. I don't even know who I'd go to about this. I don't feel—

SUSAN. No, it's okay. Sorry. I'm just.

    (*A shift.*)

So I go to the Sofitel. I stand outside Room 2806. I wander around the 28th floor. I see a hotel maid pushing a cart.

—Hi

SOFITEL HOUSEKEEPER 1 [6]. (*Limited understanding of English.*) Okay. You need?

SUSAN. No, I'm okay. I was just wondering. Do you know Nafissatou Diallo? She was a maid here. She—

SOFITEL HOUSEKEEPER 1. Oh. I no work with her.

SUSAN. Could I ask you a few questions about?

SOFITEL HOUSEKEEPER 1. Sorry. I—

> (SOFITEL HOUSEKEEPER 1 *pushes past with cart and returns to work.*)

SUSAN. I wander the other floors at random. Trying to find another housekeeper.

Hi. Excuse me. Did you work with Nafissatou Diallo?

SOFITEL HOUSEKEEPER 2 [5]. Nafi?

SUSAN. Yes. You know her?

SOFITEL HOUSEKEEPER 2. What do you want with her?

SOFITEL SECURITY GUARD [1]. Ma'am. Ma'am. Ma'am. Ma'am. Ma'am. Excuse me. Ma'am.

Are you a guest in the hotel?

SUSAN. Yes, I. Am?

SOFITEL SECURITY GUARD. What room?

SUSAN. 2806.

SOFITEL SECURITY GUARD. What's the last name?

SUSAN. …Smith…Finkle?

SOFITEL SECURITY GUARD. I'm going to have to escort you out, Ma'am.

> (*Shift.*)

This is how you're portraying us? The Sofitel employees were the ones who helped the police apprehend DSK before he left the country. We were heroes.

SUSAN. You were?

SOFITEL SECURITY GUARD. He called back for his BlackBerry.

SOFITEL FRONT DESK [2]. Bonjour. Thank you for calling the Sofitel.

DSK. Bonjour. This is Dominique Strauss-Kahn. I left my BlackBerry phone in my room.

SOFITEL FRONT DESK. Of course, Monsieur. I'll transfer you to Lost and Found.

SOFITEL HEAD OF SECURITY [4]. We pretended we had found his phone and convinced him to tell us his flight information. Then the police were able to grab him and escort him off the plane in handcuffs.

(DSK *walks off the plane, doing the Perp Walk. The rest of the ensemble boo him.*)

11. Kitchen Protocol

KARA. Where's my food for A2? They're gonna walk.

    (*To* SUSAN.)

We need to comp them a round.

MARK. Miss Kara, a porterhouse steak does not cook through in six minutes. If they were in a rush, you need to tell the guests when they place the order.

KARA. It's been 30 minutes! God damn it. You know, when the food gets screwed up, I'm the one that gets screamed at. You're salaried. You don't rely on tips!

SUSAN. This is Mark. The executive chef.

MARK. Yeah. Two years ago, I was staging in Paris at Joël Robuchon. What the hell was I thinking taking this corporate job?

SUSAN. The kitchen staff—porters, dishwashers—are back of house. Servers, bartenders, food runners, bussers are front of house, they're the people the customers interact with. Sometimes there's a lot of tension between front and back of house.

    (KARA, *tired of waiting, storms out of the kitchen.*)

MARK. We call 'em order-takers. That's all they do. These girls, they don't even try my specials during pre-shift. So how can they sell it, if they don't eat it? They're all on diets. Or they're (*Funny voice.*) *vegan.*

    (*Yelling.*)

Order up. A2 Steaks. A2.

Watch it sit in the window drying out.

    (*A moment. The food sits in the window unclaimed.* MARK *throws up his hands, indicating, "See. I told you."* MUHAMMAD *whizzes by. He grabs the food, masterfully stacking four plates of food on his forearms and hands, wiping the edges of the plates, and disappears.*)

You see Muhammad, he's running food, drinks, bussing, mopping. What do these girls do but smile and punch in a few things into Micros?

And they're making double what my guys make on the line.

    (*In the restaurant.* KARA *delivers cocktails to a table.*)

KARA. Mark said that? Sonofabitch. Chefs are all egomaniacs. Is it fair that I make twice as much as Muhammad, no, it's not right, it's not fair at all, but these Wall Street guys, they want to interact with a young, attractive woman and not a 45-year-old, short brown man.

That's just how it is. I'm just doing my job. I work hard too, and in heels for nine hours straight, and I get ogled and hit on in this stupid-fucking-minidress that makes me feel like I'm working at fucking Hooters, so Mark needs to back the fuck off or I'm going to kick his ass.

Did you bring A2 their Cab Franc?

(SUSAN *has not*.)

Come on girl, I'm working two sections here.

BALFOUR. Eh. *Mon Sou*. Did you hear they fire Namgal?

SUSAN. NO. What? She's about to have her 20th anniversary.

JANSEN. Shit. You guys talking about Namgal?

I heard it was raining, and she took one of the umbrellas from Lost and Found. But later a guest called and asked for it back.

BALFOUR. (*Sucks teeth*.) Who calls back for umbrella two months later?

SUSAN. Do you have any idea how many super valuable things I've taken home from Lost and Found over the years? That's so unfair.

JANSEN. I think Dennis fired her because she's been here too long and her hourly is too high and the GM wants to make cuts.

SUSAN. That's awful. I mean, she was probably going to retire soon.

BALFOUR. Her? No, she loved working. She would have worked here till she was a hundred.

JANSEN. It's a real shame.

SUSAN. Oh sorry I forgot—This is Jansen.

JANSEN. (*To audience*.) Howsit.

SUSAN. There's a lot of weird ethnic hirings that happen at the hotel. Sometimes it's situational. I'm from Hawai'i. I bring in one of my childhood friends, Jansen.

JANSEN. I just moved here to the Big Apple.

SUSAN. Please don't say Big Apple. Jansen brings in Alvin.

ALVIN [6]. Sup.

SUSAN. Suddenly there are three Hawaiians at The Lux. There's a large group of Nepalese housekeepers. Brazilian front desk clerks, Trinidadian housemen, and so on. Most of the engineers are from the Dominican Republic, and the porters are from Ghana. My favorite thing about working here is all of the languages I get to hear every day. The Lux is our micro-United Nations utopia.

This is Jason, the shy Chinese Sous Chef. I love watching him interact with Jen, the Vietnamese Human Resources Assistant. He has an epic crush on her, but neither of them speak much English and they don't speak each other's language. Their flirtation and ensuing awkwardness makes my day.

JASON [1]. Here Jen, I picked out an apple for you.
JEN [6]. Thank you Jason, but there is a big brown spot on that apple. I would not want it.
JASON. But I picked it out for you.
JEN. But why would I want an apple that has a spot on it?
JASON. (*Unraveling.*) It was a joke. That I would give you an apple…with a spot on it.
Because I am a chef…and I know good apples?
JEN. So that is what you think of me? That you would give me a bad apple?
JASON. No! I would give you a good apple. But??
JEN. That's okay, I would not like any apples today.
JASON. You don't get my joke.
JEN. Did you tell me a joke? What was it?
JASON. No, the apple was the joke.
JEN. How can an apple be a joke?
JASON. Arugh!!!

> (JASON *runs away, tail between legs.* JEN *shakes her head, confused by the whole ordeal.*)

12. The Jewish Mystic

> *Two fashionistas run over to* SUSAN. *They all exchange kisses on cheeks.*

SASHA [2]. Heeeey!!! We're back!
SUSAN. Hiiiii! Soooo great to see you!
JOAN [5]. We brought you that tea we talked about last time!
SUSAN. You guys are the best! Here, I'll show you to your spot.
SASHA. Hey! You remembered our table.
SUSAN. Mimosas on me, kay?

> (JANY *walks past.*)

Jany, holy shit. I have no idea who those women are.
JANY. Sasha and Joan. They come every fall for fashion week.
SUSAN. That's right.
JANY. How'd you know their table?
SUSAN. D7's the corner booth. It's everyone's favorite table.

> (JANY *exits.*)

Guests come and go. It's a blur. But.

—A memory, ten years ago. The hotel guests I will never forget.
An Israeli man with a magnificent beard comes into the restaurant with a striking woman in her sixties. They order water only. Inside the glass, they place the woman's ring and begin to read passages from an ancient holy text.
Naturally, this is very un-hotel-like behavior. We're used to City Hall yuppies and film pricks, but not Jewish mystics. Jansen goes over. I watch the man with the beard speak with Jansen. They talk for a long time while I run around, covering his tables. Suddenly, Jansen is sobbing.
I hardly ever see men cry like that, I can count the times on my fingers.
Jansen! Who was that? Why are you crying?
JANSEN. That man told me to call my father and forgive him.
I just spoke to my dad for the first time in five years.
Everything that man said about my dad was true. I need some air.
SUSAN. The man's wife comes over, asking for Jansen, and so I speak with her thanking them for the kindness she and her husband had done for him—
MYSTIC'S WIFE [6]. Do not thank us, David, he just sees things that some other people might not see as quickly. He sees it from God. Would you like to meet him?
SUSAN. She takes me by the hand to their table. David looks at me, then writes down a series of numbers and circles them.
JEWISH MYSTIC [3]. How old are you?
SUSAN. Twenty-four.
He shows me the first number he had written down, a circled 24.
JEWISH MYSTIC. What month were you born?
SUSAN. November.
He and his wife speak back and forth in Hebrew.
JEWISH MYSTIC. There is a man in your life that is causing you trouble, yes?
(SUSAN *does not reply.*)
How old is he?
SUSAN. Thirty-two—David smiles, he has also written down 32.
JEWISH MYSTIC. This man...you can never trust him. He likes many women. There is a second woman in his life, even if he is not with her now, he will never give all of himself to you.
MYSTIC'S WIFE. This is true?
SUSAN. I'm not sure. I often have a hard time trusting him.
JEWISH MYSTIC. He is not a bad man but he is not your soul partner. If you are free, and only if you are free, a 28-year-old man will come into your

life. He is better looking, smarter, and kinder. This is the man for you. He will come in the summer.

SUSAN. At that moment, only one face flashed in my mind, a face an ocean and a continent away. —And things with the man I'm with now, that will never work out? Will he ever change?

MYSTIC'S WIFE. People don't change so much. And why waste your time, your most precious life on this man? David has already seen he is not the one for you. God is going to send you real happiness, very, very soon.

SUSAN. What about my writing?

I've been struggling for a long time.

JEWISH MYSTIC. You are strong but you choose to doubt,

you choose to be weak.

You know that one day you will succeed

or you will stop writing.

You know this man is not the man for you

and yet you stay with him.

You ask me, a stranger,

these questions as if you do not know the answers.

But you do.

You always have.

    (SUSAN *wipes away tears.*)

SUSAN. Uh. Right.

Well.

    (DAIRY DELIVERY GUY [4], *is leering at her.*)

Um. Can I help you?

    (DAIRY GUY *sucks his teeth and exits with a dolly full of milk crates.* SUSAN *and* TENZIN *near the security base.*)

That new dairy guy is an asshole. Tenzin, what happened to the other guy, who would tell jokes?

TENZIN. Freddy?

SUSAN. He has a mustache?

TENZIN. Freddy.

SUSAN. I haven't seen him around.

TENZIN. He was killed.

SUSAN. Oh my God. What happened?

TENZIN. He saved up all his money and moved to Mexico to be near his mom. He was going to open up a taco truck or something. First week he was there, he was robbed at gunpoint, and shot and killed.

SUSAN. That's so unlucky. That's awful.

JANSEN. Oh shit. You guys talking about Freddy?

TENZIN. I figure, it was an inside job. I mean, how else do they know some random dude had so much money? I bet he got killed by one of his friends or like, a cousin. Probably a cousin. Fucking Mexican bullshit.

SUSAN. That's awful.

JANSEN. Are you still looking for stories?

SUSAN. Yes. Jansen, will you help me with interviews? People like you more than me.

JANSEN. People like you...

SUSAN. Ehhh...

JANSEN. You should talk to DreShawn, the head bellman.

DreShawn got stabbed by a psychotic man in front of the hotel. He was out of work for over a month and nearly bled to death.

SUSAN. Would you be willing to talk about that?

DRESHAWN [5]. Listen, my Hawaiian comrades. I don't mind talking about getting stabbed. But at the end of the day, all I have to say is,

"God is good. God is good and ain't nothing to complain about."

(JANSEN *and* DRESHAWN *exchange an elaborate fist bump.*)

JANSEN. Susan's writing about the hotel.

DRESHAWN. That's some juicy stuff, right there. The hotel's a village. Everybody's got a position. The bellmen are the athletes. We can go anywhere. This key card here? Opens every single door in this joint

Guests are a trip, man. Staying in a hotel turns folks into helpless, difficult children, and it also lowers their inhibitions. You know the number of times guests have tried to put the moves on me? Or get this—straight up asked me for hard drugs or whores, two minutes after they meet me? It's shocking.

JANSEN. We tried to interview Fernando. He does receiving at the hotel. He wouldn't, because his English isn't good enough.

But here's his story.

FERNANDO [3]. (*In rapid Spanish.*) En Colombia, yo era abogado por muchos años. Mi padre tambien era abogado. El fue el que me enseño sobre el coraje...de como ser valiente, y por eso me encontré un dia frente a la cartel, peleando un caso para el estado...

[In Colombia, I was a lawyer for many years. My father was also a lawyer. He taught me to be fearless. One day I was fighting a big case for the state against the cartel...]

(JANSEN *gently steps in and tells* FERNANDO*'s story.*)

JANSEN. He was a lawyer back in Colombia. He was defending a case against the cartel. They threatened his life. Now, he checks in deliveries of apple juice, milk, cleaning chemicals, and two-ply napkins. He got word his mother was dying, so against the advice of every, single person he knew, he bleached his hair blond, and flew back to Colombia to see his mother. He barely left the house the whole time. And for two months, no one here knew if he was alive or dead.

And then, one day he was back in the hallway moving boxes, smiling his gentle smile, just like that.

—Hey. Fernando, how was your trip?

FERNANDO. (*Smiling. Barely understanding the question.*) Hello...Was good.

(SUSAN, *upset, looks at her phone.*)

You. You good?

SUSAN. No. DSK just got acquitted of all pimping charges. He got off scot-free. Again. Not that it's a surprise at all. But just once I would like to see—

(FERNANDO *gently pats her arm.*)

FERNANDO. Okay. Be okay.

(*He exits.*)

13. Shit That Went Down in the Hotel

SUSAN. Other random things that went down in the hotel.

JANSEN. There was a gay room service prostitution ring that went on for years. Actually, it might still be going on.

JANY. There was this weird security guard. He started fires and then put them out. He would get promotions for putting out the fires. Eventually, he moved to a different hotel, and the same shit kept happening.

But finally, he got caught, and now he's in prison for a long time.

PATTY. You know who else is in prison? Ousman. He loved weapons.

He became friends with an amateur rap group and loaned them his gun collection for their music video. But then they put it on YouTube, and the police realized the weapons were real, and so he went to prison.

JANSEN. Noooo! Ousman has like five kids.

RICH. I've waited on many celebrities over the years. It's not a cool hotel anymore. It's like a 45-year-old blond with an amazing bod that doesn't want to let go.

TENZIN. Once an engineer was cleaning something with a machine and he didn't fan the exhaust, so a conference room got flooded with carbon monoxide. The room had to be evacuated and people were crying and calling their loved ones.

JANSEN. The meeting was almost over too. That's the part that kills me. Service recovery.

ALL. Service Recovery.

SUSAN. If you're feeling lonely, The Lux will send a companion goldfish to your room.

The goldfish are imported from China. They die very quickly because guests feed them pizza and tap on the glass.

How lonely do you have to be for this to make a difference?

ALLISON [2]. Once, a guy checked in with no luggage. He seemed so sad. He asked for help closing the blinds. I wondered if I should call someone about him. I had a bad feeling. And yeah. He killed himself.

SUSAN. So is the hotel haunted?

(NAFISSATOU *appears.*)

NAFISSATOU. All hotels are haunted. It's a strange sad thing to do, I mean, killing yourself at all. But then going to this place and asking strangers, asking "servants" to clean your mess.

14. An Unproductive Interview with Spencer

SUSAN *and* SPENCER *nurse drinks in a cocktail lounge.*

SUSAN. I interview Spencer, the richest person I know, who's in town for a wedding. I think he's a venture capitalist or maybe a land baron. He's a board member at a theatre.

SPENCER [3]. So, this is where you work?

SUSAN. Sort of. I mean. Yeah.

SPENCER. You aren't going to record this, are you?

SUSAN. Well. I was about to ask your permission.

SPENCER. You can't.

So you're writing about DSK and international economic policy?

SUSAN. I want to explore morality in America. How a perceived sex scandal can destroy a political career, meanwhile, other politicians have killed people. Ted Kennedy killed a woman with his car yet continued to serve in the Senate. Dick Cheney shot his friend while quail hunting.

SPENCER. Cheney shot his friend IN THE FACE. Cheney didn't even issue an apology. The friend, who also suffered a heart attack, publicly apologized to Cheney. THAT'S power. Ahh. It's so good.

SUSAN. How can DSK advocate for economic aid to the poor and immigrant classes, yet degrade and abuse women?

SPENCER. I hate to burst your bubble—

SUSAN. —You love to burst my bubble…

SPENCER. But the idea that the IMF helps poor people is bogus. The IMF gives loans for neoliberal reforms that allow European companies to profit by disrupting local economies and drowning poor countries in debt. So the notion that DSK heads this fund and abuses a refugee woman is actually entirely fitting. I do remember that the maid was unreliable. Wasn't she a prostitute, with a boyfriend in prison or something?

>   (NAFISSATOU DIALLO *appears*.
>
>   SUSAN *looks at* NAFISSATOU.)

NAFISSATOU. Here are some of the allegations.

DSK DEFENSE LAWYER 1 [1]. Ms. Diallo lied about her immigration.

DSK DEFENSE LAWYER 2 [4]. Ms. Diallo told a compelling story about being "gang raped" in Guinea and her husband dying in jail.

DSK DEFENSE LAWYER 1. Later she revealed the story was memorized from a cassette recording.

DSK DEFENSE LAWYER 2. Just a sob story to get political asylum—

SUSAN. But she did say she had been raped in Guinea, just not in the way she reported to immigration.

>   (*The* LAWYERS *snort. Rapid speech in following section.*)

DSK DEFENSE LAWYER 1. She lied about her income to protect public housing.

DSK DEFENSE LAWYER 2. She lied about a dependent on a tax form.

DSK DEFENSE LAWYER 1. She changed her account of what she did after the encounter with Strauss-Kahn multiple times.

SPENCER. That's right. Unreliable.

SUSAN. What about the attack?

Her vagina was grabbed so hard it was red and bruised hours later.

DSK DEFENSE LAWYER 1. An irritation from her pantyhose.

SUSAN. The recurring pain in her shoulder, where DSK threw her against the wall.

DSK DEFENSE LAWYER 2. A work-related injury. Perhaps from repeated movements using a heavy vacuum cleaner.

SUSAN. And the semen?

DSK DEFENSE LAWYER 1. Is abandoned tissue alone a determinant of consent? No, it is not.

DSK DEFENSE LAWYER 2. And then.

DSK DEFENSE LAWYER 1 & 2. The smoking gun phone call!

DSK DEFENSE LAWYER 1. Diallo speaks with an ex-boyfriend in prison where she said in an obscure African dialect—

NAFISSATOU. "Don't worry, this guy has a lot of money. I know what I'm doing."

>(NAFISSATOU *winks*.)

SUSAN. But that could have been a bad translation.

DSK DEFENSE LAWYER 1. In just a few short weeks, her credibility crumbled. From the perfect victim—

DSK DEFENSE LAWYER 2. Pious, devout Muslim woman, shattered by this experience to—

DSK DEFENSE LAWYER 1. Liar,

DSK DEFENSE LAWYER 2. Extortionist,

DSK DEFENSE LAWYER 1 & 2. Prostitute.

>(*Triumphant, the* LAWYERS *fling aside their briefcases and begin making out. A shift. The* LAWYERS *and* DIALLO *exit.*)

SPENCER. Even logistically, this case makes no sense.

Okay. Not to be crude here, but how does a senior citizen force a 32-year-old robust woman to perform oral sex? I mean, the woman has teeth.

>(SPENCER *chomps his teeth. Disgusted,* SUSAN *downs her drink.* SPENCER *tries to order a round from* MUHAMMAD.)

SUSAN. That's not our waiter. Can you imagine how many times he must have done this kind of thing, for him to think he could get away with it? How difficult and scary it must have been for Diallo to come forward in the first place?

>(KARA *brings the drinks. He smiles winningly at her.*)

SPENCER. (*To* KARA.) Thanks, sweetheart. Maybe it was a transaction.

Sounds like a womanizer and a con artist had a meeting.

SUSAN. She might not be perfect. She might have lied at some point. She may have thought about capitalizing on the rape. The truth may not be simple. Doesn't mean she's not a rape victim.

SPENCER. Then I toss out a rejoinder about your transparent liberal feminist agenda.

SUSAN. You say that like it's a bad thing.

SPENCER. I change the subject with a long anecdote about meeting Sarkozy's brother, Olivier, in a ski lodge in Trois Vallées.

SUSAN. I can't remember most of the things you said. Not that it was that useful. There was a veneer of power and status over everything.

SPENCER. Tonight I had dinner with Ed Snowden's lawyer.

SUSAN. You told me that three times.

SPENCER. I had dinner with Ed Snowden's lawyer earlier tonight.

He wants to move to Maui, but in New York, he plays squash with the culture editor of *The New Yorker*, and how can you beat that?

SUSAN. It's strange when men like you open up. Everyone I know is in theater.

You are the only person I know who is like you.

SPENCER. I had—

SUSAN. I get tired. I don't remember what you say.

SPENCER. By the way, before I saw you, I had dinner with Ed Snowden's lawyer.

—No. I didn't. You're mischaracterizing me. I told you about my friend Benny, at Princeton. A girl falsely accused him of molesting her. She had a powerful father who ruined Benny, had him registered as a sex offender, even after the girl admitted he was innocent. And then he hung himself—

Another round please.

SUSAN. I can't. Just the check.

SPENCER. I got it.

SUSAN. No please, you're helping me.

SPENCER. They already ran my card. Seriously, playwright. Put it away.

SUSAN. Thanks.

SPENCER. Let me ask you, have you ever, for one instant, entertained the notion that Dominique Strauss-Kahn is the true victim? He had the most to lose. Whatever happened to the presumption of innocence?

(SUSAN *pauses*.)

15. Big Pharma

JANY *discreetly signals* SUSAN *over.*

SUSAN. Jany! I thought Friday was your last day.

When are you going to the Academy?

JANY. I can't be a cop. It's my eye. My vision is too jacked up. I didn't pass the physical. They said I'm a liability. I guess. I gotta figure out what to do instead.

I guess…keep working here.

SUSAN. ...

Oh man. I'm so sorry—

JANY. Copy. Send it.

Talk later?

(SUSAN *starts to go into the door.*)

Can't go that way. You know who's in there?

SUSAN. Sign says—

JANY. No, it's not what the sign says. It's Novagen. Big Pharmaceutical Company. That guy, Jimmy? He's a nice guy. But he's a security guard for their paper. He gets paid bank just to guard their documents and materials. Nothing is allowed out of the room.

SUSAN. And the fake sign?

JANY. People come to protest, when they learn Novagen is here. Michael Moore came once. This one time, I was standing outside, and this guy, he was kind of wobbling funny. He wore a long jacket. He tried to go into the room.

(PACKAGE MAN [5] *enters, wearing a long coat.*)

Sir. Can I help you?

PACKAGE MAN [5]. Novagen in there?

JANY. Can I help you with something?

PACKAGE MAN. Sure. I got a package delivery for Carl Finkley.

(*The* PACKAGE MAN *holds up an ominous, lumpy package, wrapped thickly with tape.* JANY *eyes the package.*)

JANY. Sir. All deliveries go to security in the back.

PACKAGE MAN. Sir. I need to put it in his hands, directly, sir.

JANY. I can't allow that. Sir.

—He protests. Louder. We continue to argue.

He realizes we're at an impasse.

(PACKAGE MAN *grabs onto* JANY's *arm.*)

There are oozing open sores on his arms. He's wearing shorts under his long coat, and I could see the sores covering his legs.

PACKAGE MAN. You're a black man.

You're like me.

Why are you helping the people inside there?

Don't you know the people inside of that room right now are making decisions that make it impossible for me to be well?

I can never be well.

I can never get the medicine I need.

I can never afford the medicine I need because of the people in that room.
Why—
Why you helping them?
How much they paying you?
JANY. Sir, I need to ask you to leave or I'm going to have to call the police.
—White powder spills out of the package, and lands on my arm.
The man runs off.
I tell people in Novagen what happened. The contact says
NOVAGEN REP [2]. (*Sweetly.*) Don't worry. Happens all the time.
JANY. I need to report this to the police. It could be Anthrax or—
NOVAGEN REP. We would really prefer you didn't. But thank you *So* much.
JANY. So I wash the powder off my arm and go back to work.
SUSAN. What if you had let him in? Do you ever wonder?
JANY. Don't cause trouble.
SUSAN. You aren't curious what would have happened?
What he would have said?
What was in that package?
JANY. I'm just doing my job. They're just doing theirs.
SUSAN. I don't think that's true.
Why do they always get to win?
JANY. Who is "they"? Susan?
They just people.
On their coffee breaks, all they do is talk about their kids.
I'm not going to let some crazy man in there, just to prove a point.

>(JANY *exits.* SUSAN *looks at the* PACKAGE MAN. *She walks to the meeting room door and opens it. They exchange looks. The* PACKAGE MAN *goes through the door. She follows him into the room. A very bright white light.*)

End of Act I

ACT II

16. Big Pharma

> SUSAN *is inside the meeting room.*
> NAFISSATOU *watches her.*
> SUSAN *finds the* PACKAGE MAN*'s package on the floor.*
> *She opens up the package. It is full of anti-pharmaceutical protest pamphlets and posters with slogans such as "Healthcare is a Human Right," "PHARMA GREED KILLS," and "Healthcare for PROFIT not for People."*
> SUSAN *pulls out a large, cartoonish pill. It says* GREED. *She rubs her hands. This was the source of the white powder.*

NAFISSATOU. What did you think was going to happen?

> (*Disappointed,* SUSAN *throws the package and materials in the trash.*
> JANSEN *offers* SUSAN *a shot.* SUSAN *clinks, dejectedly. They shoot their drinks surreptitiously.*)

SUSAN & JANSEN. (*Hawaiian toast.*) Kāmau.

> (SUSAN *and* JANSEN *watch* ADJO [4], *the bartender, serve women at the bar.*)

SUSAN. Jansen, what are those women doing here? The event ended 30 minutes ago.

JANSEN. They're here for Adjo.

SUSAN. This is not at all surprising. Adjo is a bartender, a bassist, and a single dad. He's also strikingly beautiful. His father was an intellectual in Liberia who fled to Norway. Adjo had a part in one of Norway's most iconic art films.

ADJO [4]. I don't usually like to say which one. But if you're a cinephile then you've definitely seen it.

TRISH [2]. Hello…

SUSAN. I think you're being summoned. Don't go. They're just trying to get laid on—

JANSEN. Ladies. Happy Valentine's Day.

> (ADJO *pours shots.*)

SUSAN. We can't drink on camera.

ADJO. There's no cameras in this corner. Come on. Live a little.

SUSAN. Shit. You're right.

> (*Everyone but* JANSEN *drinks.*)

RICH. You ladies work for Merrill Lynch?

TRISH. That's right. I—
SUSAN. I completely forget what you tell me.
TRISH. It doesn't matter because I'm not interested in you anyway. Hey. Jansen. Adjo, be our dates!
RICH. Ladies. You don't have any plans on V-day?
TIFFANY [6]. Hell no. New York men are terrible. There's that ratio. The 1.5 single, never been married woman to every one single man.
APRIL [5]. I feel that ratio every day…
ADJO. Hey now. Being single just means you're strong enough to wait for who you deserve.
APRIL. Mm.

 (ADJO *makes another round of shots.* TRISH *clinks glasses with* ADJO.)

TRISH. Adjo, you are fucking beautiful
TIFFANY. Fucking beautiful.   **APRIL.** (*Echoing.*) beautiful…
TRISH. —But all bartenders in places like this are.
SUSAN. Actually, I think Adjo is pretty unique.

 (*A face-off between* TRISH *and* SUSAN.)

APRIL. There are so many beautiful, amazing people living in this city. And if you start comparing yourself…
TIFFANY. Yer fucked.
RICH. The average span of a New Yorker is five years. In that time, they burn through their savings or their trust funds. They party. They get work experience and then they move somewhere else, where they can actually own things, like cars, and houses. We who stay on with nothing. The artists. We're the crazy ones.
TRISH. Another round!

 (*Everyone but* JANSEN *drinks.*)

SUSAN. Shit. I feel drunk. Jansen, are you not drinking?
JANSEN. I'm avoiding all sugars.

 (TRISH *slams back a second shot and winks at* ADJO. RICH *sulks.*)

TRISH. Where are you from?
RICH. San Fran.
TRISH. What part?
RICH. (*Disappointed.*) You know it? I'm from San Jose.
TRISH. Susan, where are you from? So exotic. Look at her cheekbones.

 (*Everyone looks at* SUSAN*'s cheekbones.*)

SUSAN. Trish, stop. *You're* beautiful.

TRISH. No. You are. Beautiful.

SUSAN. I hate doing this with women. You are in fact quite attractive and I wish I could own a handbag like yours.

TRISH. It doesn't matter because I'm only hitting on you to get attention from the men.

SUSAN. —I'm from Hawai'i.

TRISH. Wow. Hawaee. And you?

ADJO. New York.

APRIL. Wow. Really?

SUSAN. Adjo's lying because he doesn't feel like explaining that he's from Norway. And I shouldn't have said Hawai'i. It always prompts more conversation.

(TRISH *almost speaks*)

Let's skip the part where Trish tells me about her last trip to Maui.

TRISH. Jansen, where are you from?

JANSEN. *Hawai'i.* (*Hah-vai-e*)

APRIL. Wow, you too? Are you guys related or something?

SUSAN. We're cousins—I really like this lie. I've known Jansen since we were four. We went to kindergarten together and he's one of my best friends. I still question if I should have gotten him this job at The Lux. Once you start working here, it's hard to quit. —I'm heading out.

TRISH. Byeee!

SUSAN. (*To* JANSEN.) Did you still want to take the subway together?

TRISH. (*To* JANSEN.) Do you do hula? I find men that do hula incredibly sexy. Like those Hawaiian football players?

JANSEN. Well…as a matter of fact, I—

SUSAN. Jansen.

(SUSAN *and* JANSEN *exchange looks.*)

Uh. Okay. Bye everyone.

(*The* ENSEMBLE *drinks and hangs out without her.* SUSAN *leaves.*)

17. Serving Coffee

SUSAN *approaches* PETER [3] *in the restaurant.*

SUSAN. Okay. So, we are told most emphatically not to fraternize with hotel guests. But.

(SUSAN *grabs the coffee pot out of* KARA's *hands.*)

—Sir, can I top off your coffee?

A memory. Me at 22 serving coffee to a famous man.

PETER [3]. I'm good.

SUSAN. I'm sorry. I could get into a lot of trouble for speaking to you, but I'm a huge fan of your films. And your stage plays. I studied abroad in London, and I saw your play *Forcible Entry*, at The Young Vic. It was ah-mazing!!!!

PETER. Thanks. I felt good about it.

SUSAN. How is your stay?

PETER. It's just grand. I'm just trying to figure out what to do in New York on a Monday night. Can't see a play on a Monday night, can you?

SUSAN. If you like films, well, of course *you* do. Ha Ha! There's that French film with Isabelle Huppert at IFC? I heard that was good.

PETER. So, when are we going?

SUSAN. Me?

PETER. Join me at the cinema. We can grab a drink after. You are 21, aren't you?

SUSAN. Ha Ha! 22! So yeah! Ha Ha Ha!

PETER. See you tonight.

SUSAN. Wow. Great. Thank you so much. Wow.

    (SUSAN *walks to the bussing station.*)

My heart soaring, I tell the news to Rizal. He's from Indonesia. He's a drag queen/food runner.

RIZAL [1]. What's up baybee?

SUSAN. Rizal. Oh my God. Do you know who that was? We're going to see a movie. Oh my God. I grew up reading his plays.

RIZAL. A little old for you, no?

SUSAN. No no. It's not like that. He's like a mentor. He's older than my dad. There's no way he could think it was a date.

RIZAL. Did you mention your boyfriend?

SUSAN. No, we talked about film. Shit. He can't be interested, right? I mean, he's so much older than me.

    (ABDUR [5] *eats a muffin.*)

RIZAL. Hey! You eating muffin!

ABDUR [5]. So?

RIZAL. Aren't you ashamed? *Tumi roja rako na?*

ABDUR. I fast on my days off.

SUSAN. Oh right. It's Ramadan. You can't even drink water all day, right?

ABDUR. It's hard.

RIZAL. Oh yeah? Then how do I do it, baybee? I calling Ramadan police on you, man. You still hungry? Eat this bacon, man.
ABDUR. Shut up. *Kisu mone koiro na.* [Please don't mind.]
RIZAL. Don't be *munafiq*, okay? [Two-faced, non-observant.]
　(ABDUR *hurls his muffin in the trash and storms off.*)
See. He only eats when he thinks no one's looking.
SUSAN. Rizal. You speak Bengali too?
RIZAL. Just a squirt, baybee, so I can tell off these assholes. How many languages do you speak?
SUSAN. Well. Uh. You know.
Actually. It's a damn shame. My mother grew up in the time when it was important to seem as American as possible. So my grandparents never taught her. I should totally be fluent in Korean and maybe like Cantonese?
　(RIZAL *rolls his eyes.*)

18. Down the Rabbit Hole

Sound of a computer restarting.
SUSAN. Aw, man!
JANY. You okay Susie?
SUSAN. My computer crashed, so I had to re-create this scene and I think the original version was better.
JANY. Man, I hate that.
SUSAN. In this version, we fight.
JANY. Man, that's a bummer, we never fight.
SUSAN. I'm wrapping up my shift soon. You wanna grab a drink at the Tavern?
JANY. I'm on a double. Next time for sure!
SUSAN. Hey, can I ask you a dumb question?
JANY. No question is a dumb question.
SUSAN. I'm trying to gather public records about the DSK case. Figure out what I'm missing.
JANY. You still working on that thing?
SUSAN. Why do you say it like that?
JANY. Nothing. It's just, you never seem happy about it.
SUSAN. Writing plays doesn't make people happy.
JANY. Huh. Well maybe you should do something that does.
SUSAN. I'm not done yet, okay?

JANY. All right, well, you can always ask the NYPD office of Public Information.

And I'd characterize this as like a minor misunderstanding. Why you gotta make everything a big thing?

    (JANY *exits*.)

SUSAN. I send a request with the DCPI.

DCPI [1]. Incorrect Filing. You must send a FOIL request.

SUSAN. FOIL?

Okay. FOIL Request sent.

FOIL [5]. Dear Sir or Madam. In response to your letter requesting access to certain records under the New York State Freedom Of Information Law, further review is necessary. Your request has been assigned to Detective Halk.

SUSAN. This is so cool. Waiting on you, Detective Halk!

DETECTIVE HALK [4]. Reply from Detective Halk.

Dear Madam: I must deny access to the records you requested on the basis of Public Officers Law Section87(2)(a). These records are sealed under court order, pursuant to Criminal Procedure Law Section 160.50. Furthermore—

DSK. Suzanne, you are what the French call "Les incompétent."

    (SUSAN *shakes her fist at* DSK.)

SUSAN. Grr.

19. Shati

SUSAN. Hi. Are you new? I'm Susan.

SHATI [6]. I'm Shati. I'm trailing.

SUSAN. Can I ask you a few questions for an immigration project?

SHATI. You can ask me anything. At LaGuardia College, they put me on the cover of the adult continuing education catalog to encourage other adults.

SUSAN. Where are you from?

SHATI. I'm from Tibet. When I was eight, my uncle and I walked across Himalayas to India. I didn't get to say goodbye to my parents. My parents were in the village but I was in city. No phones. They didn't know we were going.

SUSAN. My god. And you were eight?

SHATI. My uncle lied to me. He said it'd only take five days. But it took thirty-eight days. We had to pretend we were visiting monasteries or we'd go to prison.

SUSAN. I wish you could have met Namgal. She had to do the walk too.

(DENNIS *approaches. He has witnessed* SUSAN *recording and interviewing.* SHATI *stiffens.* SUSAN *hides her notebook and phone.*)

SHATI. Hello Mr. Dennis.

DENNIS. You had a good day today? Did Aida help you?

SHATI. Yes, we went through everything in detail. Thank you.

DENNIS. Good. We be in touch.

(DENNIS *looks at* SUSAN. *He debates talking to her, he keeps moving.*)

SUSAN. I hope you get the job.

SHATI. Thanks.

SUSAN. How is housekeeping? It seems very tiring.

SHATI. I'll finish nursing school in three years. It's hard for making money while taking classes.

SUSAN. I was in school for a long time.

SHATI. You finished?

SUSAN. I'm done. Masters Degree.

SHATI. That's good!

SUSAN. Yeah.

SHATI. And you, you still work here?

SUSAN. Yep.

20. Serving Coffee Part 2

SUSAN *hides in the service hutch.*

RIZAL. Hi baybee, are you hiding back here?

SUSAN. A memory. Me at 22.

—Rizal. You see that guy?

RIZAL. Oh. Famous Guy.

SUSAN. I'm an idiot—God! We barely talked about theater.

RIZAL. Mmhm.

SUSAN. He didn't ask a single question about me or my writing.

RIZAL. So why didn't you just have sex with him, or did you?

SUSAN. Of course not! Two minutes in, he put his hand on my knee. And then he stroked it slowly for the entire film. I was totally frozen. I didn't know what to do. I didn't want to offend him. He's a legend. But I didn't want him to touch me. And I really, really didn't want him to finger-bang me in the IFC. I crossed my legs, and then kept shifting my body, until I was pressed as far away from him as possible, but he wouldn't get the hint. When the credits rolled, he told me to stay in my seat until everyone else had left.

But I jumped up and made an excuse and ran out.

RIZAL. Just have sex with him, baybee, and make him your daddy, then maybe he will be interested in your writing things. Who's he sitting with?

SUSAN. I think that's his wife.

RIZAL. Okay baby. You fret back here. I gotta get back to work.

(SUSAN *hides in the hutch. She grows disgusted with herself.*)

SUSAN. I'm not a kid anymore. I'm a grown-ass woman. I'm going out there. I'm going to tell that pompous jackass off. Right in front of his wife.

(*She goes forward. She chickens out.*)

Aw fuck, I'm such a coward.

I can't even name him in this play over a decade later.

RIZAL. It's okay baby. You going to be okay. It's harder for us girls.

(RIZAL *exits.*)

SUSAN. Rizal abruptly quit, so I never had a chance to interview him.

As a drag queen, he looks beautiful in makeup, utterly convincing as a woman, and once he did my makeup for a theater gala. In passing, he mentioned that right after he emigrated here from Indonesia, just after 9/11, he spent ten months in a Muslim Detention Center in Brooklyn, but he wouldn't say anything else about it.

(RIZAL *appears.*)

Rizal, you changed your number. Where did you go?

Are you safe? I'm never going to see you again, so I'll never know.

I miss you already.

If this were a real village, people wouldn't keep disappearing.

21. Write-Up

SUSAN *in the Human Resources office with* JEN. JEN *has an apple on her desk.*

SUSAN. Hi Jen, You wanted to see me?

JEN. Susan. You receive complaints that you've been distracting other workers.

SUSAN. Who made the complaint? Was it Dennis?

JEN. I'm not allowed to say. Can you explain what you were doing?

SUSAN. I was talking to other coworkers. Briefly.

JEN. All over hotel? Why you were recording them?

SUSAN. It's for. It's for school.

JEN. If it a personal matter, you should talk only on your scheduled breaks, in the employee cafeteria and not where guests might see you. Here is the write-up about the incident. You can add your version on form if you like.
You are on temporary probation.

SUSAN. Whatever. It's fine. I don't care.

(SUSAN *gets up to go.*)

JEN. You need to sign.
Here's your copy of the form.

SUSAN. I don't want it.

JEN. I have to give to you.

(SUSAN *takes the form. She crumples it up.*

DENNIS *walks past with a clipboard.* SUSAN *follows. He does not slow his pace.*)

SUSAN. Dennis. Hey. Dennis. Dennis. Dennis. Can I talk to you?

DENNIS. Yes, Miss.

SUSAN. My name is Susan.

DENNIS. Did you need help, Miss?

SUSAN. Do you have a problem with me?

DENNIS. That depends. Do we have a problem?

SUSAN. What? No. I don't know?

DENNIS. I have problem with you distracting my team while they are on the floor.

SUSAN. I've barely taken five minutes of anyone's time.
I don't want to get anyone in trouble, so. Forget it.
I'm done doing interviews anyway. It's finished.

(*She walks away.*)

DENNIS. Hey. Miss.
You don't want to interview me?

SUSAN. Excuse me?

DENNIS. You interviewed everyone else. Not me, because I'm a manager?

SUSAN. Do you want to be interviewed?

DENNIS. I'm busy.

SUSAN. I don't know anything about Dennis. Here's maybe what he might say.

DENNIS. My name is Dennis. I'm probably about 48 years old. I'm from China or maybe Thailand?

(*Turns to* SUSAN.)

Really?

I wear a wedding ring, so I'm married. Probably for awhile.

I probably have a couple of kids, I think I mentioned them before?

This job probably means a lot to me.

It took me a long time to work my way up to manager. I probably worry about being respected by the higher-ups because of my accent. So I always follow my superiors and obey protocol to the letter, and expect everyone under me to follow me, absolutely. I don't have friends here. I distrust the young people in the restaurant who come and go. My team stays. Some of them have been here 19 years, since the opening of the hotel. I lead by example and I work longer and harder than anyone realizes.

SUSAN. So then why did you fire Namgal?

DENNIS. That's confidential.

SUSAN. Bullshit. You made up an excuse to fire a woman who'd been working here for nearly two decades.

DENNIS. You don't know why we let go Namgal.

You can make me look like Bad Guy in your story,

but if you not going to ask me to my face,

what's the point?

22. A Pattern of Behavior

SUSAN. Tristane Banon is beautiful—white, wealthy, and well-spoken. In 2003, when she was a 23-year-old aspiring journalist, she tried to interview DSK, a family friend. As she entered his home, she alleges he jumped her like a "rutting chimpanzee," grabbing her breasts and forcing his hand down her pants.

She believes she would have been raped if she hadn't fled the room. Her depiction of the attack is chillingly similar to Nafissatou's. Continents and years apart. Banon was from the same social circle as DSK. *She* might have been believed. —Why didn't you come forward?

TRISTANE BANON [2]. Put yourself in my place. My mother told me, if I go to the police, for the rest of my life I am the girl who had a problem with the politician. It's terrible to turn on the television and hear them say, he is the superhero, a savior, capable of everything. He'd revive the country, lower taxes, and bring happiness to each French household. But then on the news, I see the story about how the baboon attacks the chambermaid. Just in the same way. So I come forward.

But it has been too many years. I am too late.

So I am still the girl who had a problem with the politician....

And I did not help anyone else.

SUSAN. But Banon was young. Piroska Nagy is in her late 40s and a globally renowned macroeconomist. She was DSK's subordinate at the IMF. In 2008, he was accused of an inappropriate relationship with her. But the IMF ruled it was consensual.

PIROSKA NAGY [6]. Consensual? I was damned if I did and damned if I didn't. He's undeniably a brilliant analytical mind but his lack of interest towards other people makes him prone to make terrible mistakes of judgement. He's ill-equipped to lead an institution where women work under his command.

SUSAN. So then why did you stop the sexual harassment investigation?

PIROSKA NAGY. I did not fully trust the internal process at the IMF. And I had suffered enough public humiliation, and so had my husband. So I had no choice but to resign. I did write a private letter, warning the IMF about DSK.

SUSAN. What aren't you saying about him?

PIROSKA NAGY. How many times must I be punished and humiliated by the same man?

SUSAN. The Nagy affair happened three years before DSK attacked Nafissatou. Nafissatou is not glamorous and rich like Tristane Banon. She's not powerful or educated like Piroska Nagy.

In fact, Nafissatou cannot read or write in any language. She was placed in the Sofitel by a relief organization after she was granted refugee asylum from Guinea. But still she came forward.

After two months of silence, she gave an interview on national television about what happened in Room 2806.

NAFISSATOU. I say, "I'm so sorry."

He comes to me and grabs my breasts.

— "Sir, stop this. I don't want to lose my job,"

— "He say, 'You're not going to lose your job.'"

I don't look at him. I am so afraid. I didn't expect anyone in the room. He pulls me hard to the bed. He tries to put his penis in my mouth, so I shut my mouth, and turn my head. I push him. I get up. I wanted to scare him.

—Look, there is my supervisor right there!

But he say there is nobody out there, and nobody is going to hear. I keep pushing him away. I don't want to hurt him. I don't want to lose my job. He shoves me hard. He push up my dress and tear down my panty hose. Then he. He grips my crotch, it still stay red at hospital, hours later. He push me to my knees and grabs my head, so hard here. And he. He push himself into my mouth.

He is going like, "uhh, uhh, uhh." He say, "Suck my"

—I don't want to say.

I feel something wet and sour come into my mouth and I spit it on the carpet. I run. I run out of there. I am running and spitting. I run to the hallway. I so scared. I don't want to lose my job. I hide in the hallway. I'm standing there spitting. I felt so alone. So scared.

Then I see the Man come out of 2806 and head for the elevator. I don't know how he got dressed so fast, and with baggage. He looks at me like this.

(*She inclines her head and stares straight ahead.*)

Like he know I don't matter. That he know I won't say a thing.

He does not say a word. Just keeps walking.

SUSAN. Less than ten minutes after he left the hotel room, Strauss-Kahn made a call to his daughter to arrange lunch.

The criminal case against him was thrown out when the Manhattan District Attorney moved to dismiss the sexual assault case.

—How could you drop this case?

DISTRICT ATTORNEY [4]. We were all rooting for her. Dominique Strauss-Kahn's behavior seems odious at best and criminal at worst. But even victimhood is not a license to lie. If we do not believe her beyond a reasonable doubt, we cannot ask a jury to do so.

SUSAN. Dominque Strauss-Kahn was never required to testify under oath about what happened in Room 2806. Nafissatou Diallo put herself out in the open. For what?

Because just after he was released, he said this in a CNN "exclusive interview."

DSK. The only thing that remains clear is that I have suffered a terrible injustice. What happens in a room is a private thing unless prosecutors find something to tell you that you are going to be charged, and they have proof of that. And then, if they don't have proof, then it becomes a private thing again, and nobody has to say anything about it.

23. Fucking Trolls

SUSAN. Here are things said about Nafissato Diallo by Internet trolls.

[1]. – What a fucking bitch. She's a liar who wanted to get money. She should be kicked out from the States and go back to Africa.

[3]. – She's a French intelligence operative used by political opponents of DSK.

[2]. – You know the owners of the Sofitel have ties to Sarkozy.

[6]. – It was Putin.

[4]. – Oh please. She's a little piece of shit who's trying to extract money from a rich man. All he "did" is consensual sex. If you have a problem with that, I suggest you consult a shrink.

[3]. – Black women have never found white men attractive so the white men have to rape them as they did in history when they were slaves.

[6]. – He does not deserve that humiliation…he is a family man…

[1]. – I like Strauss-Kahn. I'd have voted for him.

[4]. – Absolutely disgusting woman. Send her back to…wherever…

[2]. – Look at her cunt face. She is a liar and she is—

SUSAN. Enough. —This is what the women's locker room sounds like when the housekeepers finish their shift.

(SUSAN *plays a recording of the housekeepers in the locker room.*)

24. Things I Did to Get into This Country

The ensemble become the WOMEN OF HOUSEKEEPING *with aprons and vacuums.*

NAFISSATOU. Things I did to get into this country.

[2]. I was sponsored by my Aunt.

[1]. Cousin.

[6]. Father's second wife.

[4]. I found a large nugget of gold in the Birim River. My sister and I had been looking every day for two years, and then there it was, glittering under the silt. It paid our way here. No one here believes me, but it's true.

[1]. I lived apart from my daughter.

[4]. My parents.

[6]. My village.

[3]. My friends.

TANYA [6]. My husband was very abusive to me but doted on our child. I won the green card lottery to come here. He wouldn't let me take my son. But I couldn't stay.

I had to leave my son, I'll never see him again. I have another son now, he's eight months old, I have a hard time leaving him to come to work, so I get write-ups for being late.

NADINE [2]. (*Moroccan.*) My husband and I were mid-divorce in Marrakesh. We married young. I made plans to come here. Everything was in order. My sponsor. All of my money. Every favor was called in. A month before my flight, I found out I was pregnant. My parents would never approve, no one would let me leave if they knew. So I got an abortion, where I learned I had been carrying twins.

NAFISSATOU. The things we do. Sometimes for our families, for our future.

[2]. Sometimes for ourselves.

[1]. I lost the ability to speak my own language every day.

[4]. Or articulate complex thoughts.

[2]. I am so smart in Albanian. I was a writer. You have no idea.

[3]. You have no idea.

[5]. You have no idea.

[3]. I haven't been home in

[2]. 2 years

[5]. 5 years

[1]. 8 years

[4]. 14 years

[6]. 24 years

I want to go back.

DIWATA [1]. I went back to Palawan only once, when my parents arranged a marriage for me. The ceremony lasted a week. I claimed I got bit by a rabid dog to get an extra two weeks off of work. Only time I ever lied at work. Now we have five children.

[3]. After my father was killed, my mother brought us here on a freighter ship from Panama. We had a tough time here. I tried to work hard and be a leader for my siblings. After my brother was arrested, he got deported. And sometimes I wonder, what was it all for?

[4]. I want to retire there, one day. I hope.

NAFISSATOU. I will never go back.

25. Zoo Animals

SUSAN *and* JANSEN *fold napkins.*

SUSAN. Jansen, I haven't seen Adjo in forever. What the hell happened to him on Valentine's Day with the Merrill Lynch girls?

JANSEN. Oh right. He finally told me.

ADJO. Oh hey. Well. Valentine's Day? It was eventful.

I left with April. The quiet one. We were kissing on a bench, but she didn't want to go home with me that night. So I put her in a cab, and promised to call. A moment later, I realized, we'd forgotten to exchange information. I ran after it, but it was too late.

I walked around SoHo. Witnessing love everywhere. Thinking about life and my daughter. I felt so full of love and I wanted to share it with someone. I ended up going to a bar and getting very drunk. The next morning when I woke up, the sink was full of cookies and milk, and milk-soaked money. I don't know why.

JANSEN. I told him he must have gone to a bodega and bought some cookies.

SUSAN. Poor Adjo.

JANSEN. Is it a poor Adjo story? I'm not sure.

SUSAN. Yeah. I don't know. I'm not sure he's handling the divorce as well as he claims.

JANSEN. Hey. Um. Can I talk to you about something?

SUSAN. Uh. Sure. Of course.

JANSEN. I read the pages you sent.

SUSAN. Thanks for reading.

JANSEN. The thing is…The actual people are so much more interesting than what you depict.

SUSAN. There isn't time to…it's about trying to get their stories heard, even a little.

JANSEN. I mean, I helped you interview our friends, our colleagues.

But you've put us all on display. Like we're zoo animals.

These people are your friends. They trust you.

SUSAN. Shit. That's really not my intention. Well…thanks for your feedback…I.

JANSEN. Also…I don't like the way I was portrayed in the play. I was definitely drinking on Valentine's Day. We did a shot together.

SUSAN. Oh yeah…

JANSEN. Otherwise, I wouldn't have gone home with Trish.

SUSAN. You went home with Trish?

JANSEN. Well. Yeah.

But there's a bunch of other things too. Like the call with my dad. That's private. Are we just sidekicks on your big quest?

SUSAN. No. Of course not.

JANSEN. I mean. Why do you need our stories to tell yours?

SUSAN. It's not my story. I'm trying to figure things out. Are you mad?

JANSEN. I feel used. And two-dimensional.

SUSAN. I'm sorry you feel that way.
I can change your name and some of those details.
Or, I could flesh you out?
…Or would you rather just not be in the play?
JANSEN. I don't want to be in the play.
>   (JANSEN *exits the play.*)

26. Rules for Finding a Husband

KARA. Hey girl. You okay? No crying in the locker room.
SUSAN. Hey. I'm ok.
KARA. I wanted to say goodbye. It's my last shift.
SUSAN. Girl. Is that a ring on your finger?
KARA. Nikolai and I got married.
SUSAN. That's awesome!
KARA. I'm pregnant with twins, so you know, time to stop cocktailing.
SUSAN. How can you even fit into that dress?
KARA. I have to seriously suck it in. I'm 14 weeks.
SUSAN. I'm really happy for you guys. The fact that you met each other here, it's incredible.
For all these years at The Lux. I've seen honeymooners, hookups, and now coworkers fall in love. I've seen friends leave to pursue their dream jobs and others get fired over nothing, like "stealing" a disposable umbrella.
The woman who hired me died years ago.
I've trained dozens of people since.
Am I the new Evelyn?
The only thing that matters is music
>   (SUSAN *cues the music.*)

and lights.
>   (SUSAN *cues the lights.*)

Through it all, I've held onto the words of the Jewish mystic like a lucky penny.
Believing that God, fate, what have you, will send me real happiness and success very, very soon.
In life, in love, in writing.
If you are free, and only if you are free, a 28-year-old man will come into your life. This is the man for you.

He will come in the summer.

But ten years later. I'm still unmarried. No children. No career.

At least, not in a conventional sense. Then, the 28-year-old man comes to town.

28-YEAR-OLD MAN [3]. (*British.*) Oh hiya! Wow! This is where you work?

SUSAN. —Only now he's 38. He has smile creases around his eyes, a hint of gray in his hair. His shirts are never wrinkled.

38-YEAR-OLD MAN [3]. (*He looks around.*) Very posh. Hello my friend. It's been awhile.

SUSAN. Hi.

38-YEAR-OLD MAN. Are you flourishing?

SUSAN. He always asks me that. I always reply

—Yes.

But today I say

—No.

38-YEAR-OLD MAN. Why not?

SUSAN. —I don't want to worry him. I just can't muster up the lie anymore.

(*His phone buzzes. He gives it a quick glance.*)

What's that on your screen?

(*He holds up his mobile.*)

38-YEAR-OLD MAN. This is Hazel. My little girl.

SUSAN. A daughter! Show me.

(SUSAN *looks at photos of the baby,* 38-YEAR-OLD MAN *looks around the restaurant.*)

Oh my God, those dimples.

(*Notices ring.*)

Oh! And uh how long have you been married?

38-YEAR-OLD MAN. Few years now. It suits me. It's so beautiful here.

SUSAN. Is it?

KARA. Drinks for you. On the house.

(KARA *winks.* SUSAN *shoos her away.*)

38-YEAR-OLD MAN. Must have a lot of perks, working in a hotel.

SUSAN. Ha.

38-YEAR-OLD MAN. So what's wrong?

SUSAN. I'm not…happy here.

38-YEAR-OLD MAN. So why don't you leave?

SUSAN. The hotel or the play?

38-YEAR-OLD MAN. Both?

SUSAN. Did I ever tell you about the holy man—at least, I thought he was a holy man—that I met here? Actually, we sat at this table.

(*He gently takes her hand.*)

38-YEAR-OLD MAN. You did. I thought about that story a lot, for awhile. Life is funny.

(*He releases her hand.*)

But that prophecy of yours wasn't only about love.

JEWISH MYSTIC. You are strong but you choose to be weak. You choose to doubt.

SUSAN. It's actually very unhelpful when you're full of doubt to be told to trust your instincts. Basically…what you're saying is, the only reason I'm not succeeding is myself.

JEWISH MYSTIC. Yes, my child.

SUSAN. I haven't taken down DSK. Not even in my own fantasy.

DSK. How could you? It is preposterous. Besides. There is an endless supply of men like me, right? Men like me that you want to deny the due process afforded to every citizen.

SUSAN. You want to pretend you're a normal citizen? Your heiress wife paid your six-million-dollar bail then you served house arrest in a luxury townhouse with a full staff, and millions of dollars worth of art.

DSK. Why shouldn't I be comfortable in my lifestyle before I am charged?

SUSAN. I cast you out.

I cast you out of this play.

DSK. I'm late for a meeting anyway. It's exhausting playing an abstract and frankly, generic proxy for your feelings about septic patriarchy.

SUSAN. I hope you're in hiding under a rock somewhere.

DSK. Yes, if it please you, I am laying low. I remarried. And I'm taking it easy, playing chess and serving as an advisor for the Serbian government and opening up banks in South Sudan until my comeback.

(DSK *exits the play.*)

SUSAN. A comeback?

This is the part of the play where I'm supposed to talk about me, I guess.

This is the part of the play, where if I was a fictional character,

I would admit that I want to talk about Nafissatou because I don't know how to talk about my own rape.

And how powerful men take our narratives.

That men can have facts.

And women have stories.

But I haven't been raped.

I've never experienced a tenth of what Nafissatou Diallo had to endure.

In her native Fulani, Nafissatou said the reason she would do anything to come to America, is so that her daughter could escape the genital mutilation she suffered.

NAFISSATOU. I had a bad thing happen when I was young, when I was a little girl. I got cut on my private parts. I won't let them to do that to my daughter. I bring her here when she is seven years old.

To get her to America, where she would be safe, I would tell any lie.

SUSAN. Every generation has a dream to push the next generation forward. My great-grandmother was a picture bride from Korea.

In Hawai'i when men working on the plantation wanted to get married, they sent photos of themselves back home, hoping to entice a wife with a new life in Paradise.

When she was 17, my great-grandmother took a one-way trip from Korea to Hawai'i. She married a man nearly 30 years her senior. He had sent her a photograph of himself as a much younger man. They worked on the plantation together. She had nine of his children, then he dropped dead. She struggled the rest of her life to feed her kids, and eventually worked as a cleaning lady at the military barracks.

She asked again and again to go back to Korea. But there was never enough money or time to make that happen. She wanted to be buried in Korea. But she rests in O'ahu Cemetery. I think about her as I think about Nafissatou.

I'm the first generation in my family that didn't work on the plantation or in the cannery. When *I* was 17, I took a one-way trip to New York, to pursue a Bachelor of Fine Arts degree at an overpriced private school we couldn't possibly afford. We may never pay off those loans.

My mother is in the audience today. She flew all the way from Hawai'i to see this play. She sees all of my plays.

Mom, I'm sorry I spent 12 years at this crappy job that I hate and didn't even try to get a better one. Sometimes I feel like I failed you by working here. Because your dreams for me are so big that I'm afraid I can never measure up to them.

What if I told you.

Mom.

Grandma.

And to all the women who came before.

I am not worthy of your sacrifice.

I am not worthy of the collection of things you had to endure.
> (*The* WOMEN OF HOUSEKEEPING *reappear.*)

WOMEN OF HOUSEKEEPING. (*Staggered or in unison.*) I am a warrior,
so my daughter may be a merchant,
so that her daughter may be a poet.
> (SUSAN *drinks.*)

SUSAN. I can't do this anymore. I stop writing.
I take a leave of absence from work. That's a lie. I still go to work.
And by absurd, improbable, stupid chance,
I meet a truly incredible journalist from the U.K., who covered the DSK trial.
She's staying at The Lux.
—Kate. How do you convince powerful men to speak with you?
Hell. How do you convince someone like Nafissatou to speak to you?
Someone who's been attacked by the press over and over?

KATE [2]. Well, I have a different approach for every person I interview. A different strategy. You must read each person very, very carefully or you will blow the whole thing. I have a notebook in every size. Sometimes, big men, they need to feel important, I pull out a notebook that's the size of the 10 Commandments Tablet. And then, for some people, sometimes women, but really it's not a gendered thing? Anyone who's skittish, I have a notebook about the size of a thumb. And I touch their arm, and look into their eyes, and I say, "Love, do you mind if I just jot some of this down?"

SUSAN. And they keep talking?

KATE. Mostly.

SUSAN. Tell me more about Nafissatou Diallo.

KATE. Why?

SUSAN. Because it matters what happened to her.
Her life is not salacious headlines. Her life is not a footnote in the life of a famous man.
Her life is not three minutes in a terrible, exploitative movie.

KATE. What are you trying to prove?
> (KATE *touches* SUSAN*'s arm.*)

It's all right, love, you can say it.

SUSAN. Nafissatou Diallo's name has over 720,000 hits on Google.
Every single article references one of the worst days of her life.
Her name is forever entwined with his. When asked why she chose to come forward, publicly, despite all of the terrible consequences she faced, Nafissatou said

NAFISSATOU. What happened to me…I don't want to happen to any other woman.

SUSAN. I think about that, all the time.

KATE. Nafi is a lovely person. What I observed was how much pride she had for her work. It's so frustrating, the moment they go to trial. With these women, who are accusing powerful men of rape, once the jury sees that they lied once, and of course these women have had to lie at some point to get into this country. They are caught on one smaller, unimportant lie, and then their entire case is out the window.

SUSAN. I want to think that if this went to trial today, things would be different.

KATE. You know she's still here. In New York.

SUSAN. Where?

KATE. She probably won't talk to you. But you could try.

27. A Restaurant in the Bronx

SUSAN. And so, I try.

Just opened in the Bronx is Chez Amina.

Nafissatou Diallo opened it with the money from the civil suit.

The restaurant is a small, clean 60-seater. It's a favorite of cab drivers and stays open from 5 a.m. to 3 a.m., daily. Chez Amina is also popular with the congregants of Masjid Sidiki, the mosque upstairs, who flock there after the noon call to prayer.

When a reporter dined at her restaurant and tried to interview her,

NAFISSATOU. Hello, how are you?

    (*The* REPORTER [4] *flashes a camera at her.*)

REPORTER [4]. Ms. Diallo? Just a few questions.

NAFISSATOU. Sorry, no, no…

REPORTER. For a divorced Muslim single mother of a teenage daughter from the impoverished West African nation of Guinea, opening a restaurant in New York with that sort of money is the epitome of the American immigrant dream. Now it seems Nafissatou Diallo wants to let her food, and not her story do the talking.

    (*This scene takes the time it needs.*)

SUSAN. Hi…

…Are you open?

NAFISSATOU. Yes.

Sit anywhere you like.

Would you like some water?
SUSAN. Yes.
NAFISSATOU. Here is a menu.
SUSAN. Thank you.
NAFISSATOU. Do you know what you want?
SUSAN. What's.
What's your favorite dish?
NAFISSATOU. Thiebou Djeun and Yassa Chicken.
SUSAN. Okay. I'll uh. I'll have that.
You're the owner?
NAFISSATOU. Mm. Yes.
    (SUSAN *begins to ask* NAFISSATOU *a question.*)
SUSAN. I was—
Could I—
    (SUSAN *stops herself. She looks at* NAFISSATOU.)
This is a beautiful place.
NAFISSATOU. Thank you.

End of Play

MARGINAL LOSS
by Deborah Stein

Copyright © 2018 by Deborah Stein. All rights reserved. CAUTION: Professionals and amateurs are hereby warned that *Marginal Loss* is subject to a royalty. It is fully protected under the copyright laws of the United States of America and of all countries covered by the International Copyright Union (including the Dominion of Canada and the rest of the British Commonwealth), the Berne Convention, the Pan-American Copyright Convention and the Universal Copyright Convention, as well as all countries with which the United States has reciprocal copyright relations. All rights, including professional, amateur stage rights, motion picture, recitation, lecturing, public reading, radio broadcasting, television, video or sound recording, all other forms of mechanical or electronic reproduction, such as CD-ROM, CD-I, information storage and retrieval systems and photocopying, and the rights of translation into foreign languages, are strictly reserved. Particular emphasis is laid upon the matter of readings, permission for which must be secured from the Author's agent in writing.

Required royalties must be paid every time this play is performed before any audience, whether or not it is presented for profit and whether or not admission is charged.

All inquiries concerning rights, including amateur rights, should be addressed to: United Talent Agency, 888 Seventh Avenue, 7th Floor, New York, NY 10106. ATTN: Rachel Viola, Viola_R@unitedtalent.com

ABOUT *MARGINAL LOSS*

> *This article first ran in the* Limelight Guide to the 42nd Humana Festival of New American Plays, *published by Actors Theatre of Louisville, and is based on conversations with the playwright before rehearsals for the Humana Festival production began.*

When shell-shocked colleagues John and Allegra report for work in a cavernous, unfamiliar New Jersey warehouse, they're still reeling in the wake of calamity, and barely know where to begin. It's only been 48 hours since the offices of their investment firm were destroyed in the attack on the World Trade Center, and nobody yet grasps what's happening—except that luck has spared these few traders, while most of their coworkers remain missing. Along with Cathy, their self-appointed leader, they stumble their way through grief as they brace for the overwhelming task of recouping their losses. Aside from the records in this storage facility, they've got one computer, pen and paper, and untold missing transactions. But there's also a temp: enter Margaret, a recent college graduate eager to help. Will the team be ready when the stock market reopens in mere days—and can things ever return to normal? *Should* they?

Capturing the precariousness of this moment with fascinating insight, Deborah Stein's *Marginal Loss* unfolds in the days following the 2001 devastation of the Twin Towers, as a group of grieving coworkers try to piece their business back together. Stein traces this exploration back to her own assignment as an office temp the week after the tragedy. "I was sent to this warehouse, and there were three or four people there from a company that had been located near the top of the North Tower," she recalls. "These were the employees who hadn't been at work that day, for whatever reason. They wanted me to sort unlabeled data tapes that were the backup for old computers, but didn't have machines that could read them. So I made coffee, and got lunch, but after a few days they let me go, because there was no work to do. I remember feeling like I had no idea what they were experiencing, and it was absolutely none of my business. And anything I could say would not be enough."

But it didn't occur to Stein to write about this experience until years later, when she told the story to her husband—who'd watched the second plane hit from his office across the street. They had often spoken about that day, but she'd never mentioned her temp job. Confronted with his surprise, she explained, "It didn't feel like my story to tell." The New York native had been out of town on 9/11, and had watched the crisis on television while calling friends and family. "I felt uncomfortable trying to claim it as something I'd experienced," she admits. A conversation ensued about what gives someone the right to tell a story like this one, and the many narratives that had glossed over the confusion of the tragedy's aftermath, trading on comfortable hindsight—so Stein's husband encouraged her to write her own version. "9/11 so quickly got co-opted for political propaganda, and processed sentimentally by Hollywood," Stein contends. "Now we know that it was an event in isolation, but then, nobody knew what was going to happen next. New Yorkers were very gentle with each other, but that kindness was undergirded with this sense of absolute terror and uncertainty."

So in *Marginal Loss*, when a jet flies overhead or a siren is heard through the warehouse walls, the feeling that the city might be under siege is still fresh. And as a theatrical space, the warehouse reflects this new emotional reality. "It becomes a metaphor for the way that any cataclysmic event dislocates us," Stein observes, "and the world you live in after the cataclysm is never going to be the same." In the quartet of coworkers facing this tenuous existence, no one processes their shock in the same way. But showing up for work might give the chaos some form—or at least an answer to the question of what to do next.

Stein created these four sharply observed characters very intuitively. "I knew that Margaret, the temp, was going to be the interloper," she explains. "The other three are based on anecdotes I've heard about the utterly random ways that people missed work that day, or how this experience altered their path in life." The playwright also delved into research on World Trade Center companies and what it took to revive them, which led her to the tale of a CEO who'd made a controversial decision in order to provide for the affected families. "I was interested in the person in a leadership position whose way of dealing with crisis is to use their business savvy," says Stein.

As the team rallies around the colossal task of rebuilding a business, they've got no time to waste. "These companies were working around the clock to be ready for the bell when the stock market opened the next Monday morning," Stein relates. Capturing the suspense of that make-or-break moment, and "creating drama out of the minutiae of trading stocks and bonds," both seemed like thrilling challenges to tackle. But in raising the question of what returning to "business as usual" really means—for these characters, and the country—*Marginal Loss* provocatively complicates this story of a financial firm reaching for a comeback. "The people we're rooting for," Stein notes, "are also the people who destroyed our economy seven years later. I find that paradox so fascinating."

—Amy Wegener

BIOGRAPHY

Deborah Stein is a playwright and director. Most recently, her play *Marginal Loss* premiered at the Humana Festival. She is one half of Stein | Holum Projects, a collaboration with Suli Holum that has resulted in two critically-acclaimed plays, *The Wholehearted* (world premiere at Center Theatre Group and La Jolla Playhouse) and *Chimera* (HERE Artist Residency; Under the Radar premiere; Gate Theatre in London). She directed and co-created Keith Wallace's widely produced *The Bitter Game*, a commission from La Jolla Playhouse that has toured internationally. Her work has been produced and developed at theaters including Playwrights Horizons, Clubbed Thumb, Berkeley Repertory Theatre, Boston Court, Seattle Repertory, The Orchard Project, Kelly Strayhorn Theater, Bay Area Playwrights Festival, Minnesota Jewish Theatre, and Workhaus. She got her start devising plays with Pig Iron Theatre Company and subsequently worked with some of the country's leading devised theater makers, including Joseph Chaikin, Lear deBessonet, and Dominique Serrand. Her writing has been published in *TheatreForum, Play: A Journal of Plays,* and *The Best American Poetry*. Stein currently teaches at the University of California, San Diego and has previously taught at Yale, New York University, Princeton, and The New School. She received her MFA from Brown, under the mentorship of Paula Vogel, and has received two Jerome Fellowships, a McKnight Advancement Grant, a Bush Fellowship, and grants from NEFA and NYSCA. She is a member of Center Theatre Group's L.A. Writers' Workshop, the Playwrights Union, and an alumna of New Dramatists. Born and raised in New York, she currently lives in Los Angeles.

ACKNOWLEDGMENTS

Marginal Loss premiered at the Humana Festival of New American Plays in March 2018. It was directed by Meredith McDonough with the following cast:

ALLEGRA PARK .... Nancy Sun
JOHN DAVIES .... Ted Kōch
MARGARET GALE .... Carla Duren
CATHY LAMB .... Jessica Wortham

and the following production staff:

Scenic Designer .... Andrew Boyce
Costume Designer .... Kathleen Geldard
Lighting Designer .... Paul Toben
Sound Designer .... Stowe Nelson
Media Designer .... Philip Allgeier
Stage Manager .... Stephen Horton
Assistant Stage Manager .... Leah V. Pye
Dramaturg .... Amy Wegener
Casting .... Paul Davis, Calleri Casting
Properties Director .... Mark Walston
Assistant Dramaturg .... Meghan McLeroy

CHARACTERS

JOHN DAVIES, 50s. Born and raised New Yorker, outer borough. Financial middle manager. Thought by now he'd be further along in his career. But, well, he is where he is. Overwhelmed and lost, but trying to lead.

ALLEGRA PARK, 30s. Extremely good at her job. One rank below John but her star is on the rise, so she acts as if they're professional equals. Her sharp competence and anger masks a deep sadness she hasn't even begun to comprehend, and which she will not show at any cost.

MARGARET GALE, 22. Recently graduated from a not-quite-Ivy-League school. Eager, earnestly professional. She's very capable but doesn't have direction in her life. Yet. But she thinks that she does. Pleasant, a go-getter, wants to be part of the team, quick to learn and adapt.

CATHY LAMB, 40s or 50s. Has worked extremely hard to get to where she is, and is not going to let go of an inch. One rank above John but has taken on the responsibilities of chief executive. Buries her feelings in order to be the most effective leader in a crisis.

SETTING

A warehouse in New Jersey, near the mouth of the George Washington Bridge.

TIME

This play takes place over eight days, September 13–20, 2001.

NOTE ON CASTING

There are four characters in this play. Please cast it in a way that looks like New York City in the early twenty-first century. At least three different races or ethnicities should be represented in the cast.

NOTES ON THE TEXT

A slash (/) in the middle of a line means the next line starts there. When (/) occurs at the beginning of the line, the line after should start at the same time.

Nonstandard punctuation and capitalization (or lack thereof) is intentional.

This is a play in which most things are left unsaid, or are said quietly, or are broken off mid-thought.

Words and phrases in (parentheses) are spoken, but not as to draw attention or even be heard.

Everybody in this world wakes up in the morning hoping that the previous day had been a bad dream, and then they remember it was real. And then they have to deal with it all over again.

There are as many ways to deal with shock and grief as there are people in the world.

For Andy.

Ted Kōch, Jessica Wortham, Carla Duren, and Nancy Sun
in *Marginal Loss*

42nd Humana Festival of New American Plays
Actors Theatre of Louisville, 2018
Photo by Dana Rogers

MARGINAL LOSS

DAY 1 (Thursday, September 13).

A cavernous room in an anonymous warehouse. Cement walls, cement floors, exposed HVAC tubes racing across the ceiling, a slop sink upstage. Normally a storage facility, this room has been repurposed as a makeshift office space. Long white folding picnic tables and plastic folding chairs have been strategically placed to say "this is a functioning office," although it isn't. Not really.

A single computer perches on one of the tables; on another table, a couple of file boxes stuffed full of accordion files.

Elsewhere: a couple of six-packs of Coke, an empty pizza box or two. Or three.

JOHN and ALLEGRA hover over the computer as if it might be a magic 8-ball. They're holding their breaths. Silence. Then—

The wailing moan of an old telephone modem trying to connect. They watch the computer, listening to the sound the way people used to "watch" the radio. The monotone wail goes on for a long time. The suspense of it. Maybe ALLEGRA grabs JOHN's shoulder, it's so tense.

And then, finally! The clang of the modem connecting. They whoop and holler.

ALLEGRA. / YES!

JOHN. We're in!

ALLEGRA. Whoop whoop!

>*They high five and then hug, a huge rush of adrenaline.*
>*It's awkward, they separate quickly.*
>*That was weird.*
>*Sorry. Sorry. These aren't people who usually hug each other.*
>*What now?*

JOHN. I'll call Cath, let her know.

>*He picks up the phone, and then drops it like a hot potato.*

Shit!

ALLEGRA. Shit!

JOHN. I—

ALLEGRA. Drop it! Drop it! Put it back!

JOHN. I put it back!

He does.
Are we—
ALLEGRA. Hang on hang on—
She presses some buttons.
JOHN. oh god
ALLEGRA. yeah we're good
JOHN. oh thank god
ALLEGRA. thank GOD
JOHN. right?
ALLEGRA. that was close
JOHN. right?
ALLEGRA. fuck.
JOHN. fuck.
ALLEGRA. You gonna call her?
JOHN. What?
ALLEGRA. Lamb.
JOHN. Oh—
ALLEGRA. Here use my phone.
She rummages in her purse for her cell phone.
JOHN. We're not supposed to use personal—
ALLEGRA. John.
JOHN. Right.
Beat.
ALLEGRA. You really think / they opened?
JOHN. you saw / on CNN
ALLEGRA. / you watched it?
JOHN. that the BMA[1] wanted it yesterday
ALLEGRA. No!
JOHN. It's business.
ALLEGRA. I couldn't watch
JOHN. that was lucky
ALLEGRA. I mean CNN
JOHN. She did good.
ALLEGRA. I'm sure she did.
JOHN. (*"can you believe it?"*) "Woman Saved By Muffin…"

---

1. *Bond Market Association*

ALLEGRA. I heard.

JOHN. ...I mean...

    She hands him the phone.

ALLEGRA. Here you go.

JOHN. Do you have her number?

ALLEGRA. Who?

JOHN. Lamb. Her cell phone number.

ALLEGRA. No, why would I—

JOHN. well

ALLEGRA. oh.

JOHN. oh.

ALLEGRA. Well she said she'd call us to check in, so.

    They both look at the computer.

    If she calls while the modem is connected, she'll get a busy signal.

JOHN. well

ALLEGRA. well

JOHN. okay

ALLEGRA. well let's see if this even connects

JOHN. To what?

ALLEGRA. The the the server. You know. The network, the client lists. We can email her so we don't have to disconnect the modem.

    She pokes around with the outdated mouse.

JOHN. So is it there?

ALLEGRA. What?

JOHN. The network, the network, can / you get into the network?

    She's clicking the mouse like something's jammed.

ALLEGRA. hang on, I'm trying—

JOHN. sorry

ALLEGRA. it's ok

JOHN. well?

ALLEGRA. No network.

JOHN. What?

ALLEGRA. I'm telling you

JOHN. Let me see

    Something pops up on the screen.

ALLEGRA. (*Re: the screen.*) error message

JOHN. but

ALLEGRA. I guess, the wires, everything must have just / (gone out)
JOHN. what wires?
ALLEGRA. The network. The wires. You know, the *web*.
JOHN. I thought it was more like waves. Like, radio waves.
ALLEGRA. maybe
JOHN. anyway
ALLEGRA. I don't think so
JOHN. well anyway
ALLEGRA. So
JOHN. So

> *The siren of a fire truck wails in the distance. They both turn and look. Wait for it to fade away.*

ALLEGRA. So we're just going to have to do it the old-fashioned way.
JOHN. Yeah.

> *Beat.*

Do what?
ALLEGRA. Let's see what they have here

> *She starts unpacking one of the file boxes.*

JOHN. Backups?
ALLEGRA. Paper files.
JOHN. I thought / there'd be
ALLEGRA. What
JOHN. tapes. You know, like those old
ALLEGRA. sure yeah data tapes
JOHN. Right
ALLEGRA. Well I think we should just start with what we have here.

> *ALLEGRA heaves a file out of one of the boxes and opens it. There are scraps of legal paper, and old computer printer paper with the spool holes on the side.*

JOHN. You think / it's okay to
ALLEGRA. Why else would they tell us to come here?
JOHN. I haven't really been thinking straight.
ALLEGRA. Nobody is.
JOHN. They said, do you want to work. I said of course I do. They said, go to Jersey, so. Here I am.
ALLEGRA. well we're still together, so
JOHN. something's the same

ALLEGRA. Yeah

> *Beat.*
>
> *They both look at the box full of random papers.*

JOHN. so what is this, like old receipts and things?

> ALLEGRA *starts to look through the box.*

ALLEGRA. …receipts…bills…contracts…

JOHN. …relics…

ALLEGRA. Sure but we can use these paper files to put together a list of clients. I bet that's why they told us to come here.

JOHN. An excavation.

ALLEGRA. Sure, yeah. And then once we have the list, we can call them.

JOHN. Okay.

> *Beat.*

Wait, why?

ALLEGRA. Why what?

JOHN. What would we say?

ALLEGRA. We tell them we're—we're still here. We're still in business.

JOHN. Are we?

ALLEGRA. Of course we are

JOHN. We should ask Cathy.

ALLEGRA. Paris is still open.

JOHN. true

ALLEGRA. Boston, too, I think? And Cathy said she was going to New Milford, so. Let's focus on making a complete list of clients so we can be, you know, ready.

JOHN. I—

ALLEGRA. John. We're still a business. That means we have to tell our clients that they can still trade with us. Bonds are already trading, that means we're already behind.

JOHN. you're right, you're right

> *They start paging through the paper files. It's a mess of paper: chaotic, disorderly. They don't know what they're looking at. They don't know what they're looking for.*
>
> *But it's better to do something than nothing, so.*
>
> *They make piles.*
>
> *A helicopter draws close, and then passes into the distance. They look and listen. Then, return to work.*
>
> *After a while:*

ALLEGRA. I heard they're moving us to Midtown.

JOHN. That's been in the works for a while.

ALLEGRA. You would know.

JOHN. It's not secret.

ALLEGRA. Some people know some things, is all I'm saying. Other people know other things. Knew.

JOHN. I'm telling you what I know. So now we both know.

    Beat. ALLEGRA *looks over the nonsensical piles they're making.*

ALLEGRA. You use the computer, I'll go see if there's / any paper back there

JOHN. you sit I'll do it

ALLEGRA. I need to keep moving

    ALLEGRA *exits.*
    He starts typing information from the pages into the computer.
    It's kind of soothing.
    We can't see it, but it's a pathetic document—just a list of names and phone numbers, with no orderly principle.
    JOHN *types alone for a minute or two.*
    He gets up and gets a can of Coke. He brings it back to his station.
    He pops the tab. It explodes all over him—and all over the keyboard, all over the pile of papers.
    Shit. Now what?
    Just then, MARGARET *appears in the doorway.*

JOHN. shit!

MARGARET. Hello?

    JOHN *doesn't see her; he is trying to salvage the pile of papers, and the computer, and his shirt—*

JOHN. / shit shit shit shit shit shit

MARGARET. oh—oh, hold on, hold on—

    She grabs the pile of papers and rushes them to the sink, tries to dry them off. Wipes them down with a wet paper towel.

JOHN. I can't believe—I'm sorry, I'm so sorry—

MARGARET. it's okay, it's okay, here—

    She awkwardly hands him a wad of wet paper towels and tries to help him clean his shirt and pants. He takes the wad and tries to clean the keyboard.

oh—oh—ok—you focus on, you do your, um, and—I'll—

    She gets more paper towels and tries to salvage the keyboard. He presses a few keys.

JOHN. it's sticking.
MARGARET. We should wait until it dries and then try it.
JOHN. I'm so sorry.
MARGARET. / don't apologize to me—
JOHN. / I'm such an idiot.
> *He sinks into a chair, despondent.*

MARGARET. no—no—it's fine, it happens to everyone—we'll wait until it dries, it's probably fine.
> *She gathers up the spent towels and throws them in the trash. She takes the stack of pages and lays them out on the picnic tables to dry them out.*

The good news is, / most of the ink didn't run, only on a few.
JOHN. ...great...
MARGARET. what is all this?
JOHN. receipts, and bills..."deep storage."
MARGARET. okay...
JOHN. we're looking for addresses, phone numbers, you know. The clients. Name of company, and contacts, you know, who to call.
MARGARET. call about what?
JOHN. tell them we're "back in business"
MARGARET. tell who?
JOHN. clients. Who might think, you know, because of the, uh, the planes, and—. / well.
MARGARET. Right.
JOHN. that uh maybe it means the company's closed, but we're not, we're open, we're trading, we're going to keep trading, so, we're. Yeah. Going.
> *Beat.*

MARGARET. (*Extending her hand.*) I'm Margaret?
JOHN. (*Shaking her hand.*) John hi. Equities.
MARGARET. I'm looking for Mr. um, Davis?
JOHN. pardon?
MARGARET. (*Reading from a slip of paper from her pocket.*) I'm looking for Mr. John Davis? At Lipman Kennedy?
JOHN. Oh! That's me. Dav-*ies*. Hi. John.
MARGARET. Nicky sent me? I'm Core?
JOHN. oh you're Nicky's!
MARGARET. Core Staffing

JOHN. You're the temp!

He extends his hand again. She shakes it more formally this time.

MARGARET. Margaret. Hi.

JOHN. Love Nicky.

MARGARET. she said to say / she's very sorry for—

JOHN. tell her thank you.

MARGARET. I will.

JOHN. I've never met her / actually, just on the phone.

MARGARET. She's really nice. Core is the best. Not that I've been through a lot of agencies, ha ha, I just graduated / in June actually

JOHN. no no it's okay, I know how it is.

MARGARET. I'm sorry, too—I wanted to say. I am so sorry. I am so, so sorry—I can't imagine what you're going through.

JOHN. um. yeah. thanks. So.

MARGARET. What can I do?

JOHN. nothing, really

MARGARET. I mean. I'm here to help. / Whatever you need, I—I can do it.

JOHN. Oh! Of course. Right. So.

Remembering that he has a job causes a small physical transformation—he is able to take charge of the moment, slightly.

We're trying to reassemble / the client lists, we have teams

MARGARET. right, you mentioned

JOHN. we have a team in New Milford, they're doing the bond trades, the BMA decided / to open today

MARGARET. BMA?

JOHN. so, that's happening. Bond Market Association. I have no idea how but. We're just going with it.

MARGARET. so I'm making lists. of names of companies?

JOHN. yes. Please. Thank you.

MARGARET. just tell me how.

JOHN. oh! Of course. Okay. Um. This is our backup location, where we send old files, like, every August the admins pack up the paper files and send them here, to Jersey. So, the good news is that the paper files should be pretty current.

MARGARET. (*Too much enthusiasm.*) Great!

JOHN. so, I guess, start here.

He hands her an accordion file from the box.

MARGARET. just, make a list? based on this paperwork.

JOHN. I started a list. Lipman has—I don't know, 50, 60,000 clients. Hopefully we can find them all / by Monday.

MARGARET. wow.

JOHN *presses a button on the keyboard.*

JOHN. stuck.

MARGARET. we should let it dry / before

ALLEGRA *returns with a stack of yellow legal pads.*

ALLEGRA. Never say I never did nothing for you

JOHN. ah, perfect timing! Amazing!

ALLEGRA. That's right I am amazing.

MARGARET. Perfect.

ALLEGRA *extends her hand.*

ALLEGRA. Allegra Park. Equities.

MARGARET. Margaret. I'm the temp.

ALLEGRA. Pardon?

MARGARET. / From Core? Nicky sent me?

JOHN. I ordered a temp.

ALLEGRA. Core what?

MARGARET. Core Staffing? The agency name. Like, I'm the "core" of your business. Although, obviously, I'm not.

Beat.

JOHN. Could you make us some coffee?

MARGARET. / Oh. Sure. Yes. I would love to.

MARGARET *efficiently sets to work by the sink.*

ALLEGRA. I already made some.

JOHN. there's something off

ALLEGRA. It's office coffee

JOHN. maybe it's old?

ALLEGRA. (*"duh"*) It's office coffee

MARGARET. Is it too sour? Or / is it more bitter sort of?

JOHN. sour

MARGARET. then it's the way you're brewing it. Bitter means the grounds are off, but sour is usually because you're / scalding it.

ALLEGRA. uh huh

MARGARET. oh! I'm sorry! I didn't mean *you* you, I meant like general you. / It's really common, overcooking coffee.

ALLEGRA. ah

JOHN. why don't you try making us a new pot.

MARGARET. I didn't mean to offend—

JOHN. no offense taken. We're all a little on edge.

MARGARET. of course. Of course you are. After what you've been through.

ALLEGRA. John.

JOHN. what?

ALLEGRA. We don't need a temp.

JOHN. We need help. We're going to need—

ALLEGRA. It would be one thing if she was a professional, like, a volunteer from another firm or something—but. I mean. We can't / have a temp, like, calling clients

JOHN. you want to do it all yourself

ALLEGRA. I am not having a temporary employee call my clients.

JOHN. first of all, they're not / your clients—

ALLEGRA. They're all my clients now

JOHN. —and second of all, she can make lists of numbers for us, and we can still make the actual calls

ALLEGRA. this isn't how we / do it.

JOHN. none of this is how we do it.

ALLEGRA. I'm sorry. I just don't see how it's a good idea to / bring in a temp when

JOHN. when two-thirds of our workforce is gone?

ALLEGRA. the safe list is growing every day.

JOHN. We're missing / over two-thirds of

ALLEGRA. Fine. But I'm not teaching her, you can do that.

ALLEGRA gets back to work. Beat, then—

I'm just saying. This is a business, not a blood bank.

MARGARET. (*To* JOHN.) I'm not looking to take anyone's job.

JOHN. you're fine. Thank you. So you're all set?

MARGARET. I think so, yeah. Thanks.

JOHN. ask me if you need anything. If you're not sure what to do, don't try to figure it out on your own. Ask me.

MARGARET. I will. Thank you.

They each settle in with a stack of papers to make lists on the legal pads.

They work side-by-side for a while.

The low rumble of a truck passing outside the building. They look, listen, wait for it to be gone before returning to their tasks.

ALLEGRA *gets up and pours herself another cup of coffee, goes back to her seat.*

They fall into a rhythm of picking up papers and writing down names.

Maybe here there is a silent dance of side-by-side office work.

Eventually:

ALLEGRA. should we order lunch?

JOHN. is there anywhere?

ALLEGRA. there's some menus—

MARGARET. I can take the orders.

ALLEGRA. what's the place we did yesterday?

JOHN. you mean pizza?

ALLEGRA. was that pizza?

JOHN. That was pizza.

ALLEGRA. I don't even remember actually

JOHN. I'm not hungry

ALLEGRA. Me neither

Beat.

More working.

MARGARET. you guys were here yesterday?

ALLEGRA. afternoon, yeah

JOHN. yesterday morning, the call went out, it had been 24 hours since the—uh, the planes—and uh. They said, any workers out there, call the Boston office

ALLEGRA. we're just the ones who responded

JOHN. they sent some to Connecticut, some here to Jersey

ALLEGRA. and we don't know how many are still—

JOHN. Allegra

ALLEGRA. they might find more, is all I'm saying.

MARGARET. They said on the news that Morgan Stanley has accounted for over 90% of their workforce.

ALLEGRA. see?

JOHN. Morgan's in the 60s.

MARGARET. what does that mean?

JOHN. their offices were on 63 through 68.

MARGARET. where were you?

JOHN. …higher than that.

MARGARET. were you there?

JOHN. what? of course, we—

ALLEGRA. that's not what she means, John.

JOHN. I don't understand.

ALLEGRA. she means, were you there. There there. In the building. She wants to know, were you there when it happened.

JOHN. oh—no—god no! (ha ha) Nowhere near.

ALLEGRA. dropping his daughter off at school.

JOHN. I live just over in Englewood. I guess that's why they sent me here.

MARGARET. That's amazing, I mean, you are so lucky, right? Like, so lucky. I guess maybe you don't feel lucky.

JOHN. I don't feel much of anything actually.

MARGARET. You're probably still in shock.

ALLEGRA. See? She thinks she's a therapist.

MARGARET. I saw what happened. On TV. It's like, something you can't even imagine. I still can't, like, I'll forget it happened and then I'll look at the skyline, where the buildings should be, and / then I'll remember

JOHN. if we don't contact these clients and get them to start trading with us, we're done

MARGARET. Really?

    JOHN *responds with a shrug, like, what can I say.*

ALLEGRA. We should start calling.

    They look at each other, look at their lists, look at the single landline.

We're gonna boot it offline.

JOHN. I spilled soda on the computer.

    ALLEGRA *emits a large laugh, maybe a snort-type laugh.*

ALLEGRA. You did not.

JOHN. I did. I'm sorry.

ALLEGRA. oh honey it's fine. It is so fine. You use the landline then, I'll use my cell.

JOHN. thanks

MARGARET. should I use my cell too?

JOHN. You keep making the list of client phone numbers, and we'll make the calls.

MARGARET. Got it.

JOHN *and* ALLEGRA *scan their lists.*
With a deep breath, ALLEGRA *takes out her phone and dials.*
JOHN *rests one hand on the receiver of the landline, reading through his list carefully.*
He does not make a call.

ALLEGRA. Hi, may I speak with Donald Rogers please?
...
Hi, this is Allegra Park at Lipman Kennedy
...
...
Oh, yes, uh—thank you—
...
Yeah I really, we really appreciate that. Um. So I just wanted to call and let you know that we're still in business, despite what you may have heard, this morning we resumed trading bonds and we'll be ready on Monday when the stock market reopens. We'll be open for business and we hope—
...
Who?
...
Oh. No. I haven't heard—
...
we don't know, we—
...
...
I'll let you know if...when... Ok. Thank you.

She hangs up.
She is silently weeping.
She takes a pack of cigarettes from her purse and exits.
JOHN *puts his notepad to the side. After a few beats, he follows her.*
MARGARET *continues to work alone.*
The phone rings
MARGARET *looks around, assumes someone else is going to get it.*
No one does.
The phone is still ringing. Finally, she picks up the receiver.

MARGARET. Lipman Kennedy, how can I help you?
The voice on the end is clearly distraught.
...
...
...

Oh, um—
...
No, I—
...
...
I'm so sorry, no, I don't know who—
...
Yes. I understand.
...
...
Yes of course. Hold on. I'm gonna—
...
I'm gonna write that down? Hold on, um—
> *She drops the pen.*

Shit.
...
Sorry! That wasn't about you! Um! Let me take your name, hold on.
> *She writes.*

Okay. Okay. And where can we reach you? Okay. Yes ma'am. If we hear anything—okay. Okay. Okay.
> JOHN *returns with three cups of ice.*
>
> *Over the following, he opens a can of Coke carefully over the sink and pours it into the three cups.*

JOHN. (*"good news"*) There's an ice machine down the hall.

MARGARET. Oh, great. Um, there was a phone call. she was, um. She's the wife of—do you know someone named Leonard Fontana?

JOHN. Lenny? Sure. Oh.

MARGARET. She wants to know if we've heard from—

JOHN. she's gotta call the crisis center.

MARGARET. do you have that number? In case—

JOHN. oh, uh, somewhere…no, actually, I haven't needed it, it's for, it's for the families…

MARGARET. Also, um, do you know a guy named Jeff Lasky?

JOHN. From Lipman?

MARGARET. A trader?

JOHN. Friend of yours?

MARGARET. …boyfriend. Kind of. I mean—

JOHN. oh jesus. I'm so sorry.

MARGARET. it's okay. thanks.

JOHN. That's awful.

MARGARET. Thank you.

JOHN. this thing doesn't end, does it? It just keeps going and...which desk was he?

MARGARET. Sales I think?

JOHN. wouldn't know him, sorry.

MARGARET. it's okay. thanks.

JOHN. how can you be here?

MARGARET. I needed work, I—

She senses that just needing work is not a sufficient answer.

I mean I had to do something I told Nicky, I wanted to help—that way I could, I don't know, be close to him? Or something? I couldn't just sit at home.

JOHN. well, I hope he's okay.

MARGARET. I don't think he is.

ALLEGRA *returns.*

ALLEGRA. don't think who is what?

JOHN. Jeff—I'm sorry, what's the name?

MARGARET. Lasky? Jeff Lasky?

ALLEGRA. what desk?

MARGARET. I don't know.

JOHN. boyfriend.

MARGARET. sort of—I mean, we weren't, uh—

ALLEGRA. I'm so sorry.

MARGARET. thanks.

Beat. What now?

The sound of fighter jets flying over the city. They listen, tense. But the sound fades away and nothing else happens.

ALLEGRA. (*To* JOHN.) So I finally got Lamb on the phone.

JOHN. Icy cold Coca-Cola?

He gives her the drink.

ALLEGRA. oh my god thank you you're my hero.

JOHN. Lamb's here?

ALLEGRA. are you kidding? no. I called my buddy in the Paris office. he called New Milford, who found her—somewhere—anyway, she says, yeah, keep trying to make a master client list, we're going to have to settle all the trades from earlier this week. DTC gave us an extension til Monday on the clearance deadline.

JOHN. oh my god I didn't even think about that

MARGARET. I'm sorry—what's a clearance deadline?

JOHN. the way it works is, you take a trade, you clear it with the DTC, they confirm you have enough money to cover / the trade—

MARGARET. DTC?

JOHN. Depository Trust Company. They're like the middleman, for all the firms like Lipman, Merrill, Lehman.

Beat.

MARGARET. What happens if you don't settle all the trades?

ALLEGRA. That's not going to happen.

MARGARET. But—

ALLEGRA. Our clients pay us to make them money. They're counting on those deals to be done. So if we can't close the loop, and they *lose* money they think they already made?

JOHN. it's not good.

Beat.

MARGARET. So, the trades you took in on Monday weren't settled yet?

ALLEGRA. also Tuesday

MARGARET. How did you trade anything on Tuesday?

ALLEGRA. Bond market opens at eight.

JOHN. On TV Lamb said almost a billion in business

MARGARET. On Monday and Tuesday?

ALLEGRA. Just Tuesday

MARGARET. a billion dollars? just on Tuesday morning before 8:00?

ALLEGRA. 8:46, but. Yeah.

MARGARET. whoa.

ALLEGRA. Welcome to Lipman.

They settle in to work.
But then—

MARGARET. Okay, so—uh. Where can I find the list of trades from Monday and Tuesday?

ALLEGRA. ...

JOHN. ...

ALLEGRA. ...

MARGARET. You don't have a list?

JOHN and ALLEGRA look at each other, like, "oh shit."

JOHN. oh my god.

They realize they are missing the records for all those billions of dollars.

DAY 2 (Friday, September 14).

Morning. Same as yesterday, except now there is a cooler by the door; every once in a while one of the workers will get a Coke from the cooler.

Empty pizza boxes litter the table, more than before. Maybe some fast food taco wrappers too. Maybe they were able to find a taco delivery place nearby.

MARGARET *enters. She's the first one here. She looks around, not sure what to do. She starts gathering pizza boxes, piling them in a corner of the table. Maybe she boots up the computer, checks to see if the keys are sticking.*

A fire truck siren wails in the distance. She stops what she's doing, listens. It gets close. Then fades away.

The phone rings. MARGARET *is prepared for this—she feels like she knows what she's supposed to do.*

MARGARET. (*Answering the phone.*) Hello, Lipman Kennedy, this is Margaret speaking.

...

Oh, uh, no, I'm so sorry but this is a storage facility. You'll need to call the crisis center.

...

No, I, I'm sorry, I can't—

...
...

Yes that's right. The Bond Market opened yesterday.

...

I'm actually not sure how they—we—did, I—

...
...

Oh, I, I. I don't know anything about—about paychecks, I'm just—

CATHY *is there. Where did she come from?*

—let me, um, I can take your name and—

CATHY *stands in front of* MARGARET *and motions with one hand: give me the phone.* MARGARET *hands it over.*

CATHY. This is Cathy Lamb, who's this.

...

Oh Jenny. Jenny. Hi honey. I'm so, so—
…
No we haven't heard anything, have you tried the crisis center?
…
Yes it's 212-741-4626…

        MARGARET *writes down the number as* CATHY *speaks.*

To tell the truth, we didn't do very well yesterday, we got crushed if you want to know the truth—
…
I know. I know.
…
…
Jenny, listen to me. Adam was—. Yes. He was—he was instrumental to, I don't know what I'm gonna, I mean, my loss is nothing compared to what you and Britt but—he was a mensch, is that the word? A mensch.
…
We got a line on the crews down there, and—
…
No of course I—
…
I will say this though. Lipman Kennedy is gonna come back from this thing, we're gonna provide—'cause that's what we do, yeah? What did Adam always say, he's a rainmaker? Yeah. Yeah. And that's what we're—. Everything we do from now on, we do it for you. We do it for Adam. You hear me? We're gonna make it rain. We are. We are. That's a promise, you hear?
…
Okay. Okay.
If there's anything—
…
…
…
You let me know, you hear?
…
Bye love.

        She hangs up.

Fucking disaster is what this is.

MARGARET. Yeah, I—

CATHY. You're gonna be getting a lot of those calls / and you're gonna have to handle it.

MARGARET. I got one yesterday, they said to tell them to call the crisis center but we didn't / have the number—

CATHY. You have it now though, right?

MARGARET *holds up the notepad.*

MARGARET. Yup, got it—

CATHY. You tell them, Lipman's gonna provide.

MARGARET. Great.

CATHY. But more importantly, we gotta—we got to get this business—These widows, and they're mostly widows, do you understand, a lot of them, they don't know where the checkbook is or how the mortgage gets paid—and now the one who knows, the man of the house, you know? Just—down there—there's no way to describe, if you haven't—So you see they're not gonna understand that the chances of, well, it's just very very small.

MARGARET. Oh. Right. I mean. Sure.

CATHY. I went to the firehouse yesterday, they tell me, they have crews working 24 hours looking for survivors and you know how many they found alive yesterday?

MARGARET. (I—no)

CATHY. One, that's how many. And how many bodies?

MARGARET. I heard it's at least 5,000.

CATHY. Also one. One intact body in that whole pile.

MARGARET. / oh. wow.

CATHY. That's what they're calling it, The Pile.

MARGARET. I heard "ground zero."

CATHY. That just means the site of an explosion. The firehouse boys, they're saying The Pile.

MARGARET. That's more—visceral?

CATHY. It's specific is what it is. A pile. And that's what we gotta—. Be specific. Be precise So widows like Jenny Lockhart call up, want to know why she's not getting his paycheck this week, / he could still be out there.

MARGARET. Wait do you mean—

CATHY. It takes money to make money, first lesson in this business, am I right? You know what I need? A shower. You got a toothbrush?

MARGARET. I have mouthwash.

CATHY. (*Extends her hand.*) Give it here.

MARGARET *rifles through her backpack and finds her travel-sized mouthwash.*

Smart girl.

CATHY *goes to the slop sink and gulps down some mouthwash.*

> *Then she sticks her head under the water and washes her hair, face, neck.*
>
> *A police siren wails.* MARGARET *turns her head towards it. It passes by.*
>
> *Just then, the phone rings again.*

MARGARET. um, excuse me—the phone—um—

CATHY. Take it, you got it, right?

> MARGARET *picks up the pad with the crisis center number and picks up the phone.*

MARGARET. Thank you for calling Lipman Kennedy. Our crisis center number is—

…

Oh! Oh, I thought you—okay, no, wait, hold on—

…

Let me write that down—you want, I'm sorry, is that 2 U.S. Treasury what?—2 million?—uh, shares or—oh okay, right right, *dollars* yeah okay—

…

Okay, right, sure, as soon as the market opens. Okay. Yeah. Let me read that back to you—Hello?

> *The line is dead.* MARGARET *scribbles down everything she can remember from the call, not sure what to do.*
>
> JOHN *and* ALLEGRA *enter together—we can hear them offstage—*

JOHN. (*Offstage.*) That bus, I'm telling you, Sardine City!

ALLEGRA. (*Offstage.*) You think it's always like that?

JOHN. (*Offstage.*) Always before or always now? New normal, I'm telling you—

> *They enter and see* CATHY *washing herself at the sink.*

Oh!

ALLEGRA. What? —oh!

JOHN. Cathy?

ALLEGRA. Lamb!

JOHN. (*To* CATHY.) You're here!

ALLEGRA. (*To* MARGARET.) You're here?

MARGARET. I'm sorry, I thought—the agency said—

JOHN. no it's good, we just weren't sure if you'd want / to, you know

MARGARET. I'm here to help.

JOHN. Thank you for being here.

> ALLEGRA *breezes past* MARGARET *to start setting herself up with a file box and legal pad.*

By the sink, CATHY *dries her hair and face with paper towels.*
MARGARET. I got—there was a phone call?
She hands her notepad to JOHN. *He tries to make sense of her notes.*
JOHN. what's this?
MARGARET. It was, um, Josh Felderman, at—
JOHN. yeah, but what's this about two million?
MARGARET. He said—he wants to buy two million dollars? Of U.S. Treasury bonds? When the market opens at eight.
JOHN *looks up, startled.*
CATHY *listens while combing her hair. Maybe she puts on some make-up.*
JOHN. That's not possible.
MARGARET. He said I wrote it down—
JOHN. that's, well. I don't expect you to understand.
MARGARET. I'd like to try.
JOHN. It's just. This is a good trade—I mean, under the best of circumstances, it's solid, and. Well. I mean.
MARGARET. I'm so sorry. Maybe I misheard. I can call him back.
JOHN. No I'll do it. I'm sorry we left you hanging. We should have been here at seven.
ALLEGRA *pipes up from the other side of the room.*
ALLEGRA. I would've been here, / if I hadn't stopped to pick up your late ass—
JOHN. Hey, how could I know / I'd have to wait for three full buses to go by before—
ALLEGRA. *(Teasing.)* ...if that's the story you need to tell yourself...
JOHN. I see someone's developing a sense of humor.
ALLEGRA. Out of the ashes rises a phoenix.
Beat.
sorry.
MARGARET. no it's good, humor is good in times of hardship.
ALLEGRA. Yeah I think Oprah told me that once too.
JOHN. Let me call Felderman and get this sorted before the bell.
He picks up the landline, starts to dial.
CATHY *hangs it up.*
Wait, I—
CATHY. Gotta keep the line open.

JOHN. The bell isn't for 30 minutes.

CATHY. We did basically no business yesterday and you want to risk us missing a call?

> *A standoff.*
>
> *Finally,* JOHN *turns to* ALLEGRA—

JOHN. Can I please borrow your cell phone?

> *She gives him her phone, and he goes to the hallway to make his call.*

CATHY. (*Extending her hand to* ALLEGRA.) Cathy Lamb, VP Corporate Bonds.

ALLEGRA. Allegra Park. Equities.

CATHY. Dave's assistant?

ALLEGRA. Trader. I work with Dave. And John.

CATHY. Of course, we've met.

ALLEGRA. A couple of times.

CATHY. I'm sorry, it's—my head

ALLEGRA. it's ok

CATHY. (*To* MARGARET.) You're EQ too?

MARGARET. I'm—what am I?

ALLEGRA. that's a temp John got

MARGARET. (*Extending her hand.*) Margaret Gale, Core Staffing?

> JOHN *returns, beelines for* MARGARET.

JOHN. I owe you an apology.

MARGARET. Me?

JOHN. (*To the others.*) Guess what Felderman wants?

CATHY. To steal our business?

JOHN. To buy two million U.S. Treasury.

CATHY. He—but—

> CATHY *is dumbstruck.*
>
> *This is really good news.*
>
> *No one is expecting good news.*

CATHY. / No.

ALLEGRA. No way.

JOHN. He does.

CATHY. You see? Our phones barely ring yesterday, and today we're doing real business. I told you we'd be back.

MARGARET. Congratulations!

JOHN. yeah

CATHY. But it's still not going to make up for the money we've been bleeding since Tuesday.

JOHN. Come on, Cath, a little good news—

    CATHY *addresses the room as if she's giving a presentation.*

CATHY. The bond market opened yesterday. And it was a disaster for us.

JOHN. sure, but—

CATHY. We have no infrastructure, no records—we barely have a staff—and the staff we do have, well let's be honest, the staff has undergone some extreme trauma, so—

ALLEGRA. We're finding new people / every day—

CATHY. Every single person associated with processing our loans is dead.

ALLEGRA. Missing.

MARGARET. The whole department?

CATHY. Municipal bonds: we've found 1 out of 36. Corporate bonds: 4 out of 86. EQ, 16 out of 140. Human Resources, 1 out of 9. Mortgage-backed securities, nobody from management. Clearance, nobody. Whole desks we haven't heard from. / Loans, too. This is a desk that borrows and lends 20 million a day.

ALLEGRA. They're missing. We're missing a lot of people.

JOHN. (...I don't know if I can, I just. I need a minute.)

    JOHN *stands up abruptly*
    Goes to the sink. Splashes his face with water.
    The rumble of heavy trucks passing close by.
    ALLEGRA *shakes a cigarette loose out of a soft pack of Camels. She nervously taps it on the table as she speaks.*

ALLEGRA. What about Len ..or Ryan...or his brother, what's that kid's name? / The intern?

    CATHY *plows on, commanding the room.*

CATHY. So that's what we know as of today. There are things we know, and things we don't know, and things we don't even know yet that we don't know. For example: will our customers come back to us? I went on television, I said, Lipman Kennedy is gonna come back from this thing. But nobody even knew where to call us.

JOHN. yesterday, we called clients, we told them

CATHY. Yeah, what did you say?

ALLEGRA. We told them, we're back in business, we—

CATHY. If there's one thing we learned yesterday, it's that our clients aren't gonna come back to us in pity. If we're gonna survive, we gotta get back to doing our job. / And our job is to make our clients money.

ALLEGRA. All I want is to get back to doing my job.
CATHY. But right now, I got a stack of trades just sitting / in New Milford—
JOHN. What do you mean just / sitting there?
CATHY. We have no way to process them.
>   *Beat.*
>   CATHY *lets it sink in.*

JOHN. good God.
ALLEGRA. We have no backend.
MARGARET. What's a backend?
ALLEGRA. shh
CATHY. Our back office is in pieces. Clearing anything is going to be, well, it's going to be an ordeal.
JOHN. (*To* MARGARET.) Remember yesterday, the clearance deadline?
MARGARET. The system where you enter the trades you did?
JOHN. That's the backend. We have a whole office tracking that stuff.
CATHY. Had.
ALLEGRA. It's done electronically.
CATHY. Was.
>   *Beat.*

The system was wiped out.
JOHN. We can't do anything without a clearance desk.
CATHY. You're gonna do it by hand.
ALLEGRA. How?
CATHY. Figure it out.
JOHN. I'm sorry, what?
ALLEGRA. *We're* the backend?
CATHY. For now. Boston tells me they'll have the systems back up and running, but that's a week away at least. And we have to start conducting business today. Yesterday. So here's what we're gonna do. New Milford is gonna keep taking the bond trades, and then they'll call it in to you, here.
ALLEGRA. Then what?
CATHY. Then you process it by hand. Call the DTC, file the forms, get it done.
JOHN. What do we know about clearing trades?
ALLEGRA. We haven't even begun to reconstruct the missing trades—
CATHY. We can do that over the weekend. Right now, if we can't figure out the backend, don't even think about paying out any of the bonuses to the widows. I mean how is anyone gonna get paid when all our earners are—.

Beat.

MARGARET. So...what can I do? How can I help?

CATHY. You'll get a phone call from New Milford, they'll have just taken a trade. You write it down and you call it in to the DTC.

JOHN. We're at least gonna need some turrets.

MARGARET. / What's a turret?

CATHY. We're gonna need to improvise, is what we're gonna need.

JOHN. (*To* MARGARET.) oh you couldn't miss it. It's like a phone, with all the lines, / buttons, and it's recording

MARGARET. Oh, sure sure. I've seen those, yeah.

JOHN. (*To* MARGARET.) Lipman has us recording everything— (*Turns to* CATHY.) What if there's a dispute, if the DTC comes back with a conflict, / if

CATHY. Use the regular phones.

JOHN. We only have one phone.

ALLEGRA. We can use my cell.

CATHY. Great, see? Now you have two.

MARGARET. How will I know who to call?

CATHY. These guys'll make the calls. You're a temp, you got Excel?

MARGARET. I'm pretty solid on the whole Office suite.

CATHY. Great. I told New Milford to take it slow. Do a few trades, test the pipes. If we can get the system working today, we might have a fighting chance in hell of staying alive on Monday. We'll aim for a hundred today.

MARGARET. What's Monday?

ALLEGRA. That's when the stock market opens. This is just bonds.

JOHN. A hundred trades by hand.

CATHY. Over the course of a day.

ALLEGRA. We can do that.

CATHY. It's basically just data entry.

MARGARET. I can definitely do that.

JOHN. Why only a hundred? Don't we want to show them we can come back strong?

CATHY. Because there's no point in overdoing it and failing. We only get one chance to show we can do this.

JOHN. That's what I'm saying, I want to do the job to the fullest / extent that—

CATHY. Do you have any idea how hard it is to get a taxi right now? To come out to *New Jersey?* "Oh no, Miss, the tunnel, no." Oh come on. It's your job. It's your *job* to drive back and forth underneath the Hudson River as many times as I ask you to. If I'm not scared don't you be scared. Buck up and *drive*. It's your *job*. Just like it's my job to work in a mile-high tower that defies fucking gravity, it's—

    JOHN *gets suddenly woozy.*

    He sits.

JOHN. Cath

CATHY. don't

    Beat.

JOHN. Ok. I'm sorry. Yeah.

    Beat.

ALLEGRA. what time is it?

MARGARET. 7:52.

CATHY. Eight minutes.

    Long beat.

    Nobody knows what to do with themselves.

JOHN. (*To* CATHY.) So. A muffin, huh?

CATHY. "…Woman Saved By Muffin…"

JOHN. I'm just glad you. I mean. I'm glad you, uh

CATHY. (*To* MARGARET.) It's very good of you to be here with us.

MARGARET. I want to be here.

    Beat.

JOHN. (*Kind.*) Of course.

    Beat.

ALLEGRA. Of course what?

JOHN. Her—what was his name?

MARGARET. Jeff. Jeff Lasky?

JOHN. That's right. Lasky.

    Beat.

ALLEGRA. Don't know him.

    Beat.

I'm sorry.

MARGARET. thanks.

    Silence. They look at each other and sit there.

CATHY. I'll see about getting you more phones at least.

    CATHY *starts to type on her BlackBerry.*

ALLEGRA. and access to the client database.

CATHY. Boston is sending us computers that'll hook up to their network.

ALLEGRA. yeah I'll believe that when I see it

JOHN. Park.

ALLEGRA. What.

JOHN. It wouldn't hurt to give them the benefit of the doubt.

ALLEGRA. C'mon, John—Boston?

JOHN. They're not gonna mess with us now.

ALLEGRA. Yeah right.

JOHN. Tech will help.

ALLEGRA. Oh please. Me and Christine, we're always calling the tech guys—what's their names? Hey, John?

JOHN. Yeah?

ALLEGRA. What's their names, those two IT guys on 103? Always telling me and Christine that we're the problem? Remember? PIC-NIC—

MARGARET. What's that?

ALLEGRA. —Problem In Chair, Not In Computer. PIC-NIC.

MARGARET. Oh! That's funny.

ALLEGRA. remember?

JOHN. the big guy is Mario

ALLEGRA. oh my god they're so funny. Right. Mario. Or is it Marco? Oh my god he has the biggest thing for Christine. I shouldn't tell you, she'd be totally mortified if I told you. Remember though? That ice skate trip, did you go?

JOHN. That was Darcy's first time in skates. (*To* MARGARET.) My daughter.

MARGARET. Oh!

ALLEGRA. (*To* MARGARET.) Every Christmas, the Executives take the rest of us on some kind of Winter Wonderland field trip, it's like supposed to be good for company morale / or something—

CATHY. Team building.

ALLEGRA. Right. Well usually they go skiing but people like me and Christine, we can't be away so many days. I mean Christine's got a kid, so. Anyway so last year they changed it so we could go, we went ice-skating instead.

CATHY. It was a cost-saving measure.

ALLEGRA. What was?

CATHY. We went ice-skating instead of skiing to save on travel costs. It's cheaper to buy out Wollman Rink than to bus everyone up to the Poconos.

ALLEGRA. Oh.

MARGARET. It was still a really nice thing to do. (*To* ALLEGRA.) I'm really glad you got to go ice-skating.

    ALLEGRA *can't decide whether or not to take the kindness.*

JOHN. In the old days, everyone could bring their family.

ALLEGRA. I heard about that.

CATHY. John, remember, John, when Nancy?

MARGARET. Who's Nancy?

ALLEGRA. Ex-wife.

CATHY. Did *not* get along with the / plebes.

JOHN. Cathy.

CATHY. I'm right, though, you can admit it, you're divorced, you know she was a cold fish.

ALLEGRA. Harsh!

JOHN. She didn't like skiing.

CATHY. She didn't like other people.

MARGARET. So why'd you bring her?

JOHN. She was my wife.

MARGARET. But if—

ALLEGRA. Shit like that matters.

JOHN. What was the other guy's name?

CATHY. Who?

JOHN. From IT. Who worked with Marco.

ALLEGRA. Mario.

JOHN. Marco.

ALLEGRA. Are you sure?

JOHN. Yes.

CATHY. oh this is really gonna bother me, I'm usually so good / with names

ALLEGRA. Maybe it's the other one who has the hots / for Christine.

CATHY. It's on the tip of my tongue.

ALLEGRA. I wonder what happened to him.

JOHN. You should check the crisis center list.

ALLEGRA. We should definitely check for Marco. Mario?

CATHY. Vargas.

JOHN. What?

CATHY. Marco Vargas. From IT. I just remembered.

ALLEGRA. He'd remember the other guy.

JOHN. What about Christine?

CATHY. Rivera! Did you look her up?

ALLEGRA. (*"I don't need to."*) She called me.

    Beat. Everyone is quiet. MARGARET *is the last to understand.*

MARGARET. From inside?

> *Phone rings.*
>
> *Everyone jumps.*

CATHY. 8:00!

ALLEGRA. here we go…

JOHN. (*Answering.*) Lipman Kennedy.

…

Oh, hey man. How's it up there?

…

Yeah. Yeah, it's—

/ Okay, no, go, go ahead.

> JOHN *starts scribbling madly, taking an order from a trader. Ad libs on the phone: "uh huh. Uh huh. How many? Okay, got it. Thanks."*
>
> *While* JOHN *is on the phone:*

CATHY. Tell me your name again.

ALLEGRA. Allegra.

CATHY. Allegra. And Margaret. Thank you for your service. I'll be back in the morning.

MARGARET. Thank you.

CATHY. I'm going to call a car I think…

> CATHY *goes.*
>
> JOHN *hangs up the phone.*

JOHN. Some guy named Coxor—

ALLEGRA. Cockburn?

JOHN. no he said Coxon

ALLEGRA. I don't know any Cockburn

JOHN. anyway he

MARGARET. maybe he's also new

JOHN. a million Disney six and a halfs due in 2012 at 101

ALLEGRA. buyer or seller?

JOHN. …I don't remember

ALLEGRA. John!

JOHN. I'm sorry I'm sorry I'll call back—

> *He picks up the landline receiver.* MARGARET *jumps for it.*

MARGARET. no!

JOHN. what?

MARGARET. Don't use that one!

ALLEGRA. Gotta keep it open for trades

JOHN. oh—right, of course. Of course.

    MARGARET *gives him her cell phone.*

MARGARET. Here use my cell

JOHN. What's the Boston number?

ALLEGRA. You sure it was Boston?

JOHN. yes I'm sure—

    No one knows what's going on. Just then, the landline rings.

shit

ALLEGRA. I'll get it, you work on finding the Boston / number.

    ALLEGRA *picks up the ringing phone.*

Lipman Kennedy, hello?

    She starts scribbling.

/ mm hmm, yes, ok, got it, four million AT&T— (*Ad lib continues.*)

JOHN. Hello, information? Oh. Boston. Massachusetts. Lipman Kennedy. (*Takes down the number.*) Okay. Thank you.

    He dials the number.

    Hangs up.

/ it's disconnected

ALLEGRA. (*Finishing her call.*) Okay, thanks.

    ALLEGRA *hangs up. Thrusts the paper at* MARGARET. *Sees* JOHN *looking at her helplessly.*

What?

MARGARET. (*Re: the note she was just given.*) what should I do with—

ALLEGRA. (*Looking at the number* JOHN *called.*) John. That's our main office number.

JOHN. what is?

ALLEGRA. they gave you a 212—hold on, let me do this. You help her.

MARGARET. I'm so sorry, what am I supposed to do with this?

    The landline rings again.

ALLEGRA. Find out the name of the trader who took it.

    And rings.

MARGARET. —why?

ALLEGRA. You'll have to tell DTC the full name of the trader.

    And rings.

For legal. (*Answering.*) Lipman Kennedy Clearance Desk.

JOHN. what does it say?

MARGARET. CSCO-4-2028-B-500-90

ALLEGRA. (*Scribbling, listening.*) shh!

JOHN. that's 500,000 dollars worth of Cisco at four percent due in 2028 bought for 90 cents on the dollar by by—by who?

MARGARET. it doesn't say

> ALLEGRA *hangs up and thrusts the paper at* JOHN.

JOHN. who bought the Cisco?

ALLEGRA. this says Quark.

JOHN. no, the first one

ALLEGRA. I didn't recognize the voice on the Cisco. The Quark is Carver.

JOHN. Carver! Right. Not Coxon.

ALLEGRA. We have a list for Boston / if we can get through—

JOHN. Can you just ask—

> ALLEGRA *thrusts her cell phone at* MARGARET.

ALLEGRA. here you call information and then Boston for clarification. John you call DTC, and I'll answer the trading phone.

> MARGARET *finds a tattered phone tree list taped to the cabinet near the slop sink.*

MARGARET. (*Waving the list.*) Here!

ALLEGRA. what's that?

MARGARET. I think it's an office phone list

ALLEGRA. oh my god you're my hero thank you

MARGARET. ok on it.

> MARGARET *dials.*

ALLEGRA. thanks

> JOHN *can't figure out how to call the DTC.*

JOHN. should I just…call the DTC?

> *Phone rings.*

ALLEGRA. YES (*Answering.*) Lipman Kennedy Clearance Desk.

> ALLEGRA *on the landline, taking more orders* (*ad lib*).
>
> *Phone rings.*

MARGARET. (*Calling on* ALLEGRA's *phone.*) Hi, this is Margaret at the—

ALLEGRA. (*Whispers.*) Clearance Desk

MARGARET. —clearance desk—we're in New Jersey—yeah I have a couple of trades from you guys but I need clarification. First, on this 2 million Disney at six and a half, was that buying or selling?—

JOHN. (*On* MARGARET's *cell phone.*) / hello, I'm looking for the number of the DTC. Oh, uh, that's the—Depository Trust Company? Oh actually it's, give me the number for the Depository Trust and Clearing Company—hello?

> ALLEGRA *finishes her call on the landline, gives* JOHN *the paper, and then the phone rings again.*

ALLEGRA. (*Answering.*) Clearance Desk

> ALLEGRA *takes another order* (*ad lib*).

MARGARET. Selling, okay, great, thanks. And then one more question. The buyer of 500 grand of Cisco at four percent, who phoned that in? Matt Dobson? Can you spell that for me? Let me read it back to you—oh, pardon? Oh it's busy? Um, sure, yeah, you can use my number it's 917—

> JOHN's *call gets disconnected.*

ALLEGRA. (*Still on the phone, trying to multitask.*) No that's my cell. It's 609—

MARGARET. I'm sorry, actually it's 609—

ALLEGRA. 214

MARGARET. 214

ALLEGRA. 8739

MARGARET. 8739

ALLEGRA. (*Back on her phone call.*) Sorry (*Ad lib continues.*)

MARGARET. Yep that's this phone. Okay. Thanks. Okay bye.

> MARGARET *makes the changes and hands the paper to* JOHN, *who is starting to develop a significant pile.*
>
> JOHN *is overwhelmed.*
>
> JOHN *goes to the sink.*
>
> JOHN *sticks his head under the faucet.*
>
> ALLEGRA *hangs up and passes on her piece of paper.*
>
> ALLEGRA's *cell phone rings.* MARGARET *answers.* (*Ad lib.*)
>
> *The landline rings.* ALLEGRA *answers.* (*Ad lib.*)
>
> ALLEGRA's *cell phone rings again.*

MARGARET. (*Answering.*) Clearance Desk? …Who? Oh! Sorry, yeah, hang on— (*To* ALLEGRA.) It's for you.

> ALLEGRA *looks at the cell phone screen, takes the phone.*

ALLEGRA. Hey babe listen I—I can't talk, we're using this phone for—Love you too.

> *She hands the cell back to* MARGARET.
>
> JOHN *dries his hair and face with a paper towel.*

ALLEGRA. Sorry, what was that?

> The two phones continue to ring. (ALLEGRA *and* MARGARET *ad lib.*) *Taking orders, passing them to* JOHN.
>
> JOHN *returns to his desk area. He tries again.*

JOHN. Hello, information? I need the number for the Depository Trust and Clearing Company. New York. I said. New York. Yes. Thank you.

> *Phones ring.* ALLEGRA *and* MARGARET *take more orders, give the orders to* JOHN (*ad lib*). *They are in a quick staccato rhythm.* JOHN *is off rhythm, out of sync.*

JOHN. let me repeat that back to you, it's—Allegra!—212-855-1000

> ALLEGRA *dials as he speaks it. Gives him the thumbs up.*

okay, thank you. Thank you so much.

> *He hangs up.*
>
> *The effort has drained him of any energy he may have had.*

ALLEGRA. busy

JOHN. what is?

ALLEGRA. DTC. Busy signal. Did you ask for a direct line

JOHN. no, I—

> *Landline rings.*

ALLEGRA. (*Answering.*) Clearance Desk.

> JOHN *dials.*
>
> ALLEGRA's *cell phone rings.*

MARGARET. (*Answering.*) Clearance Desk.

> JOHN *hangs up.*
>
> MARGARET *takes another order*—"Ok, got it, thanks"—*and repeats the same basic phone call throughout the following as the phone continues to ring and the slips of paper continue to stack up.*

ALLEGRA. (*Scribbling.*) got it. What? you're having trouble getting through? Yeah we only have 2 phones here—

JOHN. (*Giving up.*) here

> *He passes her* MARGARET's *cell phone, which he has been using.*

ALLEGRA. you know what, actually, why don't I give you my— (*To* MARGARET.) Hey! Say your cell phone number—

> *She holds the landline up to* MARGARET's *face.*

MARGARET. (*Speaking into the phone.*) 917-722-5959.

> ALLEGRA *takes back the phone.*

ALLEGRA. / You got that?

MARGARET. (*Back on her call.*) / Sorry, that was three million dollars of what was it? Okay. Got it. Thanks.

ALLEGRA. So, that makes three phones. Three numbers you can call us on. That's right. Sure thing. Doing our best. Thank you. Thank you. Thank you. Ok bye.

The landline rings.

Clearance Desk.

MARGARET's phone rings in ALLEGRA's hands. She snaps to get JOHN's attention.

John. Heads up!

She tosses him the ringing phone. He catches and answers.

JOHN. (*Answering.*) Lipman Kennedy?

Now all three phones are going and they're taking orders (ad lib).

The yellow slips of paper are piling up. In the middle of the chaos—

MARGARET. (*To ALLEGRA.*) um, I'm so sorry, I. excuse me. Um. Don't we need to do something with, with this pile?

ALLEGRA. (*On phone.*) which pile?

MARGARET. this one. Like, are they official?

ALLEGRA. oh shit. Okay. Um. John, you take over here, and let me use that phone

JOHN. what are you gonna do?

ALLEGRA. I'm gonna hit redial until someone answers at the DTC.

A dance of passing paper, answering the phones, recording trades.

Maybe lunch arrives and they eat pizza while still taking orders.

Maybe ALLEGRA reaches the DTC while she has a big wad of pizza in her mouth.

Time passes.

Finally, it's 5:00.

MARGARET. all right then, thanks Matt. / Yep. We'll do this all again on Monday. You take care.

MARGARET hangs up the phone.

ALLEGRA gets to the last yellow paper.

ALLEGRA. Okay, yep, that's right. I think that's everything. Thanks Gail. Have a good one.

She hangs up.

JOHN. well that's that

They each take back their own cell phones.

MARGARET. it's over?

ALLEGRA. it's five

MARGARET. That's a slow day?

JOHN. No.

ALLEGRA. hell no

JOHN. most definitely not, that is not at all what a slow day is like.

ALLEGRA. that was a bonanza

JOHN. that's called killing us with kindness

MARGARET. That's good, right? You're back in business?

JOHN. I don't know what we're going to do on Monday if we don't get some direct lines.

ALLEGRA. or a fucking computer that actually connects to the outside world

MARGARET. I'm sorry I'm not faster. I'll do better on Monday. I'm starting to get the hang of it.

ALLEGRA. Nah you did great.

MARGARET. I did?

ALLEGRA. Sure you did. Didn't she do good, John?

JOHN *has been standing in the middle of the room, staring into space.*

JOHN. Sorry, what?

ALLEGRA. Margaret here. Rocked it. Right?

JOHN. Oh. Sure. Sure you did. Thank you. You did great.

MARGARET. Don't thank me, I'm just doing what anyone would do—I'm just happy to be here. I mean, not happy, I just mean

ALLEGRA. I know, honey. I know.

MARGARET. Something Jeff said to me once, he said, do something your future self will thank you for.

JOHN. (*Sincere.*) That's nice.

MARGARET. I think in the future, I'll be grateful that I got to spend this time with you guys, helping put your business back together.

JOHN. At least we have the weekend to take care of loose ends before Monday.

ALLEGRA. yeah, no.

JOHN. come on, Park

ALLEGRA. I gotta get some time with Richie. Plus the funerals.

JOHN. I thought it was only Kelly?

ALLEGRA. They added some other ones.

JOHN. Where did they find him? Kelly?

ALLEGRA. they didn't

MARGARET. then how do they know?

JOHN. I'm sorry, but how can we have funerals when there are no bodies? Seems a little…premature.

ALLEGRA. his family decided, who am I to judge?

>   *Beat.*
>
>   *Then* ALLEGRA *bursts into a strange, wide smile. She's remembering something funny.*

ALLEGRA. (*Big smile, an old joke.*) "Tom Kelly, Fucking Bastard."

>   JOHN *laughs.*

MARGARET. I'm sorry, what?

ALLEGRA. Remember?

JOHN. "I'm Tom Kelly, and I'm a Goddamn Fucking Bastard!"

ALLEGRA. Right right, that's what it was, he's a goddamn *and* a fucking bastard.

JOHN. And he *was*

ALLEGRA. Totally. What a dick.

JOHN. And he knew it.

ALLEGRA. "I'm Tom Kelly, and you know what I am?"

JOHN AND ALLEGRA. "I'm a Goddamn Fucking Bastard!"

>   *They're laughing.*

ALLEGRA. Tom Kelly. Jesus.

>   *Beat.*
>
>   *The moment is strangely light and heavy at the same time.*
>
>   ALLEGRA *heaves a heavy sigh.*

JOHN. Nancy called me. That morning.

ALLEGRA. No.

MARGARET. who's Nancy?

JOHN. my ex-wife.

MARGARET. oh right—sorry

JOHN. She was frantic. She reached me before I could even get to Kate. She started sobbing when she heard my voice.

MARGARET. That's beautiful.

JOHN. Is it? I thought it was kind of weird. I was trying and trying to get ahold of Kate, my wife, and instead there's Nancy, my ex-wife, tying up the line. I couldn't get to Kate. Everyone's calling me, I'm talking to everyone I know except for Kate. The one person I actually want to talk to.

MARGARET. She must care about you very much.

JOHN. She's my wife.

MARGARET. I mean your ex-wife.

JOHN. Nancy?

    Beat.

She just wanted to be part of the tragedy.

    Beat.

    MARGARET *seems as if she has been stung.*

    No one notices.

ALLEGRA. I'm going home.

JOHN. Yeah?

ALLEGRA. What?

    JOHN *looks back at all of the boxes of files they pulled yesterday.*

JOHN. I wonder if I should stay a while. We didn't get to work on the client lists today at all.

MARGARET. I can do that.

ALLEGRA. You don't have to.

MARGARET. I'm happy to. You go home. Go see—Darcy right?

JOHN. (*Hesitates.*) No, I—

    It's a lot of boxes.

MARGARET. I'd rather be here.

JOHN. well, I guess—thank you. That's great.

ALLEGRA. Great. You work on assembling the master client list, and then tomorrow you guys can start calling, try to reconstruct all that business from the beginning of the week.

MARGARET. That's what I was thinking.

JOHN. You're sure you don't mind?

MARGARET. I'm sure.

JOHN. all right then.

ALLEGRA. thank you. Seriously.

MARGARET. no problem.

ALLEGRA. Want a ride to the bus?

JOHN. it's not far

ALLEGRA. let me drive you

JOHN. sure, okay, thanks.

    JOHN *is lost in thought.*

ALLEGRA. (*To* JOHN.) you coming?

    He snaps out of it.

JOHN. (*To* MARGARET.) Good night.

MARGARET. Good night.

> ALLEGRA *and* JOHN *exit.*
>
> MARGARET *sits down to work.*

LATER THAT NIGHT
(Early Morning, Saturday, September 15).

Midnight.

MARGARET *is barefoot, but otherwise still wearing her awkwardly composed professional clothes.*

She's playing some music on the boom box, privately grooving to the beat as she types information from the legal pads into the computer.

Occasionally a key sticks.

But it's not so bad.

She munches on a slice of pizza clearly taken from an open box on another table.

The sound of a key in the lock. MARGARET *jumps, stuffs the rest of her pizza in her mouth.*

It's CATHY.

She's surprised to see MARGARET, *but hides her surprise.*

MARGARET *leaps up to turn off the music.*

CATHY. you're here

MARGARET. (*Mouth full of pizza.*) mm hm

> *Beat.* CATHY *is frozen on the threshold.*

CATHY. well, good. Good. I appreciate your. Ah. Work ethic.

> *Finally* CATHY *enters the room.*
>
> CATHY *goes to her purse, which she left near the slop sink.*

MARGARET. Today was so crazy—

CATHY. I heard. Well done.

MARGARET. So I've been going through the files—I did those boxes over there, oh and that one too—I'm making this list of clients as I find them, trying to keep it alphabetized—you guys have a lot of clients!—I was thinking we could start calling in the morning, see what still needs to be settled. Maybe, uh, we should start calling at 8? Or 9? I should be close to done by then I think

CATHY. (*Distracted.*) that's great.

MARGARET. Did you forget your purse?

CATHY. what? No. I—I mean—I did. Cars. They'll just whisk you away (ha ha)

MARGARET. sure, sure

>   *Beat.*
>
>   CATHY *seems lost.*

We'll get it done.

>   *Beat.*

CATHY. will we?

MARGARET. (*Overly positive.*) We will.

CATHY. You should go home. Get some sleep.

MARGARET. I don't mind. I'm pretty functional at night.

>   CATHY *nods. She looks around, not sure what to do with herself.*
>   *She had been planning to sleep here.*
>   *She makes herself a pot of coffee.*

MARGARET. okay…so I'm just gonna…

>   MARGARET *goes back to work.*
>   CATHY *watches the coffee percolate.*
>   *Eventually:*

CATHY. They let me back into my apartment for one hour, to get my things. And I asked them for how long, and no one would answer. How many things do I need, I asked them, do you mean for an overnight? A couple of days? An involuntary long vacation? Or is this good-bye Tribeca, your property has been condemned, good night and good luck? Nobody had an answer.

MARGARET. I'm so sorry.

CATHY. The level of incompetence around this thing is truly astonishing.

>   *She laughs inappropriately.*
>   *Beat.*

MARGARET. I was sleeping. When it happened?

CATHY. lucky girl.

MARGARET. I could smell it though When I woke up.

CATHY. who couldn't smell it?

>   *Beat.*

MARGARET. I went straight down to give blood.

CATHY. They don't need any blood.

>   *She's rifling through the yellow pieces of paper.*

we'll be lucky if any of these people are willing to work with us on Monday.

MARGARET. I'm sure they'll understand that—

CATHY. Can't say I'd do any different if the shoe was on the other foot.

MARGARET. But you guys did so much business today.

CATHY. That was the level of what, maybe, a pretty good day? In normal times I mean? But this—we took such a hit, you can't even picture it. We're gonna need to really strike some kind of gold to make up for the hit we've taken.

MARGARET. I'm sure you can do it.

> CATHY *flips through a large stack of papers, like a flip book.*

CATHY. This is how it was done across the industry when I started. All that paper.

MARGARET. There's still a lot of paper.

CATHY. they say it was like confetti but it was not like confetti.

> *Beat.*

MARGARET. people are saying a lot of things.

CATHY. but not about the fire in the elevator

MARGARET. the what?

CATHY. CNN cut that part

MARGARET. I—wait. You were—you were there?

> CATHY *hands her the stack of papers.*

CATHY. Did you enter these?

MARGARET. I'm sorry, I don't mean to pry, I just—

CATHY. That's gonna be a bear, let me tell you.

> CATHY *pours herself a cup of coffee.*
>
> MARGARET *goes back to typing.*
>
> *She keeps stealing looks at* CATHY—*like* CATHY *is some kind of exotic creature.* MARGARET *is in awe.*
>
> *They continue working.*
>
> *Time passes.*
>
> MARGARET *takes a nap.*
>
> *She gets up.*
>
> CATHY *takes a nap.*
>
> *She gets up.*
>
> *The two women are in a rhythm, working together.*
>
> *A fighter jet passes by overhead. They look up and listen while it passes. Then, they go back to work.*
>
> *Finally—it's morning.*

DAY 3 (Saturday, September 15).

Continuous.

Sound of a key in the lock It's JOHN. *He wears weekend clothes—jeans, a rumpled but clean polo shirt. He carries a tray of deli coffee cups.*

JOHN. Good morning, good morning!

He passes out coffees—

MARGARET. Ooh, thank you

JOHN. For you, I didn't know what you liked, so I thought, latte?

MARGARET. Perfect! Thank you.

JOHN. I know you're something of an aficionado.

MARGARET. what, me? no I

JOHN. *(Turning to* CATHY.) And for you—also a latte, this one with three shots, the way you like it.

CATHY *takes it, smells it.*

A wave of nausea.

She puts the drink aside

She puts her head down on the desk, or between her knees.

MARGARET. Thank you so much. This is really kind of you.

JOHN. You were here all night?

MARGARET. I was! I didn't mean to, but—well Cathy came back and. Well. It just made sense. We worked all night.

JOHN. You worked together?

MARGARET. Is that okay? There's so much to do.

JOHN. Of course it's okay! But—you know you didn't have to, right?

MARGARET. I wanted to.

JOHN. Okay. Thank you.

MARGARET. You don't have to thank me.

JOHN. Okay.

MARGARET *starts showing him things on the computer.*

MARGARET. I made a spreadsheet of all / the clients, here—

JOHN. oh great, great

MARGARET. —company name, address, phone, email...And here I've made a column, here you just make a check mark to show we've made contact with someone at the company, and here is the place to list any transactions from Monday that still need to be cleared, see, or Tuesday, here.

JOHN. that's very good of you.

MARGARET. So we can use this list to call the companies and try to get information about what business was transacted last week on Monday and Tuesday.

JOHN. I see.

>MARGARET *holds up three legal pads.*

MARGARET. And then I divided the client list into four sections, and I wrote out three of the lists here, so we can each be working on a section even though we only have one computer.

JOHN. fantastic

MARGARET. Of course it's Saturday, so who knows who's in the office, but we'll do our best. I mean, we're in the office, so.

JOHN. So maybe everybody's in the office?

MARGARET. I mean, probably, right? My friend works at Goldman, I know they're working today, so

JOHN. That's great.

>JOHN *seems bewildered by all of this activity.*
>
>*The intercom buzzes.* CATHY *startles awake.*

MARGARET. Oh great!

CATHY. Who's that?

MARGARET. The computers are here!

>*She buzzes them in.*

JOHN. Morning, Lamb.

CATHY. Davies.

>*Knock on the door.*
>
>MARGARET *opens it.*
>
>*It's a large platter of food.*

MARGARET. ...uh...thank you...um—

>*She closes the door.*

CATHY. What's this?

MARGARET. Maybe a charity thing?

>CATHY *reads the paperwork.*

CATHY. oh no. oh dear.

>MARGARET *reads over her shoulder.*

MARGARET. What is—oh.

JOHN. What?

MARGARET. "Tom Kelly—Lipman Kennedy Funeral."

CATHY. shit.

JOHN. why'd it come here?

MARGARET. I guess they're trying to figure out which Lipman?

CATHY. there's only one Lipman.

JOHN. Now there are many.

CATHY. I'll bring it.

JOHN. I'm planning to go later—

CATHY. me too

JOHN. I can just take it in my car.

CATHY. We'll bring it with us. That's what we'll do.

JOHN. All right then.

MARGARET. It's really beautiful.

CATHY. Pardon?

MARGARET. How you're—coming together, how you. How you're taking care of each other.

JOHN. I'll put this in the cooler until we go.

> *He does.*
>
> *He is suddenly very tired.*

CATHY. All right, let's start calling clients. (*To* MARGARET.) You ready?

MARGARET. Here are the lists.

> *She hands out the three legal pads. Nobody moves.*

CATHY. You know what to say?

> MARGARET *prepares to take notes.*

JOHN. You'll be fine.

CATHY. You start with, basically hello, hi, I'm—?

MARGARET. Margaret Gale.

CATHY. "Hello, this is Margaret Gale at Lipman Kennedy"

JOHN. They're going to want to say they're sorry

MARGARET. I experienced that yesterday.

CATHY. Don't let them go on too long.

JOHN. Say, "listen, I'm calling, I hope you can help me out with something," they'll say, "sure"

CATHY. "We need to verify our records"

MARGARET. "Verify"?

CATHY. They can't know that we don't have any records. They might try to cheat us.

MARGARET. Wow. Okay. Uh. So I say, "hello, I need to verify my records."

JOHN. "Do you have any purchases or sales in process with Lipman from Monday or Tuesday?"

MARGARET. That's it?

JOHN. Yep.

CATHY. Ask for product name, amount bought or sold, name of Lipman trader, and—this is important—the exact date and time of the trade.

MARGARET. (*Reading from notes.*) Product name, amount purchased—

JOHN. or sold

MARGARET. —name of trader, date and time of the trade.

CATHY. You got it.

JOHN. She's a natural.

MARGARET. All right, so, great!

    CATHY *and* JOHN *don't move.*

I'll just get started then.

JOHN. Great.

CATHY. Thank you.

    MARGARET *takes her cell phone and a legal pad back to the sink, where she quietly starts calling clients and using her script. (Ad lib in background.)*

    CATHY *sips her coffee. It's gotten a little cold by now.*

JOHN. well then.

CATHY. What?

JOHN. Nothing.

CATHY. No tell me. What.

JOHN. You're not the boss, Cathy.

    Beat.

CATHY. Someone had to step up.

JOHN. you didn't have to go on television—

CATHY. / I was *there.*

JOHN. / —and make yourself the spokesman for—

CATHY. They asked me.

JOHN. Cath.

CATHY. It's not my fault I wanted a different kind of muffin.

JOHN. (*Not sure he heard right.*) That—that's not what I'm talking about.

CATHY. (*Fake breezy.*) It's not my fault that I know what kind of muffin I like, so I went down to get it, / and

JOHN. How can you make a joke about it?

CATHY. If I don't joke what am I supposed to do?

JOHN. You can't use the fact that you were *there* / to justify basically taking over the whole company from other people—your colleagues—of equal rank, who—who—

CATHY. Everyone is so wild about the muffins upstairs, but you're being blinded by price. The muffins upstairs are dry and small, and they got those little seeds in 'em that get stuck in your teeth—

JOHN. They're not actually that bad

> MARGARET *puts away her phone and tries to catch up with the conversation.*

CATHY. I like a good chewy corn muffin, I like 'em as big as my head. They have those down at the cart down on 78.

MARGARET. wait—you weren't in the office because you were downstairs getting a muffin?

CATHY. And that's how you get to be chief executive!

JOHN. She thinks she's being funny.

CATHY. Someone's got to be.

MARGARET. That's—that's amazing. You're a hero.

> CATHY *turns dark.*

CATHY. No. I'm not.

MARGARET. Of course you are. / you—

CATHY. I'm just a hard to please diva who knows what she wants for breakfast.

> *Beat.*
>
> *Awkward.*

JOHN. (that's not what I'm saying I)

> *Beat.*

CATHY. (*To* MARGARET.) Any progress?

MARGARET. I just got off the phone with, uh, March Capital?

> CATHY *sits at the computer.*

CATHY. Read me what you got and I'll enter the information.

MARGARET. Okay, so, on Monday there were three—

JOHN. Keenan?

MARGARET. Sorry?

JOHN. Who'd you speak to at March?

MARGARET. (*Checking her notes.*) Uh—Rick Keenan?

JOHN. Keenan! Yeah. How's he doing?

MARGARET. uh—fine, I think

CATHY. Give me what you got.

    MARGARET *reads,* CATHY *types.*

MARGARET. On Monday there were three transactions.
Tom Kelly bought a million Adobe five percents due in 2027 at 75 at 8:50 a.m.
David Marino sold two point five million Disney twelve percents due in 2019 at 101 at 2:31 p.m.
And David Marino again sold a million more of that same Adobe at 2:40 p.m.
And then on Tuesday, let's see—
It's Tom Kelly again, he's got two.
One and a half million IBM eight and a halfs due in 2020 sold at 101 at 8:22 a.m.
And then he sold stocks, 500,000 shares of Boeing stock, at 43.20 a share at 9:14 a.m.

CATHY. Wait what? For who?

MARGARET. For Lipman. / He sold—

JOHN. What's the time zone?

MARGARET. Eastern. 9:14 a.m. / Eastern.

CATHY. For who again?

MARGARET. (*Checks her notes.*) For us. For you. It says Lipman.

JOHN. Our in-house account?

MARGARET. / I guess? That's what he said.

CATHY. Must be Monday.

JOHN. / Nah, he wouldn't liquidate Boeing on a normal—

MARGARET. No it was Tuesday. Definitely Tuesday. He went through chronologically.

JOHN. Keenan?

MARGARET. Yeah. Rick Keenan.

JOHN. Well there's no way that's right. Could he have meant 8:14?

MARGARET. He was very precise.

CATHY. You must have misheard.

MARGARET. / I didn't.

JOHN. Keenan's thorough.

    The door opens. It's ALLEGRA, *carrying a heavy cardboard box and also a six-pack of beer. She wears funeral clothes and bright white running shoes.*

ALLEGRA. This was outside?

CATHY. The computers!

ALLEGRA. I don't know, I guess—can someone give me a hand? There's more back there—.

> JOHN *takes the box from her.* MARGARET *goes outside to get the rest of the boxes.*
>
> CATHY *types furiously on her BlackBerry.*

JOHN. I thought you were staying home.

ALLEGRA. I was at the funeral and I just. I don't know. It was weird to not be here.

JOHN. 'Cause you love us so much?

ALLEGRA. You know it.

> JOHN *and* ALLEGRA *return.* ALLEGRA *remembers the six-pack.*

JOHN. Can I get one of those?

> ALLEGRA *pulls off two cans, tosses one to* JOHN.

ALLEGRA. catch—

> *He does, awkwardly. Pops the can open and takes a long swig.*
>
> *A police siren in the distance.*
>
> ALLEGRA *puts the rest of the beers in the cooler, where she sees the funeral food.*

ALLEGRA. Ooh, lox!

CATHY. / For Kelly's funeral.

ALLEGRA. Love smoked fish. Wait. What's it doing here?

> CATHY *starts unpacking the box of computers.*
>
> *Throughout the following, the four of them set up three more computers, a printer, and a fax machine. (Ad lib interstitial dialogue as needed.)*

MARGARET. the delivery order just said Lipman Kennedy.

ALLEGRA. ah.

JOHN. (*Re: her funeral clothes.*) Which one?

> ALLEGRA *checks a funeral program in her purse.*

ALLEGRA. ummm…Federico Lanza?

JOHN. ah.

ALLEGRA. Did you know him?

JOHN. I think…maybe.

ALLEGRA. seemed like a nice guy.

JOHN. Manager in FX I think.

CATHY. Interesting.

ALLEGRA. What is?

CATHY. Lanza got to go first.
JOHN. (*"not everything is a competition"*) Cathy.
CATHY. What.
ALLEGRA. There's more this afternoon, and tomorrow—
MARGARET. You didn't know him? But you went to the funeral anyway?
ALLEGRA. Seemed like the thing to do. Told you, I couldn't stay home. I can take the lox to Kelly's later.
JOHN. Fucking Kelly, man.
ALLEGRA. (*Joking.*) What did he do now?
CATHY. Check this out.

> CATHY *shows* ALLEGRA *the note that* MARGARET *took about Kelly making a trade at 9:14 a.m.*

ALLEGRA. That's not / right. Who took this?
JOHN. / I know, right? Crazy.
CATHY. She did.
MARGARET. / I don't understand the problem.
CATHY. I think it's right.
ALLEGRA. (*To* MARGARET.) If this trade really happened at 9:14, it means that Kelly was still doing business on / Tuesday morning *after*—
MARGARET. oh. OH.
JOHN. Keenan's pretty thorough.
ALLEGRA. Maybe it was 8:14?
CATHY. Nah, Kelly would never do that—check out / the amount.
ALLEGRA. / oh my god—
JOHN. From our *in-house* account.
MARGARET. Why not?
ALLEGRA. You'd never sell off this much Boeing when the market's doing fine.
JOHN. Only makes sense if you know the market for—is about to collapse.
MARGARET. / jesus
CATHY. And you know Lipman's gonna need an infusion of cash.
JOHN. Holy shit.
CATHY. Right?
MARGARET. Isn't that, like, insider trading or something? / Knowing something other people don't know?
JOHN. Hah.
ALLEGRA. Kind of, yeah.

JOHN. (*Kindly.*) / No.
CATHY. (*Not kind.*) Don't be absurd.
MARGARET. I'm sorry, I'm new—
CATHY. Observation and action. Those are the core principles of what we do.
MARGARET. Okay...
CATHY. Kelly was just doing his job.
JOHN. Really, really well.
ALLEGRA. I don't know about that.
CATHY. (*To* ALLEGRA.) Think about the cash we'll have on hand when this clears.
JOHN. (*To* MARGARET.) A big part of the job here is identifying patterns and opportunity.
MARGARET. In what way?
CATHY. Act on what you see before anyone else does. This is actually a great example. Kelly didn't know anything that anyone with a television didn't also know at the exact same time. Maybe he knew even less. But he could see the impact this—event—crisis—would have on the market, / the company.
JOHN. And he had the balls to act on it. When he was in a war zone basically. When he knew—
CATHY. (*Admiring, in awe.*) Tom Kelly.
JOHN. (*Also admiring, also in awe.*) That fucking guy.
ALLEGRA. (*Totally weirded out.*) Kelly, man. Jesus.
JOHN. Right?
ALLEGRA. I don't know—like he could have been calling his family, he could have—but instead he's—I don't know, he's calling clients—trying to—what? Make one last sale—?
CATHY. He knew we'd be screwed if we couldn't get liquid.
ALLEGRA. We shouldn't clear it.
JOHN. Allegra.
ALLEGRA. What? We can't. We shouldn't. There are other ways to—we'll get a loan, we'll—

    MARGARET *pulls a phone console out of the box.*

MARGARET. I'm sorry to—but where does this one go?
CATHY. Oh, there it is

    CATHY *takes it from her.*

MARGARET. what is it?

JOHN *takes it.*

JOHN. that's a phone turret, I never thought I'd see one of these again!

 MARGARET *pulls out a shoebox-sized plastic container, opens it. It's full of unlabeled cassette tapes.*

MARGARET. And do you know what these tapes are for?

CATHY. What does the label say?

MARGARET. "Lipman Trading Floor." Didn't you say all your calls were recorded?

JOHN. Right, okay, maybe the missing trades are on here, and we won't have to make so many phone calls.

ALLEGRA. If that's what this is—amazing.

 She picks a tape from the top of the pile and loads it into the boom box, presses play. The button is stuck. At the same time, CATHY *and* JOHN *sort through the tapes.*

CATHY. Are they dated?

JOHN. no, nothing

 Meanwhile, ALLEGRA *shimmies the play button. Suddenly, static, and then the sound of chaos. The shriek of a fire alarm. People running, glass breaking. Maybe the sound of a sprinkler system, shouts in the far distance, things like "This way!" and "Come on, let's go!" and "We're going to the west stairs!" Perhaps a small snatch of a panicked voice, but nothing recognizable as a call of distress. No actor should be recorded saying things like "help me" or "I can't get out." But that's the spirit of it. It should be spare, but terrible. Maybe these are the only coherent words we hear:*

BOSTON TRADER ON THE PHONE. Hello?

 Beat.

You still there man?

 Beat.

Hello?

 After just a quick moment of this—

 CATHY *leaps on the boom box and yanks it out of the wall.*

 We've only heard enough of the tape for her to recognize it—because she was there—but no one else has put it together yet.

JOHN. What the hell, Lamb?

ALLEGRA. I don't think—

CATHY. NO.

JOHN. What the hell was that?

Long beat. It sinks in.

ALLEGRA. Oh…

JOHN. Oh…

MARGARET. Oh…

Beat.

ALLEGRA. Why would they do that to us?

JOHN. / Fucking Boston.

ALLEGRA. / Jesus.

MARGARET. What? Why?

JOHN. Trying to psych us out.

MARGARET. No, I—I think maybe they wanted you to have it.

ALLEGRA. *Why?*

MARGARET. Like as a kind of memorial?

Beat.

CATHY. (*Fake light.*) Gotta move forward. Can't look back.

Beat.

CATHY *throws the boom box in the trash.*

Beat.

ALLEGRA *takes it out of the trash and puts it on a shelf.*

CATHY. …it's not like I even think about it anymore.

They all look at the boom box.

The distant sound of a helicopter.

DAY 4 (Sunday, September 16).

JOHN *sleeps in a corner of the room, with a windbreaker pulled over him like a blanket.*

ALLEGRA *and* MARGARET *each sit at a computer, entering information from piles of paper at an efficient clip.*

Cans of Coke litter the table, empty bottles of beer, half-eaten cartons of Chinese take-out. And still those pizza boxes.

It's quiet for a very long time

ALLEGRA. She called me from inside. Christine.

Beat.

MARGARET. Wow.

Beat.

> MARGARET *waits, expecting* ALLEGRA *to continue.*
> But ALLEGRA *keeps working in silence.*
> Long beat.
> Eventually, MARGARET *goes back to her work.*

ALLEGRA. She didn't leave a message. I was home sick.

> MARGARET *pauses, ready to listen, but not wanting to call attention to herself. It's not clear if* ALLEGRA *knows that she is listening.*

Actually I wasn't sick. I mean, I was sick, but not that kind of sick.

Last weekend Richie and I fought like dogs. Seriously. Like *wild animals.* All summer basically. My mother always says, don't go to sleep angry, but what am I supposed to do when he doesn't come home for like three nights in a row? You either stay up waiting for him, or, you know, you can sleep. But then when you wake up, you reach for him, it's instinct, like your arm without a mind reaching for him, and then of course he's not there, so you have to remember all over again that he didn't come home last night, except it's even worse, it's exponential, like, I CANNOT BELIEVE THIS IS STILL HAPPENING.

So last Monday I was like, fuck this. Fuck him, fuck Brooklyn, fuck waiting around for some big breakup fight that's never gonna happen. I'm done. He wants to stay out all night, get shitfaced with his boys, feel sorry for yourself because your band isn't famous yet? Fine. You do that. But me, I'm working, I got a job, I'm putting food on the fucking table, I don't got to put up with this shit. This is what I'm saying to myself all day long, on the subway, at my desk. You know that thing where you talk to yourself out loud because you're preparing what to say? Christine was like, are you losing your mind?

So I'm on the train home Monday night and I've got it, I know what I'm gonna say, I'm ready, I'm gonna put his stuff on the sidewalk, not even page him, just be done. But then you know what happens?

I get to our stoop and I smell fucking chicken carbonara. You get me?

Asshole came home during the day and now he's cooking me dinner. And I gotta get a new script, you know? Like some kind of dressed-up Chef Boyardee is gonna make up for five nights he don't come home? So we fight, we throw things, we eat the chicken, we throw the chicken, there's spaghetti on the walls, in my hair, til we're too tired and we're sitting on the floor and we're having a real conversation. Killed one of those big jugs of wine, straight from the bottle, Carlo Rossi, nasty shit.

And then the next thing I remember is my deadbeat boyfriend, my high school boyfriend, he's trying to wake me up. You're on the kitchen floor and the love of your life is shaking you, your head is a hammer, you're probably still drunk, but he's there, he's saying, come look what happened on the TV, you gotta see what's on the TV.

It was—it was already over. I was late to work. I missed it.

> *Beat.*

MARGARET. Sometimes it's the asshole who saves your life.

> *Beat.*

I heard that somewhere.

> ALLEGRA *is mortified that she has actually shared something with this near-stranger.*

ALLEGRA. I was supposed to be there.

MARGARET. (*Sincere.*) You are so lucky.

ALLEGRA. I have a hairbrush Christine used to borrow all the time. I'm trying not to read the paper but Richie keeps showing me things. Like, cutting out little articles for me like I want to keep a scrapbook or some shit. That's how I know about the DNA. I told her mom about the brush and I was gonna bring it down to The Pile, to see if they could make a match but. She wanted to keep it. Her mom. I'm not sure why, it's not like it was hers, it's mine she just used it sometimes.

> *Beat.*

MARGARET. I have a T-shirt that Jeff let me wear when it was cold. We went to a quarry, like one of those old rock pits that fills up with water and becomes a swimming hole. We were in Vermont. There were three levels you could dive from. We were diving off the lowest one and he dared me to jump from the highest one.

ALLEGRA. Did you?

MARGARET. (*Shakes her head no.*) It was really high.

ALLEGRA. Did he?

MARGARET. He loved it.

> *Beat.*

ALLEGRA. I dunno. Maybe the brush smells like her head or something?

> *Long beat.*
>
> *They go back to working.*

DAY 5 (Monday, September 17).

> CATHY *and* MARGARET *both on the phone.* CATHY *is disheveled and barefoot and nearly asleep, running on fumes. Her crisp work clothes have been transformed into something: Like, if before she had*

been wearing a crisp white shirt tucked into a pencil skirt, now the shirt is untucked, it's flapping open over her camisole and the sleeves are scrunched up to her elbows. She's practically falling asleep in her chair.

MARGARET is also in some version of work clothes turned into pajamas, but she seems to have adrenaline and is more at ease.

JOHN is asleep in a corner of the room, maybe on a desk, on the floor in the corner or on two chairs pushed together to make a bed.

There are more empty pizza boxes, more taco wrappers. A couple of empty Chinese take-out containers. Lots of empty cans of Coke.

CATHY answers two phones at once, scribbling notes madly. She's taking the information about bond trades happening in real time. Elsewhere, MARGARET is set up with a large stack of paper, and is reading off a list to the DTC. After each call, CATHY passes the information to MARGARET, who has a growing stack of trade slips that she's not dealing with right now.

CATHY. (*On phone.*) / Yep, okay, yup got it. Thanks, bud.

Phone ringing throughout.

Continued, answering a call:

Clearance Desk. Yeah hi Stu, whatchu got? Mm-hm, yup, yup, okay. Got it. Yup.

...

Clearance Desk. Yeah ok, ready. Mm-hm, yup, yup, okay. Got it. Yup. (*Etc., continues as ad lib.*)

MARGARET. And then, this is everything I got from Feinstein West, I have— Ok on Monday September 10th I have Leonard Fontana buying 10 million IBM 2012 five percents at 95, yep uh huh uh huh
Ok great and then it's—
Hello? Hello?

She's been disconnected. Calls back.

Hi, hello, this is Margaret Gale at Lipman Kennedy? We just got disconnected?

...

Oh—uh, hang on, I think it was—
I was talking to Charlie Dunbar?

...

Okay, yeah, great, thank you. I'll hold.

CATHY continues (*ad lib throughout the following*). *MARGARET is on hold.*

JOHN wakes up.

Makes coffee.

CATHY. (*On phone.*) Yep, that's great, thank you—

(Good morning, John!)

Both of her phones ring.

Answering one phone:

Clearance Desk, please hold.

(*Answers the other.*) Clearance Desk, please hold.

Hands one of the phones to JOHN. *He doesn't know what to do with it.*

JOHN. I—

CATHY. (*Back on the phone.*) Thanks for holding, give it to me. (*Ad lib continues.*)

MARGARET. (*Still on hold.*) Those phones are New Milford, the bond market opened at eight.

JOHN. Is it eight already?

MARGARET. It's after nine. (*Back to the phone.*) / Oh hey, you know what, that's okay, I don't need Charlie, if you can take this info for me—I really need to get these settled by the end of day, and with the stock market about to open, I was really hoping to—

…

Okay, yeah, I'll hold.

JOHN. (*On phone.*) Hello?

…

Oh hi Matt. Yeah, yeah, we spent the weekend trying to reconstruct—

…

Oh sure ok, hang on, let me get a pencil…

He looks around, lost. MARGARET *clocks this.*

MARGARET. Actually, John, you know what? Here—I'm on hold with the DTC, and all you need to do when they pick up is just give them the trades on this list, it's the trades from last week that need to be cleared? The work we did over the weekend?

JOHN. Oh, yeah, sure—

MARGARET. And I'll take in the new trades.

They switch phones.

JOHN. Hello?

But no one's there (he's on hold). He hangs up. Goes to pour himself some coffee.

MARGARET. (*On phone.*) Hello, thanks for holding—

But they have hung up too. The phone rings in her hand.

Clearance Desk, this is Margaret. Yep we're—

...
Uh, hang on—
John? Hey, John!

JOHN. (*Startled.*) Over here.

MARGARET. Are we the backend for equities too?

CATHY. Yes!

MARGARET. Thanks!
(*Back on phone.*) Hi, thanks for holding—oh you heard that.
...
Okay great, talk to you at 9:30 then.

> *Hangs up. Sees that* JOHN *is still stirring his coffee. The phone rings in her hand.*

Clearance Desk, please hold. (*Calls over to* JOHN.) John, can you help? Cathy told me to get everything cleared with the DTC before the stock market opens at 9:30, but that's in 20 minutes, and—(*Back on phone.*) Thanks for holding.

> *She starts to take notes. Just then,* ALLEGRA *arrives. She's full of bright energy like a breeze, carrying a coffee tray with four lattes.*

ALLEGRA. Good morning, good morning! Everyone ready for the bell?

JOHN. I—uh—

> ALLEGRA *looks around. Clearly, no one looks ready for the bell.*

ALLEGRA. (*To* MARGARET.) Tag me in.

> MARGARET *hangs up her call and lets the phones ring. Now* CATHY *is answering both phones.*

CATHY. (*Answering phone.*) / Clearance Desk. (*Ad lib continues.*)

MARGARET. Oh thank god, you're back. Okay. So this stack of paper is all of the business we reconstructed over the weekend—that spreadsheet I was making? So we just need to call the DTC and literally just run down the list. Cathy wants it done before the stock market opens at 9:30—

ALLEGRA. Great, so why don't we split it into four parts—

> ALLEGRA *splits the sheaf of paper into four parts, giving herself and* MARGARET *larger piles than what she gives to* CATHY *and* JOHN.

MARGARET. We're already getting bond trades from New Milford.

CATHY. I'm on with New Milford—

ALLEGRA. That can wait til later. Twenty minutes, let's bombard the DTC, get this done.

CATHY. (*Speaking into both phones.*) Give me twenty. / Call me back in twenty minutes.

ALLEGRA. Here's the number—

> *She pulls a sticky note off the pile and plants it on the desk or the back of the computer.* CATHY *and* MARGARET *dial.*

CATHY. / This is Cathy Lamb, I have some Lipman trades for you… (*Ad lib.*)

MARGARET. / Hi, this is Margaret Gale again?

…

Oh Charlie!

…

Yeah we got disconnected! (*Ad lib.*)

JOHN. (*To* ALLEGRA.) when I think of where we were / a week ago today

ALLEGRA. I know.

JOHN. I just. it's all.

ALLEGRA. I know. But, we gotta do this.

> JOHN *dials.* CATHY *and* MARGARET *continue reading their lists.*

JOHN. Hi, yeah, hey, this is John Davies at Lipman Kennedy? / We have some backlogged trades to settle—

…

Okay great. So, uh, should I just start reading? Yeah okay um I got… (*Ad lib.*)

> *Meanwhile,* ALLEGRA *has been scanning her list, about to call, when—*

ALLEGRA. Hey—hey, what's this?

CATHY. What (sorry, hang on)

ALLEGRA. This has Kelly's Boeing sale on it.

CATHY. I told Margaret to make a list all of the business that we recorded over the weekend.

ALLEGRA. (*To* MARGARET.) I told you not to put it on the list.

CATHY. I made a call.

> ALLEGRA *looks at* JOHN.

ALLEGRA. John.

> JOHN *shrugs, like: what can I do?*

You know what Kelly was like. You know this isn't right.

> CATHY *puts her call on hold.*

JOHN. (*Holding the phone away from his ear.*) / It's a lot of money.

ALLEGRA. Things are different now, we can't just go back to / business as usual, we—

CATHY. The faster we can get back to business as usual, the better off we're going to be.

ALLEGRA. Things are different now.

CATHY. With this windfall, we might even make a / marginal profit this quarter.

ALLEGRA. There are other ways to make a profit.

MARGARET. (*Still on phone.*) Hang on a sec— (*To the others.*) Doesn't clearing this trade mean that Jenny Lockhart will get her husband's bonus?

JOHN. (*On phone.*) / hold on, I have to put you on hold for a sec—

CATHY. Not just Jen. Melissa Fontana. Abigail Wu. / Barry's wife and kids.

MARGARET. wow

JOHN. Barry.

CATHY. If Kelly hadn't done this for us, I wouldn't be able to promise those families / anything. Not a cent.

JOHN. I haven't even thought about him. Jesus. / All those kids.

MARGARET. (*On phone.*) I'm so sorry, I'm going to have to call you back—

ALLEGRA. Tom Kelly, shit, he could have called his wife, his kids—you were at the memorial, you saw them, those three little girls—

CATHY. He used his last moments on earth to provide for them, / and us, and—I don't see anything wrong with

ALLEGRA. He just wanted to win. All Tom Kelly ever wanted / was to WIN.

CATHY. Of course he wanted to WIN!

Beat. CATHY *and* ALLEGRA *stare each other down.*

MARGARET. I think he's kind of a hero, actually.

CATHY. / Sure, I can see that—

ALLEGRA. no. No. No.

MARGARET. In the last minutes of his life, he did this amazing sacrifice thing—he didn't call home, he didn't try to get out, instead he did this thing / that means his family is going to be okay without him

ALLEGRA. Instead of calling his family, instead of helping people, / he

MARGARET. He did help people. He's helping them right now.

CATHY. How about instead of disrespecting Kelly, instead of judging his choices—and you weren't there, you don't know what you would have done, you have no. fucking. / idea—

ALLEGRA. I'm not / saying that I—

CATHY. We should applaud Kelly for his bravery, his fortitude, his strength of character—

ALLEGRA. I just—

CATHY. All I'm saying is, I wasn't this brave.

Beat.

JOHN. sure you / were
ALLEGRA. of course you / were brave
MARGARET. none of us could possibly imagine—
> MARGARET's *phone starts to ring.*

CATHY. 9:30.
> *Phone keeps ringing.*

Market's open.
> *And ringing.*

You gonna get that?
> CATHY *picks up the call on hold.* MARGARET's *phone keeps ringing.*

CATHY. (*Cont'd, on phone.*) Okay, I'm back.
> *Finally,* MARGARET *answers the phone.*

MARGARET. Good morning, Lipman Kennedy?

DAY 6 (Tuesday, September 18).

> ALLEGRA *sits alone at the table.*
> *She takes the boom box off the shelf.*
> *She takes headphones out of her purse, and plugs them into the boom box.*
> *She listens to it for two full minutes.*
> *We watch her listen.*
> *We can't hear what she hears.*

DAY 7 (Wednesday, September 19).

> *The office is now furnished with more tables, more computers, more telephone consoles. The food trash has been cleared away. It's starting to look like an office.*
>
> *Everyone wears professional clothing. Maybe they've even showered. The mood is festive, although still restrained. This is still an office, and they're still in crisis. It's just—now the state of crisis has become kind of normalized; they can celebrate the small victories inside it.*
>
> JOHN *pops a bottle of champagne.*

JOHN. / ah!
MARGARET. woo hoo!
> *He pours it out into four plastic cups. It drips all over the table.*

JOHN. / oh shoot

ALLEGRA. / careful!

MARGARET. hang on, it's ok, I'll get—

    MARGARET *grabs some paper towels and cleans up after him. As soon as everyone has a glass:*

CATHY. As of this evening, we have officially cleared as much as is knowable of last week's business.

MARGARET. / Yes!

ALLEGRA. / wow

JOHN. / amazing

CATHY. We have shown Wall Street that Lipman Kennedy's not going anywhere. We came back strong on Monday, made some very smart calls as the market tumbled, purchased some securities we've long had our eye on at bargain prices. Monday, yesterday, today—our small band of warriors has processed more business than anyone thought humanly possible.

JOHN. / yeah

MARGARET. / incredible

CATHY. We did it. We're not going under.

ALLEGRA. / (whew)

MARGARET. / yeah!

CATHY. It looks like our losses will be marginal this quarter. We might even make a small profit.

JOHN. / Oh, wow.

ALLEGRA. wow

CATHY. And so I will be going on CNN in a few hours to tell the world what I'm telling you now—Lipman Kennedy will be giving 25% of our profits to the families for the next five years.

ALLEGRA. / Oh my god.

JOHN. / oh, man. just incredible.

    Maybe MARGARET *claps here.*

CATHY. The widows will get their money. And we couldn't have done it without you—and—you—and you.

    She toasts them each in turn.

JOHN. And to you, Cathy. Cheers.

MARGARET. / Cheers!

ALLEGRA. cheers

    They toast.

CATHY. Cheers, John.

They all toast and sip their drinks. CATHY *downs her glass and pours herself another.*

JOHN. can I say something?

CATHY. of course, you don't need to ask

    JOHN *clears his throat.*

MARGARET. Stand up, stand up!

JOHN. ah—okay, uh—

    He does.

um. To our lost brothers and sisters, for whom we keep this ship afloat.

ALLEGRA. / Amen to that.

CATHY. Hear / hear.

MARGARET. Cheers.

    They toast.

    ALLEGRA *chugs her glass, pours another.*

    JOHN *remains standing with his glass extended. He's not done with his toast.*

JOHN. as you know I'm not much for…I just, I want to say, uh. That I'm really, um. Thankful. to all of you for—well I think the most important thing to note here is that we've done something together, the way we all—we kept each other together in a life raft in a really bad storm, I mean "really bad" doesn't begin to—and I don't mean the storm is over, I mean, I don't know about you but it keeps coming—like—waves, like—

    He is overcome. He sits down.

    MARGARET *takes the glass from his hand and gently places it on the table.*

CATHY. Thank you John.

MARGARET. I think what John is trying to say is that you all have done something more meaningful here than just saving the business.

CATHY. Exactly. Hear, near.

    CATHY *pats* MARGARET *on the back. It's almost a back-slap, like they're teammates on a softball team or something.*

    ALLEGRA *lets out a sound that sounds something like a guffaw.*

    Only MARGARET *notices.*

CATHY. and I'd like to give a special acknowledgement to the newest member of the Lipman team, Margaret Gale, who has gone from knowing—if I can say it—absolutely nothing about our business lines to being integral to our turnaround.

    MARGARET *blushes, grins.*

MARGARET. I just wanted to do what I could do to help.

    CATHY *and* JOHN *toast her.* ALLEGRA *does not.*

JOHN. cheers. I think Jeff would be proud.

    Beat.

    A siren in the distance. No one notices.

sorry—that was his name, right? Jeff?

MARGARET. I—it's been—it's been really special to spend time with people who, I mean. Even if you didn't know him exactly, I've gotten a little sense of the people he worked with, and— /

ALLEGRA. Okay, here we go.

MARGARET. / I'm sorry—what?

JOHN. Allegra?

ALLEGRA. Lasky, right? Jeff Lasky?

MARGARET. Do you remember him?

ALLEGRA. I don't.

CATHY. Oh! Lasky? Big guy, kind of a lion head?

MARGARET. Yes! You knew him?

CATHY. Isn't he the one who got married to whatshername who used to be in HR?

MARGARET. / No, he—

ALLEGRA. Lindsay.

MARGARET. (*Genuinely perplexed.*) —I'm sorry, what?

CATHY. Lindsay. How is she?

ALLEGRA. They were engaged.

MARGARET. / Wait. No. I—

ALLEGRA. She organized a memorial last night. Like a one-week-later / kind of thing.

MARGARET. He told me they were taking a break.

ALLEGRA. Ah.

MARGARET. They were on a break. We'd only been, we hadn't been together that long. It's not like his friends knew me yet or—

ALLEGRA. (*Not buying it.*) Okay. / Okay.

MARGARET. —or I'm sure they would have invited me—

ALLEGRA. He was engaged.

MARGARET. They were on a break.

ALLEGRA. (*To the others.*) I mean…

    CATHY *shrugs.* JOHN *looks away.*

MARGARET. It's not like I didn't know him.

ALLEGRA. Okay.

MARGARET. we hooked up / right after Labor Day. The weekend after Labor Day. We met in Vermont.

ALLEGRA. stop. stop. stop. stop. stop. That doesn't mean he's your boyfriend.

MARGARET. I know that.

JOHN. But didn't you say—

MARGARET. No. Yes. No. I don't know.

ALLEGRA. You told us he was your boyfriend. / Why would you—

MARGARET. I didn't mean—I mean, it made me feel—connected, to you, and—I swear, I didn't know he was engaged. Why would he hook up / with me if—

ALLEGRA. I don't know, maybe because he's a dog?

MARGARET. He's not a dog. He's dead.

ALLEGRA. That doesn't mean he's not a dog.

JOHN. Allegra!

ALLEGRA. What! It's true!

MARGARET. I'm sorry, okay? I'm really sorry. I didn't mean to / let you think—

ALLEGRA. You thought a skanky one-night stand in the woods meant some asshole was your boyfriend?

JOHN. / (jesus!)

MARGARET. No, I'm not stupid.

ALLEGRA. He was never going to be your boyfriend.

MARGARET. I KNOW THAT!

ALLEGRA. So you lied.

MARGARET. / SO WHAT?

JOHN. Allegra.

ALLEGRA. Why would you—I just, I don't understand.

MARGARET. I'm so sorry. I didn't mean to lie—

ALLEGRA. When it seems like everyone in the world is, I don't know, trying to do good, be good, be better—why would you—I mean, why would you lie about something like this?

MARGARET. ...I didn't think I was...

JOHN. Allegra. Come on.

ALLEGRA. It's just like Tom Kelly.

JOHN. What's like Kelly?

ALLEGRA. Are we going to be people who look out for each other, who try to be good and kind and honest, / or are we just going to go on being—

JOHN. We are looking out for each other—

CATHY. We are getting things back to normal as quickly as possible.

ALLEGRA. Things are never going to go back to normal.

JOHN. I don't believe that.

MARGARET. In just one week, look at how much we've already done.

Beat.

ALLEGRA. Okay. You know what? Take it. Take Jeff Lasky, take Tom Kelly, tell whatever story you want to tell about yourselves. Take this job, this money, whatever. It's yours now. This isn't for me. and I—I just—I just. I can't.

CATHY. Where are you going?

JOHN. Allegra. Come on. We need you.

ALLEGRA. yeah, but I don't need. This. There's only so many hours in a day, and…I. I gotta get out of here.

> ALLEGRA *takes her purse and leaves.*
>
> *The others sit for a long while. Probably they don't look at each other. Maybe* CATHY *finishes her glass of champagne. But the others don't have the stomach for it.*
>
> *Finally:*

MARGARET. I didn't mean to lie to you.

Beat.

It just—it just came out.

Beat.

I wanted—.

Beat.

I'm sorry.

JOHN. It's okay.

CATHY. I don't really give a shit about what you do in your personal life.

MARGARET. okay. thank you

CATHY. Just don't bring it to the office.

MARGARET. Okay. I won't. I'm sorry.

CATHY. (*To* JOHN.) Park was right about one thing.

JOHN. What's that?

CATHY. (*Re:* MARGARET.) She's more like Tom Kelly than she seems.

JOHN. (*To* MARGARET.) I think she means that as a compliment.

CATHY. Seeing opportunity in even the worst circumstances.
MARGARET. I don't think I—oh.
CATHY. See?
MARGARET. I think so.
CATHY. So we'll see you tomorrow?
JOHN. Where are you going?
CATHY. Now that we've got this office functioning, I've got to check on the progress in Midtown.
JOHN. that's still happening?
CATHY. Lucky break we signed our lease in August, right?
MARGARET. What's in Midtown?
JOHN. New offices. They were consolidating over the summer.
CATHY. Gotta keep pushing the ball forward, right?
JOHN. There were going to be layoffs.
CATHY. You two really have been essential this past week. What you have done, it has truly been heroic.
JOHN. Can we stop using that word, please?
CATHY. I'll see you.
  CATHY goes.
  Long beat.
MARGARET. I'm really sorry.
JOHN. it's okay
MARGARET. You've been so nice to me. / And after everything you—
JOHN. there have been a lot of emotions lately. It's okay.
MARGARET. it's not.
  Beat.
I wanted to be close to you.
JOHN. To me?
MARGARET. To the survivors.
JOHN. I didn't survive anything
MARGARET. You're alive. You're here.
JOHN. I guess.
  Beat.
MARGARET. I can handle the extra work.
JOHN. Good thing we found you.
MARGARET. Yeah.
JOHN. It's your lucky day.

MARGARET. You still believe in luck?
JOHN. How could I not?
> *He toasts with the flat champagne.*

DAY 8 (Thursday, September 20).

The grey light of ambient streetlight from the parking lot, an eerie glow.

The door opens—it's CATHY. *She kicks off her shoes, takes her purse out of the place she has stashed it in a corner or a filing cabinet. She changes into pajamas, cleans her mouth out with* MARGARET'*s mouthwash.*

She lies down on the table and goes to sleep.

Lights down.

Lights up.

The storage room, with 4 or 5 computers and an equal number of telephone consoles.

CATHY *is gone.*

MARGARET *is in the middle of a phone call. While she speaks she types on a computer.*

MARGARET. I know
…
I know
…
Jenny
…
Lipman Kennedy is here for you
…
…
we all lost somebody that day. We did.
…
oh I know, honey
I know
…
Listen to me Jenny
We're gonna—
> *Something beeps. An incoming call.*

Jenny? I'm so sorry, I'm going to have to call you back. Okay. Okay. Bye now.
> MARGARET *presses a button to switch calls.*

This is Margaret.

...

> *The lights start to shift to something warmer. The array of cords and computers and tables start to look like a fully functional office, on a high floor somewhere above Midtown.*

Joe. Joe. Joe. No.
I'm not selling it that low. No.

...

I'm just not. Do you know—

...

...

...

I'm going to stop you right there. no. no. no. Look. You're the ones who made us open for bond trading on September 13th, okay? And now you're telling me that we're doing too much business too fast? And that makes us risky?

...

...

Do you want a deal or not, Joe? Do you want a deal or not?

...

No. No.

...

That's bullshit and you know—

...

Well then we don't have a deal then.

...

...

Are you sure?

...

...

Yeah. That's what I thought.

...

You do that. You talk to Mel. Tell him Lipman Kennedy is open for business. Tell him Margaret Gale said so.

> *As she hangs up—*
> *Blackout.*

End of Play

GOD SAID THIS
by Leah Nanako Winkler

Copyright © 2018 by Leah Nanako Winkler. All rights reserved. CAUTION: Professionals and amateurs are hereby warned that *God Said This* is subject to a royalty. It is fully protected under the copyright laws of the United States of America and of all countries covered by the International Copyright Union (including the Dominion of Canada and the rest of the British Commonwealth), the Berne Convention the Pan-American Copyright Convention and the Universal Copyright Convention, as well as all countries with which the United States has reciprocal copyright relations. All rights, including professional, amateur stage rights, motion picture, recitation, lecturing, public reading, radio broadcasting, television, video or sound recording, all other forms of mechanical or electronic reproduction, such as CD-ROM, CD-I, information storage and retrieval systems and photocopying, and the rights of translation into foreign languages, are strictly reserved. Particular emphasis is laid upon the matter of readings, permission for which must be secured from the Author's agent in writing.

Required royalties must be paid every time this play is performed before any audience, whether or not it is presented for profit and whether or not admission is charged.

Inquiries concerning stock and amateur performance rights should be addressed to: Dramatists Play Service, www.dramatists.com. All other rights inquiries should be addressed to: APA, 135 West 50th Street, 17th Floor, New York, NY 10020. ATTN: Beth Blickers, bblickers@apa-agency.com.

ABOUT *GOD SAID THIS*

This article first ran in the Limelight Guide to the 42nd Humana Festival of New American Plays, *published by Actors Theatre of Louisville, and is based on conversations with the playwright before rehearsals for the Humana Festival production began.*

When Leah Nanako Winkler's mom was diagnosed with uterine carcinosarcoma, a rare and aggressive cancer, she would never have guessed that the difficult experience of her mother's illness would inspire a new play. Back in her hometown of Lexington, Kentucky for her mom's chemotherapy sessions, Winkler found herself passing long hours at the hospital by writing. "Sometimes when a monumental event happens in my life, I'll take that circumstance and turn it into the starting point for a play," she says. "I really did write a script during those chemo sessions. By the last one, I had a full draft." The piece that emerged was *God Said This*, a bittersweet and wry portrait of a dysfunctional Kentucky family also grappling with cancer—and discovering, to their surprise, that adversity brings them closer.

Set in Lexington, *God Said This* follows the Rose family, whose wife and mother, Masako, has carcinosarcoma. A Japanese immigrant who married a Kentucky native, Masako soldiers through her treatment with extraordinary resilience, despite chemo's debilitating side effects. To keep her company, the rest of the Roses—her husband, James, and their two daughters, Hiro and Sophie—gather in tension-filled shifts in her hospital room. Hiro, a New York transplant who hasn't visited in years, clashes with James, from whom she's been estranged. James, a recovering alcoholic, is eager to make amends for the misdeeds of his past—but repairing his relationship with his daughters, especially Hiro, isn't proving to be easy. "Some would say he's been a bad father. Some would say he was abusive," Winkler explains. "And the question is: is it too late for his redemption?" Meanwhile, born-again Christian Sophie struggles to hold the family together and help everyone reconcile their differences. "Sophie comes from a place of love all the time," says Winkler. "But she's running out of energy—she's turning to God and God doesn't seem to be answering."

When Hiro isn't at Masako's side, she reconnects with John, a former high school classmate. "When you're visiting home for a specific reason, like a parent getting sick, getting back in touch with old friends can be a lifeline," Winkler reflects. So, even though they've never known each other well, Hiro and John spend their spare time driving country roads together, trying to take the edge off. According to Winkler, John becomes a foil for James; a devoted father concerned with his son's future, he's "everything Hiro wanted James to be as a dad." In conversations peppered with local references and witty banter, John also challenges Hiro's "East Coast liberal" assumptions about people in Kentucky. "Something that bothers me about the portrayal of Kentucky in the media is that we're usually shown as uneducated and racist," asserts Winkler. "But there's a lot of beauty and smart people here. I think the diversity of the South is often ignored."

God Said This isn't the first play that Winkler's written about this part of the country—or about the Rose family. Taking place seven years earlier, Winkler's 2016 comedy *Kentucky* follows Hiro's return to Lexington to stop her sister's wedding. (Misguidedly, she believes Sophie needs rescuing from her newfound Christian beliefs.) As the highly theatrical and darkly funny story unfolds, we also encounter James and Masako among the cast of larger-than-life characters. Winkler emphasizes, however, that *God Said This* isn't intended to be a sequel. "Those who have read or seen *Kentucky* will find little gems, but this is a stand-alone play," she says. And while *Kentucky* centers on Hiro as its protagonist, Winkler considers *God Said This* "a true ensemble piece," written in a less whimsical, more realistic style. She elaborates: "This play is quieter and more subtle. It's a serious family drama about dealing with how we feel when a loved one becomes ill. It's also about the strength that it takes to seek or grant forgiveness, with or without God."

However, *God Said This* isn't without humor, either. "I hope that when they see it, people laugh," Winkler declares. "It was written from a place of pain, but there are definitely funny moments." And, although its premise comes from personal experience, Winkler stresses that the story isn't autobiographical. "About 11% of it is factual," she says. "John's based on a real high school friend, who I interviewed about his life in Lexington, but the other characters are imagined. There are some similarities between my family and the Roses: we come from the same social class, we're both multicultural, and we've both had our differences. But for the most part, the play's plot is made up. During my mom's chemo, I thought about what the Roses would do if they were in this situation, instead of me. The writing was like an escape."

At the same time, Winkler does view *God Said This* as a way of immortalizing her mother. "My mom's really excited about it, because she says that everybody gets sick, and people should know what it's like to be sick," Winkler explains. "Uterine carcinosarcoma makes up less than five percent of all uterine cancers, so I'd love to spread awareness about it. On a lighter note, though, it would be great if watching this makes people think about calling their moms."

—Hannah Rae Montgomery

BIOGRAPHY

Leah Nanako Winkler is a Japanese-American playwright from Kamakura, Japan and Lexington, Kentucky. Her play *God Said This* won the Yale Drama Series Prize, and was produced at Primary Stages and at the 2018 Humana Festival of New American Plays. Other plays: *Kentucky* (2015 Kilroys List, World Premiere: Ensemble Studio Theatre co-production with Page 73 and the Radio Drama Network), *Two Mile Hollow* (2017 Kilroys List, 2017–2018 Simultaneous World Premiere at First Floor Theater, Mixed Blood/Theater Mu, Artists At Play, and Ferocious Lotus), *Linus and Murray* (Ensemble Studio Theatre/Marathon 2017), and more. She is the 2018–2019 Jerome Fellow at the Lark, an alumna of Youngblood, a 2016–2018 Time Warner Fellow at WP Theater, a member of the Ma-Yi Writers Lab, and a member of the Dorothy Strelsin New American Writers Group at Primary Stages. She was awarded the first-ever Mark O'Donnell Prize from The Actors Fund and Playwrights Horizons in 2017. Winkler is one of the inaugural playwrights to receive a commission from Audible's Emerging Playwrights Fund.

ACKNOWLEDGMENTS

God Said This premiered at the Humana Festival of New American Plays in February 2018. It was directed by Morgan Gould with the following cast:

JAMES	Jay Patterson
MASAKO	Ako
SOPHIE	Emma Kikue
HIRO	Satomi Blair
JOHN	Tom Coiner

and the following production staff:

Scenic Designer	Arnulfo Maldonado
Costume Designer	Jessica Pabst
Lighting Designer	Isabella Byrd
Sound Designer	M.L. Dogg
Media Designer	Philip Allgeier
Stage Manager	Kathy Preher
Dramaturg	Hannah Rae Montgomery
Casting	Emily Tarquin, Actors Theatre
Casting Consultant	Vanessa Kai
Properties Master	Heather Lindert
Production Assistant	Olivia Tymon
Directing Assistant	Joan Sergay
Assistant Dramaturg	Vivian Barnes

God Said This was originally written and developed at Primary Stages in the Dorothy Strelsin New American Writers Group.

God Said This was initially developed as part of the 2016–2018 WP Theater Lab Residency.

CHARACTERS

JAMES, 50s or 60s. A recovering alcoholic. Inappropriate. Can be mean but can also be surprisingly sentimental. Seeking redemption but will never say he's sorry. Funny at times but mostly when he doesn't mean to be. Kentuckian.

MASAKO, 50s or 60s, his wife. Has cancer. A total optimist and a beam of light though when sad, the tears often don't stop. Masako's resilience is her strength—even if it's not so obvious at first. Japanese immigrant.

SOPHIE, 29, their youngest daughter. Kind, patient but imperfect. Her biggest fears have come to life and she is on the verge of a breaking point. Kentuckian. A born-again Christian.

HIRO, 36, their eldest daughter. New York transplant. Isn't always aware of how she affects others but is making a huge effort to be there for her family. Can be cool and collected but epiphanies hit her all at once to the point of overwhelming emotion.

JOHN, 37, Hiro's acquaintance from high school. A funny, straightforward, don't take no shit kind of person. Kind of a jerk actually. But a respectable one. Sometimes has a dark anger behind his eyes. Kentuckian.

TIME

Now.

PLACE

The play takes place over four-ish days—mostly at the Markey Cancer Center in Lexington, Kentucky. Sometimes the characters are in cars, hallways and Alcoholics Anonymous but lighting and chairs can indicate the location.

PLAYWRIGHT'S NOTE

James, Masako, Hiro and Sophie are a mixed-race family from the South. And though the play might not deal with "specifically Asian" issues—that's the power. My own family is mixed race and when we gather, we don't sit around talking about how we are mixed race. We just exist and live our lives. Give the AAPI performers the opportunities to play deeply flawed, complex people who are different from one another—who are not defined by their race. Don't let any of these roles be stereotypes. Don't put John in flannel.

Other things: John and Hiro are not meant to be romantic, that angle is too clichéd. Think about what they get from each other. Masako is the smartest, strongest person in the room. Sophie's Christianity is not a joke and should never be the butt of one. Her faith has helped her greatly in her life. Also—remember that Kentuckian doesn't always mean white. Red State doesn't always mean dumb. Poor doesn't mean uncomfortable. This is also a family who doesn't know what to do with each other. They don't know how to love each other but the love is there. Don't rush through it. Also, remember that James isn't a hero. He's done terrible things. Hiro isn't shallow or bratty—she's trying to be there. And most importantly, Masako is full of life.

Jay Patterson, Satomi Blair, Emma Kikue, and Ako
in *God Said This*

42nd Humana Festival of New American Plays
Actors Theatre of Louisville, 2018
Photo by Jonathan Roberts

GOD SAID THIS

Act One

Scene One

DAY ONE. Sudden lights up on JAMES. *He's at an AA meeting. He speaks with a Kentucky drawl.*

JAMES. Hi. Well y'all know my fucking name. But I'm James. James Rose. And I am an alcoholic.

(*Pause.*)

Today I just wanted to say what I've been thinkin' about. And what I've been thinkin' about is women. Damn women! There was a time in my life when every fucking woman in my life was hard on me. I dunno if they were all on their periods at the same time or what but they were hard on me. My wife. My mother. My daughters—the eldest especially. She never comes 'round that one. Even when I was sick she never came around. But now that Masako, that's my wife—now that she's sick—she's back. Least for the next few days. Wanted to be with her at the hospital.

(*Mocking.*)

Women stick together. Tee hee. Hee.

So, all the women in my life are together again in Kentucky. Well minus my mother. Don't miss her much, may she rest in hell. But every other woman is here. And it's making me wanna. It's making me wanna drink.

I ran away from problems before I was sober. I liked to disappear. I liked to forget everything and have me some fun I couldn't remember. And now? I feel everything! My wife's sickness. I feel that. My eldest daughter's hate—I feel that too. And well—the younger one—the baby—she loves Jesus so she don't hate. But I can feel her looking at me with this sympathy which gets to me more 'cause well—I don't need nobody feelin' bad for me.

What else?

Oh.

Been tryin' to sell some of my shit down at the flea market. Y'all should come by. I got these cool ass rocks. I got a Facebook page about it. People seem to like it. Or actually, they do "like" it. Clickity clack.

(*Pause.*)

So yeah. That's what I've been thinking about. And I thought I'd let you know.

(*We hear a Japanese choir sing a gospel song. This takes us into...*)

Scene Two

Same day. Hospital. MASAKO *lies in the hospital bed. The Japanese choir music plays from her phone. She's relaxing, wearing a soft cancer-specific hat. She's connected to a chemotherapy drip.* SOPHIE *is on the couch, reading something like* <u>Gone Girl</u> *and she's riveted. A few beats. Then,* MASAKO *rises, unbeknownst to* SOPHIE. *She takes her hat off, scheming. We see her balding head for a brief moment before she puts on another hat—a cute funny one with two long braids attached. She speaks with a Japanese accent.*

MASAKO. (*Softly.*) Sophie.

(SOPHIE *doesn't hear her over the music.* MASAKO *turns off the music.*)

MASAKO. (*Dramatically.*) SOPHIE!!!!!

SOPHIE. (*Scared.*) WHAT. WHAT. MOM WHAT'S WRONG?

MASAKO. …My hair growed back.

(SOPHIE *sees her mother with the fake braids and laughs.*)

SOPHIE. Wooow.

MASAKO. It's miracle!

SOPHIE. With God—anything is possible! Thank you Jesus.

MASAKO. Thank you Jesus!

(*They laugh.*)

SOPHIE. Feelin' okay?

MASAKO. Just little nausea.

SOPHIE. Already? The chemo's not started yet on the drip I don't think. Want me to call the nurse?

MASAKO. No no. I just feel nausea when I come here. It's the thinking about hospital food. Just seeing lady with hospital food I feel nausea automatic.

SOPHIE. Well she isn't very nice.

MASAKO. *Colleen.*

SOPHIE. *Right. Colleen.*

MASAKO. See. I say her name right. But she cannot say mine.
She call me

(*With a country accent.*)

Maseiiiko.
And One time, Yoko! I can't wait for this be over.

SOPHIE. Well, just think—by Friday—no more chemo!

MASAKO. And no more cancer.

(*A sad pause* SOPHIE *doesn't respond to this but instead looks at* MASAKO *with worry. Her mother's future is uncertain and the optimism can be heartbreaking.*)

MASAKO. Cancer no baka.

SOPHIE. Cancer no baka!

(*Pause.*)

It's been a long six months of treatment huh.

MASAKO. Sooo looong.

SOPHIE. They say the last stretch is the toughest but you won't be alone. Not for a second.

MASAKO. I so sorry I worry everyone. Such inconvenience!

SOPHIE. You *love* that everyone's here. You love it.

MASAKO. (*Coy.*) Maaaybe.

(*Pause.*)

I hope everyone get along!

SOPHIE. Me too. I've been praying on it. Actually let's pray again. Just to make sure.

MASAKO. Okay.

(SOPHIE *closes her eyes.* MASAKO *does too, but then opens her eyes about halfway through—watching her daughter with warmth.* MASAKO *isn't a born-again Christian like her daughter—but she likes the idea of God. And she likes making her daughter happy by participating in the ritual of religion.*)

SOPHIE. Lord, I know you're here. I feel your strength through the resilience you give us as we fight this horrible disease. Please let us get through the next few days with courage and perseverance and grace. Please help us heal. And Lord, please help our family get along. Please help Hiro have a peaceful time in Kentucky and let her open up her heart to *everyone*—including Dad. And please help Dad continue his growth and change and thank you for the blessing you gave him in the form of his alcoholism being forced to come to an end through liver failure because too much of something doesn't do anyone no good. Unless of course—it's you Lord.

(*Pause.*)

Oh. And we pray for Colleen.

(MASAKO *rolls her eyes. She really hates Colleen.*)

For a woman with such a bad attitude must be suffering in her life with her own struggles. Amen.

MASAKO. Amen.

(*A pause. They look at each other.*)

MASAKO. Sophie.

SOPHIE. Yes Mama?

MASAKO. Are my eyebrows still on?

SOPHIE. You could use a touch up.

MASAKO. Give me give me!

SOPHIE. Okay!

(SOPHIE *gets an eyebrow pencil. She climbs into bed and touches up her mother's hairless eyebrows.*)

MASAKO. Yaaay.

Scene Three

Same day. JOHN's *car.* JOHN *and* HIRO *are driving on a country road.* JOHN *is packing a bowl.* HIRO's *phone beeps with a text.*

HIRO. Shit, I gotta get back to the hospital soon. Can you pack that a little faster?

JOHN. …you do it then I'm driving.

HIRO. Fine.

JOHN. You're welcome, by the way for picking you up and taking you for a dip on these beautiful country roads.

(*Pause.*)

Bet they don't have country roads like this in New York.

HIRO. I summer on the weekends upstate. There are country roads there.

(*A beat. There is a harsh casualness between she and* JOHN. *They are old acquaintances who have known each other forever without really knowing each other but are familiar anyway. Nothing between them is super sentimental.*)

JOHN. So I officiated Laura and Adam's wedding.

HIRO. Yeah I saw the pictures. I *cannot* believe I wasn't invited. I mean, I wouldn't have gone but they should've invited me—

JOHN. —I love officiating weddings actually. I've done like nine. Wanna do more—

HIRO. —How are they doing anyway? Adam and Laura?

JOHN. They got like four kids. Motherfuckers can't pull out of a parking space. And I don't talk to them that much anymore actually. Adam sold his house. Moved the family to Louisville.

HIRO. Louisville makes sense for Laura. But seems too city for Adam.

JOHN. Fuck Louisville. Fuck Rick Pitino. Fuck those flannel wearin' ghost huntin' didgeridoo playin' Louisville fucking hipsters

HIRO. Hicksters.

JOHN. Hick?

HIRO. Yeah. Like hipsters but with hicks.

JOHN. Haa hickster.

(*Genuinely kind of impressed that a woman can be funny.*)

That's actually pretty funny. Maybe Lexington's trying to be hickster now too though. They been opening a bunch of gastro pubs and shit.

HIRO. Oh yeah! I read about that on Trip Advisor.

JOHN. *Trip Advisor?* How long has it been since you've been back?

HIRO. My sister's wedding was seven years ago so…I guess seven years. And I hadn't come back for seven years before that.

JOHN. How biblical of you.

HIRO. *Why?*

JOHN. Well the Bible shows us that God uses "sevens" throughout the Scriptures to denote prophetic time. Like for example—"Behold, there come seven years of great plenty!"

HIRO. You religious?

JOHN. Not really. I mean I just read a lot.

HIRO. (*Genuinely kind of impressed that a man from Kentucky reads.*) Wow.

JOHN. Ugh. Don't be impressed because I *read* Hiro. That's so "East Coast liberal" of you. There are smart people here and dumb people here. Just like anywhere else.

HIRO. Okay okay.

(HIRO *takes a hit.*)

Shit! I forgot how strong Kentucky weed was.

JOHN. It's all from Colorado and California actually.

HIRO. Well it's such a nice way to get my mind off things.

(*A beat. He thinks about not asking—but then does.*)

JOHN. So. How bad is it? Your mom.

HIRO. (*Unsentimental.*) Pretty bad. She has this thing called carcinosarcoma which is like this rare and aggressive cancer cocktail that comes from two different types of cells.

JOHN. So she gonna die?

HIRO. It's hard to tell if she'll die soon or like in five years. They cut out the tumor from her uterus a few months ago and now they're pumping her with chemo to try to prevent it from coming back.

JOHN. Jeez.

HIRO. I'm on this Facebook group about it actually because there isn't that much research. But people on it keep dying and it's depressing as fuuuuck. Abigail Vaughn from Minneapolis wrote today:
Five weeks ago my mom was diagnosed with carcinosarcoma. This morning she died at the age of fifty-six.

JOHN. *Five weeks?*

HIRO. I guess I'm leaving the group now. Thanks for the support everyone… well except for you—@EmiliaParsons. The things you said about "holistic healing" were extremely offensive.

JOHN. Emilia Parsons. What a scrappy hoe.

HIRO. That thread was really stressful. But I like getting information from real people. The truth calms me down even if it's bad. Especially when it comes to illness.

JOHN. Hey isn't your dad sick too? I see him at Chinoe pub a lot singing karaoke and I heard that—

HIRO. He has cirrhosis. It was stage four actually but his liver like healed itself after he quit drinking and now he doesn't have to have a transplant. So unfair.

JOHN. He was pretty shitty right? I remember that like from high school that he was shitty.

HIRO. Yeah he's still shitty. But he's weaker. I'm not scared of him anymore. I feel like I could kill him at any minute if I wanted.

>   (*Pause.*)

You *know*, we were *estranged* for a long time.

JOHN. Estranged? From your dad? Haha that's so entitled.

HIRO. What? Why?

JOHN. Because that's your dad, ya dum dum.

>   (*Pause.*)

My dad was shit too. He's dead now though.

HIRO. (*Unsentimental.*) I remember that. Didn't he pull a gun out on your mom or something?

JOHN. (*Unsentimental.*) Yeah.

HIRO. (*Casual.*) How's she doing?

JOHN. (*Casual.*) Good. Great actually! She retired. She's dating a nice dude. They watch my kid for free so I can smoke weed with you.

>   (HIRO *gives* JOHN *a look.*)

JOHN. *I don't do things like this often.* Besides thirteen-year-olds are very independent.

HIRO. OH MY GOD YOUR KID IS THIRTEEN?

JOHN. Um. I'm thirty-seven. That's a relatively normal age to have a thirteen-year-old kid. You weirdo.

HIRO. Who's the mom??

JOHN. This stupid cunt I have to tolerate for the rest of my life.

HIRO. That is VERY disrespectful.

JOHN. Dude. If you knew her—you'd say the same thing. She broke down my door with *my own grandmother's cast iron cornbread skillet* and bashed me on the head.

HIRO. …well what did you do to *make* her do that?

JOHN. I wouldn't let her have my kid when she was high on fucking heroin. Thank God I have primary custody now but it was scary for a while.

(*Pause.*)

Anyway I was surprised you contacted me we were never really that close.

HIRO. Well you're like the only high school person who comments on my Facebook rants which means you're the only person I've kept in touch with.

JOHN. That's sad.

HIRO. God you're right. That *is* sad. I'm sad. I'm sad and old.

(*Pause.*)

I *had* friends here.

JOHN. I feel you. That's how it goes. There are people I was close to who I see at Kroger and we say hiiii but it's weird now.

HIRO. Nicole VanCamp. She was my best friend here.

JOHN. Don't think I saw you at the funeral.

HIRO. You went?

JOHN. Everyone went. That's what friends do.

(*This kind of stings.*)

HIRO. You don't have to hang out with me if you don't want to.

JOHN. I'm the one who asked you to hang. You just messaged me looking for food recommendations.
And don't you worry. This is *a hundred percent platonic*.

HIRO. …wow you just really had to throw that in there didn't you?

JOHN. Well you never know how someone's interpreting your intentions.

HIRO. But like *a hundred percent platonic? A hundred percent?*

JOHN. Okay ninety-nine.

HIRO. I have a boyfriend.

JOHN. Well we'll go back to a hundred percent again.

(*They drive.*)

Scene Four

Same day. Hospital. MASAKO *is asleep.* SOPHIE *is not. Maybe she's on the couch trying to read. She is caught off-guard when* JAMES *enters.*

JAMES. Hi ho.

SOPHIE. Dad! What are you doing here?

JAMES. Just felt like comin' I guess.

SOPHIE. Oh. Well it's not your turn.

JAMES. I know.

SOPHIE. I'm waiting for Hiro to come tag me out.

JAMES. Okeedokie.

(*A FEW BEATS.* SOPHIE *realizes her father is here to stay. She tries to make the best of it.*)

SOPHIE. How was AA?

JAMES. Fucking stupid. Went to karaoke afterwards. For a song.

SOPHIE. Yeah? What'd you sing this time?

(JAMES *sings the first verse of "Heartbreak Hotel."*
Pause.)

JAMES. It's Elvis. *That* is Elvis.

(HIRO *enters carrying a crafty food bag.*)

HIRO. Sophie! Mom! I got us fun gastro pub food to eat.

(*Seeing* JAMES.)

What are *you* doing here?

SOPHIE. *Hiro you're late—*

JAMES. —Just felt like comin' I guess—

HIRO. —Mom…you awake…?

SOPHIE. Don't wake her!

HIRO. (*To* MASAKO.) Want some…Collard Green Kimchi? Or Duck and Waffles?

SOPHIE. *She can't eat today. She doesn't have the appetite.*

HIRO. She should at least have something—

SOPHIE. —She *can't*—

HIRO. That worries me.

JAMES. IT'S FINE.

(SOPHIE *and* HIRO *jump. They look to* JAMES *with tension. He can be a scary guy.*)

Eat when you want. Don't eat when you don't want. Meal times are a manmade social construct. They're a scam!

(*He has nothing else to say.*)

HIRO. …Kay.

SOPHIE. (*To* HIRO.) You reek.

HIRO. Shit I do?

MASAKO. It's fine.

(*Everyone looks at* MASAKO.)

Marijuana is fine. Your father smoke it all the time. He reek too. I like it. Smells like home!

HIRO. Hiii Mom!!!!

MASAKO. Hiiii!

HIRO. Sorry! Didn't mean to wake you.

SOPHIE. Yes you did.

MASAKO. It's okay Sophie. I'm happy. My cancer bring everyone together.

(*Let a few beats go by. This is a family who doesn't know what to do with each other.* SOPHIE *faintly coughs.* HIRO *stares blankly ahead.* MASAKO *beams.* JAMES *fiddles on his smartphone.*)

JAMES. …Well. I took a picture of myself for only the second time in my life yesterday.

HIRO. Like a selfie? You took a selfie?

JAMES. Yeah.

(*Pause, this takes a little bit of courage.*)

I'll show you if you want.

HIRO. I thought you hated machines. You literally threw a computer at me once.

JAMES. I still don't like the *computer*. But I like the phone. I got my rock friends on Facebook.

HIRO. What do you mean rock friends? Like…Rock 'n' Roll?

SOPHIE. No. He collects rocks now. Heaps and heaps of rocks.

JAMES. I do.

MASAKO. He does.

JAMES. (*A huge effort to say this.*) You know Hiro. Uh. Before you leave. I'd like to sit at a table with you and I'd like to show you my rocks.

(*Pause, serious.*)

They're amazing.

HIRO. (*Prompt but kind.*) No thanks.

MASAKO. *Hiro, please be nice to your father.*

SOPHIE. Yeah Hiro. Be nice. It'll make everyone really, *really* happy. If you go to the house to look at Dad's rocks.

MASAKO. Mmmm hmm.

(*Everyone looks at* HIRO *with great anticipation.*)

HIRO. UGH okay fine. I will come over to look at your rocks.

JAMES. You will?

SOPHIE. (*To herself.*) Yes!

JAMES. Good then. Come by the house in the morning. I'll pull out the good ones.

(JAMES *is very happy. This makes* MASAKO *happy.*)

SOPHIE. (*A little frantic.*) You know Mama…Dad. When Hiro comes over to the house maybe just maybe I can sneak out of here for a few minutes too? And…and she and I can clean? Just a little teentsy bit?

MASAKO. Clean? Clean what?

SOPHIE. Just like maybe the living room and the kitchen—

MASAKO. —living room kitchen is fine.

SOPHIE. Can we paint then? *Everything's* peeling—

MASAKO. *I will do it.* I'll clean and paint when I get better. That not your job. Is my job. Plus your father has his things. Right James?

(*Everyone looks at* JAMES. *He's engrossed in his phone.*)

James. JAMES!!!!

(JAMES *looks up from his phone, startled.*)

JAMES. …HUUUUHHHHH?

MASAKO. Nevermind. Let me see selfie.

(JAMES *shows* MASAKO *his selfie.*)

Hyu hyu!!! So handsome. But you should smile more. You are more handsome when you smile.

(*A click and maybe a flash!* MASAKO *takes a selfie with* JAMES. *She smiles. She is radiant.* JAMES *is blushing, a little caught off guard.*)

Scene Five

DAY TWO. JAMES *again, at an AA meeting. You get the sense that he enjoys talking to an audience.*

JAMES. Hi again I'm James. James Rose. And I'm an alcoholic blah blah blah. Heh. Heh. Heh. So I don't like movies. Haven't been in years the last one I saw in the theater was *Groundhogs Day*. Didn't like it. But I've been thinkin'

a lot this early A.M. about movies because movies have this thing that life don't have a lot of and that is redemption. Shit people get redeemed in movies. Crackers get hearts of gold and they are forgiven and they are fixed. I used to think all that was bullshit.
But lately I'm thinkin' maybe…maybe not.

(*Pause.*)

I'm not a man who tries to change what he can't control. But I can control myself, when I try very, very hard. And so today I will participate in Serenity.

(*Maybe closing his eyes, maybe not.*)

God grant me the serenity to accept the things I cannot change;
Courage to change the things I can;
And wisdom to know the difference
Living one day at a time;
Enjoying one moment at a time;
Accepting hardships as the pathway to peace;

(*Pause.*)

Oh guess what y'all? My daughter. The eldest one who hates my guts. She's coming over to the house this morning! She's coming to see my rocks!

Scene Six

> *Same Day. Hospital.* SOPHIE *is pacing around. She is pissed.* HIRO *enters, clearly hung over.*

HIRO. …hey.

SOPHIE. (*Aggressive whisper.*) Hiro. Hallway! Now!

> (SOPHIE *drags* HIRO *to the hallway.*)

SOPHIE. *Out drinking all night?*

HIRO. …so?

SOPHIE. So?!?! SO?!?!? You were supposed to meet Dad at the house this morning to look at his rocks!!!!!

HIRO. (*Not bratty, genuine.*) Oh. Shit I forgot.

SOPHIE. Let me guess. *Because you were with some guy?*

HIRO. …yeah. But it's a hundred percent platonic!

SOPHIE. *I call a hundred percent bullshit!*

> (*A moment.* SOPHIE *and* HIRO *both gasp, they are shocked that* SOPHIE *said a curse word. It's been years since* SOPHIE *has cursed because of her religion. She covers her mouth.*)

HIRO. Oh my God Sophie Leonore Rose Williams. You cursed!!! You cursed with your mouth! I'm texting your husband RIGHT NOW.

(*On her phone.*)

Hey Da'Ran, you will never guess what sin your perfect little born-again Christian wife committed devil emoji devil emoji devil emoji devil emo—

(SOPHIE *grabs* HIRO'S *phone out of her hand and throws it on the ground. Hard.* HIRO *is taken aback.*)

SOPHIE. It's not funny!!!!!! None of this is funny. Don't you understand that it's not funny!!?!?!?

HIRO. (*Genuine.*) I'm...sorry. Sophie, I'm sorry.

(SOPHIE *is really upset.* HIRO *takes this in.*)

SOPHIE. *I really, really* wish you would have went to the house, Hiro. I wanted you to see what condition it's in. *I needed you to.*

HIRO. It's that bad?

SOPHIE. *Everything* is falling apart. And on top of that Dad's *such* a hoarder.

HIRO. (*Trying to be helpful.*) Well that's not surprising. Grandma was a hoarder. Grandpa was a hoarder. We come from a family of hoarders. This is why I throw everything away even gifts and day-old food with no sense of remorse—

SOPHIE. —and he can't take care of himself. Mama did everything. And now that she's not strong enough there's piles of dirty clothes and underwear just everywhere. And Dishes. Dust rising up from the furniture. Black mold in the bathroom. Clutter on top of clutter. But I can't do anything about it because it just upsets Mama and now Dad's gonna come back and he's gonna be mad because you didn't see his rocks and Mama shouldn't be around that kind of energy right now!!!!! GOD HIRO. WHY DIDN'T YOU LOOK AT HIS ROCKS?!?!! WHY HIRO WHY?

HIRO. I dunno I just. I'll go *now*. Okay? I'll go now.

SOPHIE. Well you can't go NOW. *I* have to go to work and you have to stay with Mama.

HIRO. Can't you call in?

SOPHIE. I don't get paid if I'm not there. And we need the money.

HIRO. Hey! Between your church and me we've been covering a lot of it. Remember—I'm an account director now with like assistants and everything!

SOPHIE. *It's more than you think.*

HIRO. I *make* more than you think.

SOPHIE. —well the chemo's only partially covered and the scans are covered every six months for the first year and then only once a year after that. But she needs to get one at least every three months for the rest of her life so you'll pay that out of pocket?

HIRO. Well—according to the *carcinosarcoma Facebook group*—

SOPHIE. I hate the carcinosarcoma Facebook group, Hiro! I wish you wouldn't have added me.

HIRO. But we can't just blindly trust everything the doctors say! The fucking healthcare in this fucking country is—

SOPHIE. Not right now.

(*Pause.*)

Hiro, remember what I said to you before you came back? Remember the mission I gave you?

HIRO. ...to make Mom happy.

SOPHIE. So please. Get your stuff together!

(SOPHIE *heads out.*)

HIRO. Okay bye I love you! SOPHIE I LOVE YOU.

(SOPHIE *stops. Turns. Looks at* HIRO.)

SOPHIE. Then why do you always need a man around?

(HIRO *is taken aback.*)

HIRO. I don't always need a—

SOPHIE. —Hiro, you're so strong and independent and I love that about you. But at home—you always, *always* need a man around. Why?

HIRO. That is *so* not true—

SOPHIE. —uhm yes it is. You brought that Adam guy to my wedding last minute. And in high school you were always hanging out with your creepy twenty-two-year-old boyfriends from Hot Topic!

HIRO. Tilford was eighteen and Blaze was *barely* twenty but okay—

SOPHIE. It's like you can't just *be here*. Well guess what Hiro? Now is the time to just *be here*.

(SOPHIE *exits. A beat.* HIRO *takes a moment. Then she salvages her phone. It still works. She sends a text. She heads to the hospital room.* MASAKO *is awake.*)

MASAKO. Hiro chan. I made you oinari san. It's in mini-fridge. So nice there is mini-fridge. So luxurious. Like nice hotel.

HIRO. Mom—you shouldn't have.

MASAKO. You love oinari san.

HIRO. You should be resting.

MASAKO. All I do is resting.

HIRO. No I mean. You should have been resting *before* chemo started up again. You don't know how to—

(*Catching herself.*)

Never mind. Sorry.

    (*Pause.*)

I mean.
Thank you.

MASAKO. Eat.

    (HIRO *eats.*)

Oishi?

HIRO. Oishii. Want some?

MASAKO. Everything tastes bad.

HIRO. Do you want some water?

MASAKO. Water tastes bad.

HIRO. Do you wanna watch a movie?

MASAKO. Movies are bad. Last one I saw in movie theater was *Groundhog Day*. I did not like.

HIRO. Then uhhh. Do you wanna like. Tell me your life story?

MASAKO. …what?

HIRO. You know. You can tell me your life story. And I can like, get to know you all over again and stuff. What was your earliest memory?

JAMES. *I waited for you this morning*

    (JAMES *has entered. He's carrying a very large garbage bag and looks* livid.)

I waited for you this morning because you were supposed to look at my rocks! But you didn't show up! So. I brought some of my rocks to you!!!

    (JAMES *slams the heavy bag on the ground.* HIRO *jumps. Then—*JAMES *begins taking some rocks out of the garbage bag. He's restraining his anger and trying hard to be kind but he's still coming in hot.*)

These are. These are some of my *favorites*. You can pick one out. And take it back to New York. If you *want*.

MASAKO. Ooooh how nice, James. *Pick a rock Hiro chan.*

JAMES. Yeah pick one.

MASAKO. (*Abrasively to* HIRO.) *Pick one.*

JAMES. Any which one you want.

MASAKO. (*Kindly to* JAMES.) Can't wait to see what she will pick!

    (HIRO *looks at her dad, then at her mom, who is looking at her with daggers.*)

HIRO. Okay.

(HIRO *quickly picks out a random rock.*)

I'll take this one.

JAMES. OH SHIT!!!!!!! The JASPER INDONESIA. DIDN'T MEAN TO PUT THAT ONE IN THERE

(*Pause.*)

Pick a different one.

HIRO. (*Irritated.*) No.

JAMES. (*Aggressive.*) JUST PICK A DIFFERENT ONE.

HIRO. (*Highly aggressive back.*) NO!

JAMES. DON'T BE SPOILT!

HIRO. HOW THE FUCK AM I SPOILT WHEN I DID EVERYTHING MY FUCKING SELF MY ENTIRE LIFE.

JAMES. THAT IS A CROCK OF SHIT. HERE. JUST TAKE THE HARLEQUIN QUARTZ.

HIRO. I DON'T WANT THE HARLEQUIN QUARTZ. I DON'T EVEN KNOW WHAT IT IS.

JAMES. THE HARLEQUIN QUARTZ IS A CRYSTAL INCLUDED WITH THE LEPIDOCROCITE FAMILY. OFTEN THE INCLUSIONS APPEAR AS TINY RED STARS OR CLOUDS WITHIN THE TERMINATION END OF A QUARTZ POINT. IT'S A REMOVER SAID TO BE A POWERFUL EMOTIONAL BALANCER OKAY? ENCOURAGING SELF-LOVE, SELF-WORTH AND HEALING OF OLD SELF-PUNISHING WOUNDS!!!!

HIRO. I GOT PLENTY OF SELF-LOVE AND SELF-WORTH AND I WANT THE INDONESIAN WHATEVER IT'S PRETTIER.

JAMES. WELL YOU CAN'T HAVE IT. IT'S TOO RARE TOO BEAUTIFUL AND YOU DON'T EVEN KNOW NOTHIN' ABOUT IT!

(HIRO, *mad as hell—takes a small bottle of bourbon from her purse. She drinks, not breaking eye contact with* JAMES. *She breathes out, making a lion's breath.* JAMES *can smell the liquor. He wants it. This is a very tense moment. They don't break eye contact.*)

MASAKO. GOLDFISH!

(*A beat.*)

HIRO. What?

(MASAKO *is trying to diffuse the situation with positivity.*)

MASAKO. My earliest memory is goldfish. Sun beam in goldfish bowl. I named goldfish Toon Chan. After toonkigou.

(*Pause.*)

Toonkigou.

Do you know what that means?
HIRO/JAMES. Treble clef.
MASAKO. Treble clef. That's right. I study music in Shimabara. Opera. Piano. Flute. I teach songs to preschool kids in small country. Then five years after study I thought—there must be more melodies to life I haven't heard. And that's when I went to America. And I met you. James. I met you.

>(*Pause.*)

And then you came along Hiro chan.
You came alo—

>(*Then,* MASAKO *starts dry heaving.* JAMES *brings her an adjacent barf bowl. She pukes what she can into it.*)

I've always loved music.

>(HIRO *pats* MASAKO's *head. So does* JAMES. *They stand there like that, patting the head of the woman they both love in a brief united moment. As we seemlessly transition into…*)

Scene Seven

>*Same Day.* SOPHIE *stands alone. Take time with this song. It's okay to take time.*

SOPHIE. (*Singing.*)
Abide with me; fast falls the eventide;
The darkness deepens; Lord with me abide.
When other helpers fail and comforts flee,
Help of the helpless, O abide with me.

Swift to its close ebbs out life's little day;
Earth's joys grow dim; its glories pass away;
Change and decay in all around I see;
O Thou who changest not, abide with me.

Not a brief glance I beg, a passing word,
But as Thou dwell'st with Thy disciples, Lord,
Familiar, condescending, patient, free.
Come not to sojourn, but abide with me.

>(*Speaking.*)

Oh sorry. Welcome to Men's Warehouse.
You're going to like the way you look. I guarantee it!

>(*Pause.*)

Oh hi Travis! How are you? How's the new baby? Come on 'round back I got some awesome suits I wanna show ya!

Scene Eight

JOHN *and* HIRO *get into* JOHN's *car. They're drunk.*

HIRO. You sure you're okay to drive? You've had a couple.

JOHN. Yeah yeah.

HIRO. You sure you sure? Everyone drives drunk in Kentucky and they like die.

JOHN. I wouldn't do that to my kid.

(*He starts the car. Then stops it.*)

Okay no you're right. I should wait a little.

HIRO. Should I order us a Lyft?

JOHN. Nah. Let's just sit here for a second.

HIRO. Okay.

(*A beat.* HIRO *tries to make out with* JOHN.)

JOHN. Woah woah woah. What are you doing?!?!!?

HIRO. Umm. Making out with you?

JOHN. You said you had a boyfriend!

HIRO. I lied.

JOHN. Why would you lie about that?

HIRO. Because you said we were a hundred percent platonic and I was like—how dare he?

JOHN. Well I meant it.

HIRO. Wow. Okay.

(*Pause.*)

I don't understand why you'd want to hang out with me then.

JOHN. Um. Because I'm genuinely interested in people? I just wanted to hang out with you. As a friend.

I just want…I just want a connection with a new person. Is that a crime? *Fucking* isn't what I want from you at all.

HIRO. Who said I wanted to fuck? I just wanted to kiss. I'm lonely. It's lonely. I get so lonely here by myself with my family.

JOHN. Okay but Hiro. Do you know how many girls I've already kissed this week?

HIRO. Uhhh.

JOHN. Three. And we did more than kiss. We fucked. God I'm so tired!!! I've already fucked three different girls this week!

HIRO. *You?* …were they pretty?

JOHN. Oh my God!

HIRO. Sorry. That was rude.

JOHN. Yes. Yes it was!

HIRO. But seriously—were they?

(*JOHN chuckles.*)

JOHN. Hiro, Hiro, Hiro. You *know* I have a Masters degree right?

HIRO. Yes. From Eastern Kentucky University.

JOHN. (*A college cheer done a little too serously.*) EKU WUT WUT?!?! GOOOOO Colonels!

HIRO. You've told me like a bunch of times.

JOHN. Because it's amazing. Seriously. Do you know how amazing it is? That I have a fucking Masters degree? Bitches love that shit! On top of that I have a good job. A nice car! And an adorable son I can take care of and support while still having a moderate amount of disposable income! Fuck! I'm a fucking Yuppie. Me. A YUPPIE. That's fucking incredible considering how bad I used to be!

HIRO. Were you really that bad though?

JOHN. YES.

HIRO. I thought you were just normal bad for like our school. Like you got arrested for shoplifting at the Liquor Barn or something

JOHN. Oh yeah. And I had to hide my weed in the grid of Justin's truck.

HIRO. Justin Alden, right? From the private school?

JOHN. (*Working himself up.*) Lexington Catholic wannabe gangster Justin. See—I was really good at shoplifting. I was slick but that rich bitch motherfucker—he was HORRIBLE at shoplifting! Just like—an untalented bridge troll. Went to the bathroom with an entire case of beer, hid it under his shirt and tried to walk out. It was his fault we got arrested not mine.

HIRO. Kay.

JOHN. And you know what? I got arrested see—and people at our school were like "oh whatever people get arrested all the time." But JUSTIN gets arrested and he goes back to that SIXTEEN-K a year classroom a fucking legend. People thought he was hard as fuck!

HIRO. Hey is Justin Alden still around?

JOHN. Yeah.

HIRO. Is he still uh…hot? Cuz if you don't wanna make out with me maybe he will.

JOHN. Oh my God. You don't remember the car accident. Do you?

(*HIRO does not.*)

We were driving in Irvine late one night smoking weed back in the day. I was drunk. Justin was going fast. Couldn't even see the fences painted black over the green. We started blasting Master P. I don't remember anything past that but Justin crashed into a tree. Told me he said John…John…you okay man? John? And I didn't answer. So he figured I died. Then he realized his face was smashed through the windshield. So he pried his face off the glass and blood was leaking out of his cheeks and his neck and he just knew he was going to die. So he went to lay down in the middle of the road, looking up at the stars and sayin' God—please tell John I'm sorry. Tell my mama I love her. I'm dead. I'm dead I'm fucking dead. I'm sorry I'm sorry I'm sorry. I'm sorry.

(*Pause.*)

But he ended up being okay. His face is just really fucked up.

HIRO. Oh my God. How fucked up?

(JOHN *shows* HIRO *a picture on his phone.*)

Holy shit.

JOHN. Anyway, he just kind of went downhill from there. Kinda sits at home all day. He's on disability not for his face but because of anxiety.

HIRO. You can get on disability for anxiety?

JOHN. Yeah and he's a former addict. Or an addict. Depends on the year. Kind of a recluse.

HIRO. God. Sounds like he really fucked up his life.

JOHN. (*Dead serious.*) It's really easy to fuck up your life. Like. Really easy. If I wanted to fuck up my life I could do it *right now.* But you know what's hard? *Getting your shit together and getting a fucking Masters Degree.*

(*Pause.*)

God if I didn't have my kid, I don't know what would've happened to me. He's the love of my life. When he turns eighteen, I have to find something else to live for. But for now, he's what I'm living for.

HIRO. (*Genuine, worried about* JOHN *driving drunk in a real way.*) Give me your keys. I'm ordering us a Lyft.

Scene Nine

Hospital. Same Day. JAMES *and* MASAKO *are asleep.* MASAKO *in bed and* JAMES *on the couch or a chair. Then all of a sudden the chemotherapy drip starts beeping. It beeps for quite a while before it wakes* JAMES *up.*

JAMES. Masako?

MASAKO. Mmm.

JAMES. Is that thing beepin'? Or is it my hearing aide?

MASAKO. Thing beeping. But it's okay. Beeping normal.

JAMES. *Well can you tell it to be quiet?*
MASAKO. It will stop. You be patient.
>   (*The beeping goes on for a while. Then stops.*)

See? I professional now.
JAMES. WHAT?
MASAKO. PROFESSIONAL.
JAMES. HUH?
MASAKO. AT CANCER. I PROFESSIONAL.
JAMES. WHAT?
MASAKO. WHAT TIME IS IT.
JAMES. GOT PLENTY OF TIME.
MASAKO. YOU HEARING AIDE STUCK. COME HERE.
>   (*Gesturing.*)

Come come.
>   (JAMES *goes to* MASAKO. *She fixes his hearing aide.*)

MASAKO. Better?
JAMES. I was hearing you! It just wasn't…clear. Didn't mean to fall asleep. It must have moved around when I was laying down.
MASAKO. What time is it?
JAMES. Nigh time.
MASAKO. Mmm. You like nigh time.
JAMES. When it's dark your imagination can start.
MASAKO. I do not like dark.
JAMES. I know it.
MASAKO. But sometime the sun and the moon are together. This side sun and this side moon. And some little stars. I like that.
JAMES. Play of Light.
>   (*Pause.*)

That's next month's theme in my Facebook group. "Play of Light."
MASAKO. In rocks?
JAMES. No that's my Facebook *page*. But I'm also in some groups. Rocks sure. But light too. And one about birds. I'm the boss of that one.
MASAKO. (*Impressed.*) You are???
JAMES. I get to choose the pictures *and* the covers.
MASAKO. You made it???
JAMES. I didn't *make it* the guy *stuck me in there*.
MASAKO. What guy?!?!? New friend??

JAMES. Guess so.

MASAKO. And you boss???

JAMES. I didn't ASK for it. But yeah he made me boss.

MASAKO. So cool!!!

JAMES. Yup.

MASAKO. I'm glad you enjoying machines.

JAMES. I told y'all. I really still don t like the computer. I just like my phone.

MASAKO. That's same thing.

JAMES. No it ain't.

MASAKO. Yes it is.

JAMES. It's not sitting at a desk.

MASAKO. But phone is tiny computer.

JAMES. I couldn't sit at a desk for so long! The little screen I can handle.

MASAKO. I happy for you James. You find joy of internet. You were late to party but you join the party.

JAMES. Ha!

MASAKO. It's fun. I listen and read many stories from internet. I read about sickness.

JAMES. *Why?*

MASAKO. Because everybody gets sick. And many people want to talk loudly about it. And I have an internet friend too. Her name Priscilla. She a wild woman. In Nevada. She been living with for seven years same cancer as me. She give me hope.

JAMES. How'd you find her?

MASAKO. Popular blog. Every single day she post about adventures. About treatment. About life. I try to read.

JAMES. What's it called?

MASAKO. "Tumor Has It."

JAMES. Heh. That's pretty good.

MASAKO. James. Will you read me last two days? My brain swiss cheese I have not checked. She getting the result of her scan soon. I want to know result too.

JAMES. Yeah. I can do that.

> (*Lights up on* SOPHIE *sitting alone in her car—also reading on her phone. She's on the Carcinosarcoma Facebook Group—upset but unable to look away.*
>
> *Then somewhere else—lights up on* HIRO *wearing workout clothes. She's going for a moonlight run.*)

HIRO. (*To herself.*) What are you living for?

(*Then—she sprints.* HIRO *sprints in place or, whatever the space allows that fits the director's vision—throughout the entire duration of the scene [the idea is that she is running, exhausting herself, feeling her body]. NOTE: This scene is a cacophony. It must be fast-paced and rhythmic.* SOPHIE *and* JAMES *are both reading from their respective phones but please note they are reading different content on separate websites.*)

JAMES. (*Reading from his phone.*) Tumor Has It. April 13th.

SOPHIE. (*Reading from her phone.*) Carcinosarcoma Facebook Group. April 13th. Lucy Jones from London.

JAMES. Hey ya'll it's Priscilla. Blogdiggity bloggin' from the Grand Canyon!

SOPHIE. To say this group has been a lifeline would be an understatement. Thank you from the bottom of my heart for your support these past six months.

JAMES. No I'm NOT on my Mac my darlings—I'm not THAT addicted to technology. I'll publish this ish later at the Yavapai Lodge.

SOPHIE. So it breaks my heart to post an update that I knew was coming but still somehow hoped I'd never, ever have to write.

JAMES. Right now I'm scribblin' in the sunshine on a notebook littered with bumper stickers from Gotcancer.org—thanks for the rec Lympho Bob. My favorite? The one that says CCKMA: CANCER CAN KISS MY ASS!!!!!

MASAKO. Cancer can kiss my ass!!!!!

JAMES. Just yelled that into the cavernous valleys.

MASAKO. CANCER CAN KISS MY ASS!!!!!!!

SOPHIE. My mum died. My strong, beautiful and irreplaceable mum. She died. It happened this morning at eight a.m. U.K. time.

JAMES. And my voice echoed like a vast angry God.

SOPHIE. I don't know what she did to deserve this pain.

JAMES. I just feel so much up here.

SOPHIE. Her body—

JAMES. My body.

SOPHIE. Her poor body.

JAMES. My strong body.

SOPHIE. Wasn't a body anymore.

JAMES. It brings tears to my eyes.

SOPHIE. It brings tears to my eyes—

JAMES. Thinking about what hell my body went through. So I'll share with you something that helped me during times of sadness.

SOPHIE. I'm just so sad. But I guess. I guess.

SOPHIE/JAMES. But I feel sad then I am still alive.

JAMES. Repeat it out loud.

SOPHIE. I am alive. I am alive. I am alive. And that means I have to live. I have to live for her.

(SOPHIE *puts her phone down, overwhelmed. She wishes she hadn't read that.*)

JAMES. Getting the results from my scan tomorrow. Think of me. Xoxo. Priscilla.

(SOPHIE *starts her car, almost in a trance.*)

Tumor Has It. April 14th

(*Getting caught up in his own reading.*)

As you know, I got the results of my scan today. I can't believe how fast this happened. The beast snuck up and spread to my lungs—Oh SHIT.

(JAMES *stops himself. He looks over at* MASAKO *who seems to be asleep. God please be asleep. He didn't want her to hear that.*)

Masako, you didn't hear none of that. Did you? Masako are you alright?

(*No answer from* MASAKO. *Meanwhile,* SOPHIE *is driving fast. Too fast.*)

SOPHIE. I am alive I am alive I am alive I am alive I am alive I am alive I am alive I am alive I am alive I am—

(*Then she gasps—seeing something coming toward her. She tries to swerve but it's too late.*

Then bright flashing lights. Realistic crashing sounds.

Blackout on everyone except for HIRO—*who is still running. Hard. Feeling her heart beat, hearing her own breath. Her strength.*

And then we hear MASAKO *crying in the darkness—then full on wailing.*

A slow fade in on MASAKO'S *face as she wails and wails for Priscilla. For her own life.*

HIRO *doesn't see or hear it. She stops running. But she keeps on taking in the Kentucky air. Breathing.*

Breathing. Breathing. Blackout.)

End of Act One

Act Two

Scene One

>*Darkness. A ringing of a phone. It rings and rings and rings and then—*

HIRO. (*Groggy.*) Sophie?

SOPHIE. (*Upset.*) Hiro.

HIRO. What's wrong? Is Mom—

SOPHIE. I totaled my car.

>*(The lights gradually come up on* HIRO *and* SOPHIE *in separate places. It's early, early morning of Day Three—before the sun comes up.)*

HIRO. How?

SOPHIE. A deer. I hit it. I hit a friggin' deer because I was so upset at that stupid carcinosarcoma group you added me to on Facebook. Unadd me!!! Unadd me now!!!!

HIRO. That's...not how Facebook groups work. You just leave the group of your own accord.

SOPHIE. This is YOUR fault.

HIRO. That's...really unfair.

>(*Pause.*)

Are you alright?

SOPHIE. NO. But yes. I only sprained my wrist. But don't you DARE tell Mama about this. It'll just stress her out!

HIRO. I won't.

>(*Pause.*)

Do you need me to come get you?

SOPHIE. I'm with my husband, Hiro. OBVIOUSLY.

HIRO. Hi Da'Ran...

SOPHIE. He *doesn't* say hi back.

HIRO. ...Do you need anything? From me?

SOPHIE. I need you to unadd me from that group. It was mean of you to add me. So, so mean. All those people dying. All those people losing their mothers. I don't need to see that. *I don't need to see that.*

HIRO. Okay. Okay.

>(*Genuine.*)

I'm sorry. I'm sorry.

SOPHIE. The deer.

HIRO. Hm?

SOPHIE. I had to watch that deer die. On the side of your road—

HIRO. The deer—

SOPHIE. She was laying there after I hit her—all bloody and scared. Her eyes were open. Her small black eyes just filled with death. And she was moving. Moving Hiro! Her breath pounding against the ground. And her legs...*her legs*. At first I thought they were twitching but then I realized...she thought she was running, Hiro. She couldn't even stand but she thought she was running...running away from me. She didn't know she was dying Hiro! She didn't know she was dying!

Scene Two

DAY THREE. JAMES enters. He's at AA again.

JAMES. Good mornin'. Hi. Guess who's back again? Me. It's me. I'm back. Heh.

(*Pause.*)

Just sucked down some macaroni and cheese. It's hard when your wife don't cook for ya.
Forgot to put the butter in. And we didn't have no milk. So, I put in some mayonnaise.
Still sucked it down but wasn't as good. Sticky.

(*Pause.*)

Reachin' the homestretch of chemo. Doctors said the drip might be done tomorrow morning. Might be the middle of the night. Hopin' for the middle of the night. Then—we just wait. Wait in the uncertainty. No. *Live* in the uncertainty.
People hate uncertainty. Drives some people mad. Which is funny 'cause everything in life is uncertain. Well. 'Cept for death.
My daughter—the one who hates me—she done shoved a drink in my face the other day! And shit. I wanted a swig so badly. It never goes away. Wanting to take that swig! But God. In that moment I thought about how anger manifests when yer sober and how it manifests when yer not.
My eldest daughter—she'd love to tell me my anger manifested onto her and her sister and my wife.

(*Pause.*)

I say—anger sure as hell manifested inside my body when I was drinkin' I'll tell ya that. I was stupid. Fuckin stupid. Didn't think beer was bad for ya.

And I still don't think it is. But drink a twenty-pack of anything every day for twenty years and then...'course it's bad. Again, I was stupid. And my body became angry at the stupid. My liver got stiff and lumpy. My skin turned yellow. And my belly—well it swoll out to here until I exploded and I bled out my mouth and ass. Oh and I couldn't walk no more. I remember all I wanted was to be able to walk. I told Masako—*I want to walk! I want to walk goddamnit, I want to walk!*
And now—by some sort of miracle. I'm walking again. And I don't take it for granted.

    (*Pause.*)

Nowadays when I feel angry I remember that I can walk. And the anger subsides. It really does.

    (*Pause.*)

Hi I'm James. And I am an alcoholic.

Scene Three

> *Hospital.* MASAKO *is asleep. She looks five times worse than she did the day before.* SOPHIE *enters. She's wearing a band on her wrist. She looks disheveled, exhausted. She looks at her mom. A beat.*

MASAKO. (*Weakly.*) tou.
SOPHIE. (*Softening.*) Mama.
MASAKO. ...arigatou. Otousan arigatou.
SOPHIE. You dreamin' Mama?
MASAKO. (*Can barely talk.*) You. Hiro chan. Little girls. Eating candy your papa got from Kroger. Candy...make you so happy. You smile so big and you say "Otousan arigatou."

> (SOPHIE *puts on a long-sleeved sweater—hiding her wrist. She forces a smile.*)

SOPHIE. I saw Colleen on the way in. She said she tried to come by and take your breakfast order but you turned her away. Still can't eat?
MASAKO. Mmm.
SOPHIE. Feelin' nauseous?
MASAKO. Mmm.
SOPHIE. Do you want me to call the nurse for some Ativan?
MASAKO. No. Makes me not poo. I want to poo. I miss the poo.
SOPHIE. Do you wanna go to the bathroom and try?
MASAKO. Mmm.

(SOPHIE *helps* MASAKO *out of bed to the adjacent bathroom. She's careful about her wrist. This is difficult but methodical.* MASAKO *drags her chemotherapy drip with her. The cord gets caught.* MASAKO *wants to close the door of the hospital room for privacy.*)

MASAKO. Close the door.

SOPHIE. It's the cord.

MASAKO. Please close door!

SOPHIE. It's the dang cord!

MASAKO. What you do??

SOPHIE. You're so weak today Ma—

MASAKO. Stop! *I said stop!!!!* Go away! Go away go away!!! I can do myself!!!

(*Then*—MASAKO *starts to get sick.* SOPHIE *gets her barf bowl. This goes on for an uncomfortable period of time. When she's done,* SOPHIE *attempts to take her mother to the bathroom but* MASAKO *stops her. She's wet herself.* SOPHIE *puts her mother back into bed. She takes off her mother's urine-soaked underwear and puts it in a plastic Ziploc bag. This isn't easy but it's methodical.* SOPHIE *then cleans her mother's urine from the floor and goes to put the barf bowl into the bathroom.*)

MASAKO. I wish time go by faster. I want it to be tomorrow now!!!

(*A beat.*)

I need...new pantsu.

SOPHIE. Yup. Mmm hmm!

(SOPHIE *reaches into a bag and gets out a fresh new pair of underwear. She puts it on* MASAKO. *This takes a while but it's clear she's done this before too. A few beats.*)

Wanna listen to a sermon on your phone?

MASAKO. No.

You can tell me. What God said.

SOPHIE. Me?

MASAKO. You.

SOPHIE. Okay.

(*Pause.*)

God said as your days, so shall your strength be.
God said my words are life to you.
God said to your old age and gray hairs I will carry you.
I will deliver you, I will preserve you I will keep you alive.
I will satisfy you with long life.

I heal all your diseases and your broken heart.
I'll bind up your wounds and your light shall break forth
as the morning God said—
your health shall spring forth speedily
God said—
Trusting Me brings health to your navel
God said—
and marrow to your bones
God said—
My joy is your strength.
I will recover you.
I'll make you to live.
I am ready to save you.
And God said this, Mama.
I love you.
Mama, I love you.

Scene Four

    CAR. JOHN *and* HIRO, *same day, afternoon. A beat.* JOHN *seems weird.*

HIRO. mmm.
    (*Pause.*)
That barbecue was good.
    (*Pause.*)
Thanks for calling me on your lunch break and taking me to barbecue.
    (*Pause.*)
But I would have never thought to go to a place called Red State Barbecue and it was really good so.
    (*Pause.*)
Yeah.
    (*Pause.*)
Eh hem.
    (*Pause.*)
John
    (*Pause.*)
John.
    (*Pause.*)
JOHN YOU'RE BEING WEIRD TODAY JOHN.

JOHN. YEAH. YEAH I *AM* BEING WEIRD HIRO.

HIRO. Well stop! It was really awkward eating ribs in silence.

JOHN. Well I feel like if I'm not silent I'm just gonna start screaming!!!

HIRO. Why???

JOHN. Because I'm pissed!!!!!

(*Screaming out the window.*)

I'm PISSED off.

HIRO. At me!?!!?

JOHN. NO. I'm pissed because I'm STRESSED OUT and feel useless as though my life has been for NOTHING.

HIRO. Oh God. Did something bad happen?

JOHN. No. Except for the fact that I spent the last THIRTEEN YEARS OF MY FUCKING LIFE just DEVOTED to my kid and he just doesn't do his FUCKING HOMEWORK. EVEN THOUGH I DO EVERYTHING FOR HIM. LITERALLY. EVERYTHING TO MAKE HIS LIFE BETTER. And yesterday I was just begging, pleading for him to stop doing this to me. To just do his homework. And he's like okay coo, I'll do it. And this morning, I checked his grades and his grades are dropping because HE'S NOT DOING HIS HOMEWORK. AND THEN LOOKED ON HIS BED AND HE HAD LEFT THE HOMEWORK HE SAID HE WAS GOING TO DO JUST, CRINKLED ON THE BED UNDONE!!!! AND I JUST DON'T KNOW WHY HE'S DOING THIS TO ME. WHAT DID I DO TO DESERVE THIS? WHY JOHN JUNIOR. WHY. WHYYYYYY. WHYYYYYYY. WHYYYYYYYYY.WHYYYYY ?!?!!!?!? WHYYYYYYYYYY. SERIOUSLY. WHYYYYYY? WHYYYYY?!!?!? WHYYYYY!!?!?

HIRO. You named your kid John Junior? Like after yourself? That…takes a lot of gall—

JOHN. WHYYYYY?

(*An awkward pause.*)

HIRO. Um. Well. I don't have children. So.

(*Pause.*)

I don't really have anything to say.

(*They drive.* JOHN *collects himself.*)

JOHN. It just…makes me crazy you know? I'm physically exhausting myself I'm so frustrated and angry. And then I calm down and the adrenaline subsides and I start shaking. More like shivering actually. See? I'm doing it now.

(JOHN *is shivering.* HIRO *looks at* JOHN *with a mixture of utter disgust and mild concern.*)

HIRO. …have you tried yoga?

JOHN. *What.*

(JOHN *looks at* HIRO *with a mixture of utter disgust and mild amusement.*)

HIRO. Again. I do not have children. Nor do I ever plan on having children. But I do know that having all that anger just…living inside of you is bad.

(*Pause.*)

Do you see a therapist?

JOHN. What? No!

HIRO. Well. I have for years. And Larry really encouraged me to find a creative outlet. So outside of my work I play music. I'm not very good but it doesn't matter. I write little songs when I'm upset and just bang it out on a banjo.

JOHN. A banjo? Ha. That's pretty cat.

HIRO. Cat?

JOHN. You don't remember we used to say that in high school? That shit's cat. That's cat. You're cat?

HIRO. …absolutely not.

JOHN. Ah. Well all the cool kids said it.

HIRO. …Is being cat *good*?

JOHN. *It's cat.*

(*Pause.*)

Wanna sing me one of your songs?

HIRO. No! They're just for me. But that's the whole point. You should find something that's just for you.

(JOHN *stops the car.*)

JOHN. Okay. Get out.

HIRO. Oh my God! I was just trying to be helpful Goddamnit—

JOHN. —shut up you fool I'm not mad I'm trying to show you something!

HIRO. Show me what? Like your penis? Because I feel like that maybe that ship has sailed!

JOHN. JUST GET OUT OF MY FUCKING CAR.

(HIRO *gets out of the car.* JOHN *also gets out. They stand side by side.* HIRO *has no idea what's going on. She watches* JOHN *look out into the distance—taking in a deep breath.* HIRO *doesn't know what to do.*)

HIRO. What are you looking at?

JOHN. WHAT AM I LOOKING AT? Hiro are you serious??? I'm looking at that fucking picturesque piece of beautiful farmland right in front of us is what I'm looking at!

HIRO. What do you mean "picturesque"?

JOHN. UM the gently rolling hills, sparsely wooded field complete with a little tiny creek running through it? THE FUCKING ADORABLE HORSE MOM WITH HER LITTLE PONY?

HIRO. Kay.

JOHN. Anyway. You said I should find something that's just for me. Well—it's my dream to buy land like this someday. Just for me. Well. Me and my kid. So maybe moving forward when I'm angry I can come here or something. I dunno.

HIRO. Places like this give me anxiety.

JOHN. Why???

HIRO. It's too remote. And honestly, I'm having a hard time understanding why anyone would choose this. Sorry I don't mean to sound like "oh I'm a city mouse," and "you're a country mouse" but yeah. Can you...help me understand why this would be something you want?

JOHN. UGH DO YOU SERIOUSLY NEED ME TO MANSPLAIN THIS TO YOU?

HIRO. I WOULD LOVE THAT.

JOHN. AWESOME. GREAT. Well. For starters—many middle-class people's assets peak like in their fifties. And I know you lived in a shitty area—

HIRO. Hey now—

JOHN. —But I grew up solidly middle class. And in OUR economic class—

HIRO. —You're so condescending—

JOHN. —the kids move out and they downsize. But nobody has an estate anymore to pass down. When they retire, everyone just uses up everything they accumulated when they were younger and don't pass a lot on, and then the next middle-class generation has to work really fucking hard to catch up to their parents. It'd be nice to pass on some financial security to my kid.

(*Pause.*)

Legacy. Is something I think of a lot. And you know what? I'm smart. I have an MBA. This isn't an impossible dream. Wow. I already feel calmer.

HIRO. Oh my God.

JOHN. I know. I'm like a good parent. It's surprising.

HIRO. No I mean. Oh my God. What the fuck am I gonna do?

JOHN. Huh?

HIRO. (*Having a panic attack.*) Like—what kind of fucking SHIT am I going to inherit when both of my parents fucking die which let's face it COULD

BE SOON. My fucking dad doesn't think about shit like legacy! And my mom—FUCK. I DON'T EVEN THINK SHE HAS A FUCKING WILL. FUUUUCK!!!!FUCCK!!!! FUUUUCK. OH MY GOD FUUUUCK!!!!

JOHN. Um can you not freak out, I just literally talked myself out of a complete meltdown.

HIRO. AHH. AHHH. AHHHH. AND THEY HAVE ALL THIS DEBT. JOHN AM I GOING TO INHERIT THE DEBT? IS THAT HOW DEBT WORKS?

JOHN. I mean?

HIRO. AND THE HOUSE. OH GOD THE HOUSE. Sophie's been warning me this whole time and I've just been ignoring her!…I'm so fucking stupid. JOHN. WHY AM I SO FUCKING STUPID? I HAVE TO GET MY SHIT TOGETHER. I HAVE TO CLEAN MY PARENTS' HOUSE. JOHN WILL YOU DROP ME OFF THERE INSTEAD OF THE HOTEL?!?!

JOHN. Hey Hiro. It sounds like you just have some planning to do and it's still early—

HIRO. But it's not fucking early!!! Don't you get it?!!? I'm running out of time. I fucked up. I fucked up John. I'm running out of time!

(*Sound of* MASAKO *crying again.*

This leads us to…)

Scene Five

Hospital room, later that day. MASAKO *is crying in bed.* JAMES *watches her uncomfortably.*

JAMES. Masako—you've been crying for an hour. It ain't gonna help nothin'.

MASAKO. My bones hurt. I hate this medicine. It makes my bones go Muaaan muaaan.

JAMES. There there.

(JAMES *touches* MASAKO.)

MASAKO. *Don't touch me.*

JAMES. Does it hurt when I touch ya?

MASAKO. I don't want you to touch because *you* gave me cancer.

JAMES. What now?

MASAKO. You gave me cancer because you were so mean. You made me so stressed out.
You gave me cancer. This is your fault. This is your fault. Anata no sei! Anata no sei!!!!

(MASAKO *starts hitting* JAMES. *He wants to shove her away or hit her back but he doesn't. He lets her hit him. We see this struggle. It's not easy.*)

JAMES. Are you finished?

(*She's finished.*)

MASAKO. Not fair.

JAMES. (*A little more bitter and aggressive than he intended.*) Nothing's fair.

MASAKO. *I know that. I'm not stupid. But this not fair mostly of all.* I take care of me. I eat smoothie. Drink almond milk. Eat Vegetables. I drink wine only sometimes. And I walk five mile every day. And still I get sick. But you! You drink osake every day. Twenty pack of beer every day. You almost die. But now you fixed. It's not fair. I cannot see the light. I cannot see the light!

JAMES. *Well of course you can't see the light Masako. Because you are the light!*

(*Pause.*)

Okay?

MASAKO. ...Okay.

JAMES. I'm just.

(*Pause.*)

I'm just glad you're as well as you are.

(MASAKO *cries again. Then embraces* JAMES. *A beat.*)

MASAKO. What did you do today.

JAMES. Flea Market.

MASAKO. Did you have fun?

JAMES. They call me the rock man over there cuz I'm a salesman of rocks. There was this guy in high school who used to carry around this big stick and he would pray about Jesus. They used to call him Stick Man. I'm like him but without God and with rocks

MASAKO. There's God in you, James.

JAMES. Ya think?

MASAKO. I know. Because I used to pray all the time when you get mean. I was not religious but I pray anyway. And when Sophie became Christian she pray and I pray with her—please let James be the James I met in California again. Kawaii quiet James too pure for this world. He is shy. Hard for him to be sunao but when he does he is so cute. And it took many, many years but my prayer come true. No? That is why I believe now. In something a little more. I believe because of the God in you.

(MASAKO *looks at* JAMES *a sweet moment. The scene melds to—*)

Scene Six

HIRO. *Alone. Talking on the phone.*

HIRO. So I wasn't planning on going back to my parents' house at all because it's filled with bad memories and I get so triggered. Plus I'm a thirty-six-year-old account director with like assistants and everything. I can finally afford the hotel of my childhood dreams: the Hyatt Regency. But my mind really went into panic mode when you mentioned all that stuff about legacy. Everything hit me all at once.

(*Lights up on* JOHN *on his phone. He and* HIRO *are talking to each other.*)

JOHN. Yeah sorry about that. I didn't mean to send you into a spiral. I just thought it was my turn to complain.

HIRO. So even before I walk in the door—the place is a fucking disaster. My dad has two cars in the driveway that don't even work plus a broken motorcycle. Nothing about the yard makes sense. Sticks everywhere. Dead trees. Dead flowers. An oddly blooming Cherry tree. Yellow grass in the Bluegrass state.

(*Pause.*)

But then I go inside and...my shoulders soften. I'm breathing normally. And I feel...comfortable? Sure there's junk everywhere but I find myself kind of liking the junk? I mean what the fuck is that becoming an adult? Liking the shit you used to hate?

JOHN. Sometimes things you hated in your childhood can morph into feeling like an old relative. A crusty dusty part of your worn-down soul. God I'm tired.

HIRO. And I noticed something I had never seen before. A photo of my mom and dad when they eloped, framed and hanging proudly like it was meant to be there. Like someone hung it.

JOHN. Why'd they elope? And how'd they even meet. Your parents? Was your dad in the—

HIRO. No my father was not in the army you basic bitch. Everyone asks me that. I know they met in California. I don't know all the details. Never cared to ask.

JOHN. You should ask.

HIRO. Anyways—I started wondering...when was the last time I saw my parents kiss? And I realized I never have until this picture. So, I'm in my childhood home, with full intention of throwing shit away and here I am staring at my parents kissing for the first time ever in my life. *God. They looked so happy.* And that's when it dawned on me that there was a time before I was born when my parents were just a couple. Independent of me. And Sophie. They were just a couple in love. And then I did the dishes. And I went back to the hospital.

JOHN. So you're not freaked out anymore?

HIRO. (*Dry.*) Of course I'm freaked out. The cycle of poverty is an endless loop of doom and I've deluded myself into thinking I've escaped it. But that's what therapy, detox cleanses and Doo Da is for.

JOHN. Da fuck is Doo Da?

HIRO. My banjo.

(*Pause.*)

I don't know what's gonna happen to my parents.

JOHN. That's just how it is.

(*Pause.*)

You know—I think a lot of times parents just get caught in the bullshit like everybody else.
I think about my dad and when he was young and…he was probably just caught up in bullshit too.

HIRO. …where are you right now?

JOHN. Home.

HIRO. I found some pot. Wanna smoke it with me? I can come over quick—

JOHN. I can't hang out tonight.

HIRO. Oh okay. One of your hoes coming over? Tammy Lynn or Chastity or something?

JOHN. Naw. I'm hanging out with John Junior. We're gonna watch a movie.

(*Pause.*)

He crashed his bicycle today.

HIRO. Oh no! Is he okay?

JOHN. Yeah just a little banged up. But he was crying. And it hurts me so bad when he cries. God, I love him so much.

HIRO. Do you tell him that?

JOHN. *Every fucking day.*

HIRO. He's lucky. I've never heard my dad say, *I Love You.*

JOHN. Well, you know what Hiro? My dad never said it either. But I know he did.
That's something I learned when I became a parent. Even when you can't express it, you are always, *always* overwhelmed with love for your kid. *God you'd do anything to protect them.* I'm so broken today because John Junior fell off his bike. I wish I was there to catch him.

(*Pause.*)

Shit I gotta go. *Transformers* is starting.

HIRO. Alright.

JOHN. (*Towards his son.*) Be right there bug!

(*Pause.*)

Bye Hiro.

HIRO. Bye John.

(HIRO *alone again. She smokes weed. Then*—SOPHIE *enters.*)

HIRO. Soph what are you doing here? It's not your shift is it? Did I fuck up?

SOPHIE. No. Da'Ran's having a bro night and I didn't want to be alone. And…I just wanna be with Mama.

HIRO. And what does *bro night* look like for Saint Da'Ran.

SOPHIE. Applebees. Half-priced apps. It's a good deal.

(HIRO *agrees. It is a good deal.*)

Are you seriously smoking weed in a hospital parking lot?

HIRO. Get this. It's Dad's. His stash was just sitting right there on his nightstand next to an Elvis statue and a mountain of rocks so I took it!

SOPHIE. You went to the house. What a mess right?

(HIRO *nods.*)

Did I tell you Dad still smoked when he was trying to get on the transplant list?

HIRO. Is that allowed??

SOPHIE. Heck no. It's hard for an alcoholic to get on a transplant list in the first place. Gotta go to AA. All that. Prove they're clean—

HIRO. Well he *did* get sober—

SOPHIE. But he still smoked. And when he got through a month of sobriety so that he could get on the transplant list the doctors were like…Mr. Rose… you tested positive for marijuana we can't put you on the list. And he was like HUHHHHHHHH?!?!?!

HIRO. What a dumbass!

SOPHIE. So he quit smoking. Got put on the list. But then boom! He magically doesn't need a transplant anymore. So he started smoking again.

HIRO. Livers are so weird.

SOPHIE. It's a miracle. I wonder why Dad got a miracle but Mama didn't.

HIRO. She still might.

SOPHIE. It's been hard not to lose hope.

HIRO. But you've always been so hopeful.

SOPHIE. Hiro, I can't. I can't have children.

HIRO. ...what?

SOPHIE. I have PCOS. It can make it difficult to get pregnant sometimes but I found out about a month ago that I can't ovulate. You haven't had anything similar?

(HIRO *shakes her head no*)

You've never had any problems? Like ever?

(HIRO *hasn't.* SOPHIE *gets upset.*)

I wanted me and Da'Ran's children more than anything else in the world.

HIRO. You can adopt! They'll still be your children.

SOPHIE. I know. I know. But I really wanted to be pregnant. I wanted Mama to touch my pregnant belly and make little blankets and hats and—

HIRO. She can still make blankets. She can still—

SOPHIE. *I know you don't want kids. You've always talked about it. Why don't you want kids?*

HIRO. Because I don't want to end up like Dad.

SOPHIE. We're not our parents! I would have been amazing—

HIRO. And I *know that* and you still will be but I don't wanna risk it. I'm so sorry Sophie. I wish I could give you my ovaries. I wish I could give you my ovaries and Dad could give Mom his immortality.

(HIRO *embraces* SOPHIE—*who is at the end of her rope. She's never seen her sister like this. But surprisigly* SOPHIE *is comforted by a simple embrace. A beat.* HIRO *offers* SOPHIE *weed.*)

Want some?

(*Pause.*)

Just kidding. I know you don't.

SOPHIE. Sure.

HIRO. What?

SOPHIE. I said sure. I'll take a hit. F it. God will still love me.

(HIRO *is filled with utter glee. She's smoking pot with her sister for the first time!!!!!!! Yeee!!"* SOPHIE *takes a hit. She doesn't cough or anything.*

She takes another one, then takes a deep breath.)

HIRO. Oh my god oh my god you're *good* at that.

SOPHIE. I used to be wild before Jesus found me, Hiro. Woke up once half naked on the roof of Rock Haven looking up at the morning stars...

HIRO. Rock Haven? The eighteen and under club!?!?!! Hahahaaaa—

SOPHIE. It was a school night. And I thought I was soooo cat.

(HIRO *registers, once again, that she was not cool in high school.* SOPHIE *takes another hit. Passes it to* HIRO.)

HIRO. I wish we would have hung out more when you were wild.

SOPHIE. You were in New York by then. I think that's part of what made me so wild. I was lonely.

HIRO. Thanks for telling me that.

(*Pause.*)

I'm afraid Mom will die. And I didn't get to tell her all the things I needed to tell her.

SOPHIE. Me too.

HIRO. But I don't even know what I need to tell her, you know? I already feel normal. Her changing body. Her vomiting in front of me. It doesn't traumatize me.

SOPHIE. Well, it traumatizes me. It's my mama.

HIRO. But Soph.

(*Pause.*)

When Mom would cry and cry and cry in bed because Dad would rage at her for doing something that wasn't even remotely wrong like turning the heat up so we'd be warm and she'd lay in the middle of us and we'd sandwich her and pat her head so that she could go muster up the strength to go apologize to him and say "sorry sorry James. I'm sorry I was wrong please forgive me," and afterwards we would be like "yaaay good job Mom!"…was that traumatizing for you?

SOPHIE. No that was normal.

HIRO. See. I'm still traumatized by that. And this is why I can't forgive him. But Sophie. I need to forgive him. I need to forgive Dad for the sake of Mom in these moments. To give her peace. And I know that. But I can't. How did you do it?

SOPHIE. It wasn't easy. That's all I can say is that it wasn't easy. God—

HIRO. Don't tell me it was God.

(*Pause.*)

Sorry. It's just.

(*Pause.*)

Sophie, did I tell you that I went to church?

SOPHIE. *You?*

HIRO. St. John The Divine. It's a Cathedral up by Columbia.

SOPHIE. What for the decorations or—

HIRO. Because I was lost.

SOPHIE. Like literally lost or?

HIRO. No Because I was *feeling* lost.

(SOPHIE *laughs.* HIRO *is serious.*)

SOPHIE. OH wait. You're serious. Sorry I'm like super high and this is like. Blowing my mind right now. Go on.

HIRO. And I walked in and...

SOPHIE. *And...?*

HIRO. Security was like. Sorry ma'am we're closing.

(SOPHIE *laughs more.*)

HIRO. But I think I wanted to feel close to God so I went to church. And I don't know God. But you know God. And I wanted to be close to you. I've lost too much time with you because I was so angry. I lost time with Mom too.

SOPHIE. But you had every right. Every right to be angry.

(*Pause.*)

Hey, you wanna know besides church—how I learned to forgive Dad?

HIRO. Yes.

SOPHIE. I forgave him by paying attention to his language of love.

(*Pause.*)

People have different ways of loving. And Dad can't love with his words. Most of the time. But he shows a lot of love and remorse through his actions.

HIRO. How?

SOPHIE. What would he always do after a blind drunken rage? How would we know the storm was over?

HIRO. He'd go to the store.

SOPHIE. And what would he always say when he was on his way to the store?

HIRO. "I'm going to Kroger. Want me to pick you up anything?"

SOPHIE. That was him saying "I'm sorry."

HIRO. And we'd say no.

SOPHIE. But he'd bring us each a candy bar anyway.

HIRO. (*A realization.*) And that was him saying "I love you."

Scene Seven

A little later. Hospital. Same. JAMES *is singing Dan Hill's hit song "Sometimes When We Touch" softly to* MASAKO *in bed.*

This goes on for a little while, through the first several verses.

SOPHIE *and* HIRO *enter; they are hiiiigh.*

HIRO. Woah woah woah woah woah whaaaaaat is going on here???

SOPHIE. I feel like I just caught you two having sex. Oh my Gosh do you remember when I actually caught you having sex? I heard screaming coming from your room and I hadn't ever seen y'all kiss so I thought someone was murdering Mama so I rolled in with my huge U.S. history book to beat the burglars away and caught you rolling naked off of Dad!!!!!

MASAKO. Ohhh yes. I remember.

HIRO. Hahhahahahahahahaha whaaat. That did NOT happen.

SOPHIE. Oh my gooooshhh I think that was a repressed memory!!!

HIRO. I didn't know you guys had sex. I've never even seen you kiss in person.

SOPHIE. Why didn't anyone ever talk to me about that?

HIRO. You guys should kiss *now*. Kiss! Kiss! Kiss! Kiss! Kiss! Kiss!!!

SOPHIE. Yeah kiss!!!!!

HIRO. Kiss!!!!!

JAMES. What the hell are you guys on?

SOPHIE. YOUUUUUUR DRUGS!!!!!!

HIRO. I STOLE YOUR STASH. Oh my god I told him. I actually told him!!!!

JAMES. My stash? You done stole my stash?!?!? Well I'll be.

(JAMES *is laughing.* MASAKO *is laughing too.*)

SOPHIE. MAMA. YOU LOOK SO MUCH BETTER.

MASAKO. I am feeling better.

JAMES. Chemo's done. She's just on potassium now.

MASAKO. Potassium like banana!

(SOPHIE *and* HIRO *celebrate vocally.* MASAKO *joins in.*)

JAMES. So we got a choice. Doctors say if she finishes the paperwork she can leave around midnight. Or we can wait 'til the morning.

SOPHIE. What do you wanna do Mama?

HIRO. Yeah what do you wanna do? If you wanna go home tonight me and Sophie can wait!

SOPHIE. Yeah lets wait!!!!!

MASAKO. Yaaaay!

SOPHIE/HIRO. YAAAAAAY!

HIRO. (*Looking at her dad.*) You can stay too.

(*Pause.*)

If you want.

JAMES. ...okay.

MASAKO. Yaaaaay. I'm so happy!!!!

(*Squealing. Celebrating Then the excitement dies down. Stillness. Quiet that goes on for a while.* JAMES *then starts playing around on his phone.*)

HIRO. So do you like. Wanna tell us the story of how you two met?

MASAKO. Why?

JAMES. I'm busy.

HIRO. Busy with what?

JAMES. I'm chatting with my rock friends on Facebook.

SOPHIE. What do you guys talk about?

JAMES. Rocks.

(*Another beat. And then.*)

SOPHIE. Daad....Mom....Dad.....Dadd....

JAMES. WHAT.

SOPHIE. Why do you live in Kentucky? You guys met in California. Why did you raise us in Kentucky? I mean I love it here don't get me wrong but why?

HIRO. Yeah California has so many Asians.

MASAKO. Kentucky has Asian. I teach piano only to Asian girls and boys. I make living.

SOPHIE. But why Kentucky.

JAMES. What is with all these questions?

HIRO. Just tell us!

SOPHIE. Yeah tell us.

JAMES. Well. Kentucky is where your Grandma and Grandpa was. And that's where I was from. So figured we'd go back.

HIRO. Is that it?

JAMES. Yup.

(*Another long pause.* SOPHIE *and* HIRO *are mystified. This is the first time this family has had an honest conversation in a while and definitely the first time they have asked their parents questions about their own family.*)

SOPHIE. Dad. Daaaad.

JAMES. WHAT?

SOPHIE. When you go to the Chinoe pub for karaoke every night do you buy anything?

JAMES. I give them a dollar for the water and I give them a dollar when I sing.

HIRO. I'm surprised they let you in.

JAMES. The owner is my friend.

HIRO. You have friends?

MASAKO. He has many friends. And I have many friends too. My best friend name is Chip.

James best friend name Morino san and he call him Mr. Trees.

(SOPHIE *and* MASAKO *laugh.*)

MASAKO. (*To* HIRO.) That nickname is bilingual double entendre. You would not understand.

JAMES. He told the bartender not to serve me beer.

HIRO. Why would you ask for beer when you know you'd like die if you drink it?

JAMES. I don't ask for beer. Sometimes people try to buy it for me because of my great singing. But the bartender knows not to let 'em.

HIRO. Well you had enough beer to last you a lifetime.

JAMES. Hmmm.

MASAKO. Hiro be nice to your father he work very hard.

SOPHIE. Mama what did you want to be when you grew up?

MASAKO. A mother.

(*A nice beat.*)

SOPHIE. Dad how about you?

JAMES. I didn't really think about it. I was too busy riding horses. Playing sports.

HIRO. Do you regret not thinking about it?

JAMES. No, *Miss Account Director.*

SOPHIE. (*Cracking herself up.*) —*with like assistants and everything*—

JAMES. —I'm having a nice ride. I meet a lot of people. Talk about whatever I want.

(*Pause.*)

When I was nineteen, I started studying business but stopped because it was so boring.

MASAKO. He's very smart.

JAMES. So I traveled with nothing in my pockets 'cept for a dime.

(*Pause.*)

You spend a lot of time at work. But if you're not interested in what you're doing with your work—your life is gonna be hell. A lot of people never figure out what they're living for. They just do stuff to stay alive. That's the world as it is.

HIRO. Did you like working at Sam's Club before being on disability?

JAMES. As a matter of fact, yes. Yes I did.
MASAKO. ...I miss you.
> (*Everyone looks at MASAKO.*)

SOPHIE. What was that Mama?
MASAKO. I was just thinking girls. How I had bad time. So, so bad laying here. But now good thing happened. And that is feeling our family together. Like Christmas and birthday. Better than Christmas and birthday. But I miss you. And I think—how can I miss someone who is here? But I think that's because...the more I'm near you the more I wish I knew you as much as you knew yourself. The more I wish I could protect you more than you can protect yourself. Ever since you were born I just wanted to protect you. And now you protect me. I am so lucky. I am so, so lucky. I'm so lucky *cancer is over. It's over!!!!* Oh I'm so lucky you are here. Oh I'm so lucky I get to miss you in this moment.
SOPHIE. We're right here Mama, we're right here.
> (SOPHIE *goes to her mom and hugs her.* HIRO *follows. They sandwich her in a group hug.* JAMES *doesn't join in, instead he looks on as the prelude to Dan Hill's "Sometimes When We Touch" plays.*
>
> HIRO, MASAKO *and* SOPHIE *freeze in a tableau as the lights fade into a BLACKOUT. The song keeps playing in the dark. We listen to a lot of it. Through the scene change and a bit into the next scene until...*)

Scene Eight

> JAMES, *alone.*

JAMES. Hi. I'm James And I'm a—
> (*Pause.*)

I'm an alcoholic.
> (*Pause.*)

I see a lot of you today that I've become...friends with.
Sorry. Words can be hard.
> (*Pause.*)

Oh! My daughters. They asked me how me and my wife met. And. At the time. I didn't feel like getting into it. But I guess now is the appropriate time to get into it.
> (*Pause.*)

I saw Masako before I met her. About seven times to be exact. And for seven days I couldn't talk to her. Because she was just so damn...

(*Pause.*)

See, it was the seventies and I had hitchhiked from Kentucky to Berkeley and was livin' outside because it was warm. And I like the earth. I showered at the port. I was clean and I was happy. And one sunny day I noticed this woman, sitting on a bench nearby my tent. This dark haired, tiny woman and I thought to myself…that is one…

(*Pause.*)

So naturally I couldn't go talk to her. And I watched her go. And kicked myself in the damn nuts. But lo and behold…the next day she came back and sat down with a book! *War and Peace*. So I knew she was smart too. Which scared me even more. I thought about starting up a conversation but I hadn't read *War and Peace* ever in my life so. I watched her go again, knowing she was out of my…

(*Pause.*)

But then the next day goddamnit there she was again! Holding flowers this time. Tulips to be exact. Purple, pink and gold. And I thought—this is it James. You gotta go talk to this woman. But fuck! Some other dipshit got to her first. Sat down right next to her and started strikin' up a conversation. He had long hair. Mustache. Looked like his name would be "Sandy" or "Sky" you know the type. So I retreated. And the next day it rained and the mood of the sky matched my damn heart. And I sat there sulking lookin' at the clouds until…right there on that bench again…there she was. Holding an umbrella—looking at the clouds too! I couldn't believe it! But…when I took two steps forward I took two steps back 'cause I saw that she was…crying. Not the way I learned Masako could cry and cry and cry 'til you wanted her to shut up but just a soft type of crying like in a painting or somethin' so I left her alone. And besides there was this voice inside of me right then. A voice inside of me that said—it's okay to leave her alone. Because she'll be back tomorrow. And the next day she was back. But she still seemed sad. I figured that fucker Sandy, Skyler or whatever—he probably did somethin'. Figured she needs some space she needs some more time.
She needs more time.
So on the sixth day when she came I still didn't approach—but I promised that on the seventh—on the seventh day I'd talk to her. And she was wearing this beautiful yellow dress on that seventh day.

(MASAKO *enters. She is wearing a yellow dress.*)

JAMES. And she looked like herself again. So before she could sit down on that bench I marched right on up to her and said Hi. I'm James. James Rose.

MASAKO. I'm Masako Shiota.

JAMES. It's nice to meet you.

MASAKO. It's nice to meet you too.

JAMES. And I asked her what she was doing right now and she said—

MASAKO. I am visiting America for first time. I am lonely but I am happy. This is my favorite place to come and sit. Think about my life.

JAMES. And she asked me—

MASAKO. What are you doing now?

JAMES. And for some reason I told her I was on my way to the record store.

MASAKO. Oh?

JAMES. I didn't want her to think I was a stalker even though I kinda was I suppose but I said yes. I am on my way to the record store to buy a record.

MASAKO. Which record?

JAMES. And the first song that came to my mind was—this song we just played for you.

MASAKO. "Sometimes When We Touch" by Dan Hill? That song I love!!!!

JAMES. You do?

MASAKO. Yes! Yes!

> (*She sings the first couple lines of "Sometimes When We Touch."*)
> *Then, speaking:*)

So romantic!!!!

JAMES. And I mustered up the rest of my courage and asked…
Would you like to come with me? To the record store?

MASAKO. Yes James. I would love to come with you to the record store.

JAMES. And off we went. And we held hands. And we held each other. And we spoke things like—

MASAKO. Suki. I like you.

JAMES. Suki too. And—

MASAKO. *Ai shiteru.* I love you.

JAMES. And—

MASAKO. OH NO JAMES I'M GETTING DEPORTED!

JAMES. NO YOU FUCKING AIN'T MASAKO—MARRY ME.

MASAKO. I do!

JAMES. I do.

MASAKO. 'Til death do us part.

> (HIRO *enters. She's wearing black.*)

JAMES. And she said things like…

MASAKO. I want children.

> (SOPHIE *enters. She's wearing black too.*)

I know I'd be a good mother, James.

(SOPHIE, HIRO *and* JAMES *all stand side by side. We realize now that* JAMES *is wearing a dark blazer or jacket.*)

And you. You would be a *good* father.

JAMES. Masako and I. We've had our up and downs but we were married thirty-seven years and she was the strongest woman I'd ever met. I mean she married me didn't she? And stayed married to me until the day she died. I think…I think sometimes I was hard on her because I knew she could take it. And Masako was a fighter. Even when the cancer kept comin' back and they kept taking out parts of her body she kept on like she was whole. And when she couldn't stand no more…she stood it. She even played the damn piano! I don't know if she ever knew she was dying because she was so full of life.

(*Pause.*)

I say. I say. Masako's strength went unnoticed sometimes. A lot of people thought she was weak because she was cute and small and she was nice and she smiled a lot but it takes a lot of strength to smile. It does. It takes a lot of strength to be nice. Being an asshole is easy. If my wife taught me anything it's the courage to be…patient and kind. And I promise I will try to live patiently and kindly for her. And Goddamnit I will try to smile more.

(MASAKO *is gone now.*)

Anyway I don't know what else to say I've never had to give no eulogy before.

(*Realizing he forgot something.*)

OH FUCK!!!!

(*He takes out a crinkled piece of paper.*)

I forgot…I forgot the shit I wrote down.

(JAMES *reads from the crinkled paper.*

Full conviction.)

MASAKO LIKED THE OCEAN. AND SHE APPRECIATED JUDGE JUDY. OKAY. Okay I'm done. That's it. I'm done. Whew—I'm finished. I'm finished. I'm fucking finished. I'm finished.

(*He takes a deep breath. A beat as* HIRO, SOPHIE *and* JAMES *look out.*)

HIRO. Well, what the fuck do we do now?

(SOPHIE *is too devastated to talk. Another beat.*)

JAMES. Well.

(*Pause.*)

I was thinkin' about rushing off to Kroger to pick up some things. Who knows when we'll get to eating—talking to all these damned people.

(*Pause.*)

Want me to get you something? Like a candy bar?

(*A beat.*)

HIRO. ...yes.

SOPHIE. Yes.

JAMES. ...Yes????

(*Pause.*)

Alright then. Off I go.

End of Play

YOU ACROSS FROM ME
by Jaclyn Backhaus, Dipika Guha, Brian Otaño, and Jason Gray Platt

Copyright © 2018 by Jaclyn Backhaus, Dipika Guha, Brian Otaño, and Jason Gray Platt. All rights reserved. CAUTION: Professionals and amateurs are hereby warned that *You Across from Me* is subject to a royalty. It is fully protected under the copyright laws of the United States of America and of all countries covered by the International Copyright Union (including the Dominion of Canada and the rest of the British Commonwealth), the Berne Convention, the Pan-American Copyright Convention and the Universal Copyright Convention, as well as all countries with which the United States has reciprocal copyright relations. All rights, including professional, amateur stage rights, motion picture, recitation, lecturing, public reading, radio broadcasting, television, video or sound recording, all other forms of mechanical or electronic reproduction, such as CD-ROM, CD-I, information storage and retrieval systems and photocopying, and the rights of translation into foreign languages, are strictly reserved. Particular emphasis is laid upon the matter of readings, permission for which must be secured from the Authors' agents in writing.

Required royalties must be paid every time this play is performed before any audience, whether or not it is presented for profit and whether or not admission is charged.

All inquiries concerning rights, including amateur rights, should be addressed to:

For Jaclyn Backhaus: William Morris Endeavor Entertainment, 11 Madison Avenue, 18th Floor, New York, NY 10010. ATTN: Derek Zasky, dsz@wmeagency.com.

For Dipika Guha: William Morris Endeavor Entertainment, 11 Madison Avenue, 18th Floor, New York, NY 10010. ATTN: Michael Finkle, 212-903-1144, mfinkle@wmeagency.com.

For Brian Otaño: William Morris Endeavor Entertainment, 11 Madison Avenue, 18th Floor, New York, NY 10010. ATTN: Luke Virkstis, 212-903-1337, lvirkstis@wmeagency.com.

For Jason Gray Platt: jplatt@woodshedcollective.com.

ABOUT *YOU ACROSS FROM ME*

This article first ran in the Limelight Guide to the 42nd Humana Festival of New American Plays, *published by Actors Theatre of Louisville, and is based on conversations with the creative team before rehearsals for the Humana Festival production began.*

"The world begins at a kitchen table," declares Joy Harjo in her poem "Perhaps the World Ends Here." Harjo goes on to evocatively describe both the everyday rituals and the extraordinary life events that occur around this familiar object. The table is a place of contrasts—a site of communion and conflict, tradition and rebellion. And coming to the table, whether we're showing up for a celebration or a reckoning, means navigating and even embracing those contrasts. Maybe that's especially true now, in an era of deep political and social divisions. In polarizing times, what does it mean—and what does it cost—to come to the table? Will it bring us together, or reveal just how far apart we really are? In *You Across from Me*, four playwrights—Jaclyn Backhaus, Dipika Guha, Brian Otaño and Jason Gray Platt—explore this surprisingly complicated act, and the many ways we connect and confront.

Bold and inventive, these writers take us to a range of theatrical worlds—from a championship foosball match to a late-night hospice lounge, from a 1950s instructional video to a borderline-dystopian apartment building. As characters from all walks of life come to the table in wildly different ways, they make space (however reluctantly) for loved ones, enemies and strangers. The many narratives and points of view in *You Across from Me* hint at the show's wide array of inspirations. Among other subjects, the playwrights investigated the quirky, unexpected role that the humble table has played in major world events. For example, peace talks during the Vietnam War were held up by disagreements about the shape and number of negotiating tables, and crucial Cold War diplomacy happened over ping-pong tables in 1970s China. The writers also explored works of art from across history that have looked at the table in new ways, including the still lifes of Dutch Old Masters, Judy Chicago's feminist sculpture *The Dinner Table*, and the striking photographs in Carrie Mae Weems' *Kitchen Table Series*.

Ultimately, however, the playwrights' most important inspiration has been the performers for whom they're writing: the twenty acting apprentices in the 2017–2018 Professional Training Company. Actors Theatre has commissioned playwrights to create a Humana Festival show for the apprentices since 2000, making *You Across from Me* part of a strong tradition of investing in writers and offering opportunities for early-career actors to learn about new play development. Central to the commission is giving the playwrights and actors ample time to work together and get to know each other throughout the season. In August of 2017, the writers traveled to Louisville, joining the apprentices, director Jessica Fisch and dramaturg Jessica Reese for a weeklong workshop. Among the highlights of the week was the sharing of stories about how the table—as a gathering place, obstacle or symbol—has showed up in their lives. Reflecting on family heirlooms and airplane tray tables alike, the group shared hilarious and moving tales of transformative meals, surprising self-discoveries and hard-fought compromises.

Then the playwrights ventured off to write, each one tasked with drafting a series of short pieces that tackle coming to the table. They returned to Louisville in December and again in February 2018 to keep developing their work alongside the actors and the director-dramaturg team, building the show from the ground up in just a few months. For the playwrights, *You Across from Me* is a unique project that invites them to experiment with short-form writing, craft a show for a large ensemble and collaborate with other writers. In the end, the wealth of material they've generated—witty and heartfelt, imaginative and satirical—has come together to form a singular theatrical experience, one that showcases both their own distinctive voices and the talent of the acting apprentices.

The process of creating *You Across from Me* has revealed that there's a certain resonance between coming to the table and entering a theatre. In both cases, we gather around in order to receive sustenance, reflect, tell stories and find community. At the same time, put a table in a space, and suddenly there are stakes: which side are you on? Who gets a seat, and who doesn't? A table can suggest not only welcome and abundance, but also hierarchy and exclusion. The phrase "you across from me," after all, is another way of summing up one of drama's central elements: conflict. And a table, like a theatre, is a place where we're often asked to suspend our disbelief, whether we're pretending (as some of the characters in *You Across from Me* do) that a comically disastrous date is going just fine, or that the powerful person at the head of the table knows any more than the rest of us. Around a table, we perform rituals or enact dramas, connect face to face or seek truth—and anything can happen. So have a seat. Here, at least, there's enough room for everyone.

—Jessica Reese

BIOGRAPHIES

Jaclyn Backhaus is a playwright of Punjabi, German, and desert botanical descent. She is a co-founder of Fresh Ground Pepper and a core member of The Kilroys' new class. Her play *Men On Boats* was a finalist for the John Gassner Memorial Playwriting Award, a *New York Times* Critic's Pick for its productions at Clubbed Thumb and Playwrights Horizons, and recently finished a sold-out run at American Conservatory Theater in San Francisco. *Men On Boats* is published by Dramatists Play Service. Her most recent play, *India Pale Ale*, received the 2018 Horton Foote Prize for Promising New American Play and was produced by Manhattan Theatre Club. Other plays include *Wives* (world premiere at Playwrights Horizons, Fall 2019), *Folk Wandering* (book writer and co-lyricist with eleven composers, produced by Pipeline Theatre Company), *You Across from Me* (Humana Festival), the *People Doing Math!* live podcast show (part of the INCOMING! Series at The Public Theater's Under the Radar Festival, 2016) and *You on the Moors Now* (Theater Reconstruction Ensemble, The Hypocrites in Chicago, published by Dramatists Play Service). Backhaus was the 2016 Tow Foundation Playwright-in-Residence at Clubbed Thumb and she is currently in residence at Lincoln Center Theater. Backhaus holds a BFA in drama from New York University's Tisch School of the Arts, where she now teaches playwriting. She resides in Ridgewood, Queens, with her husband, director Andrew Scoville, and their son Ernie.

Dipika Guha is an L.A.-based Calcutta-born playwright raised in India, Russia and the United Kingdom. Her plays include *Yoga Play* (South Coast Repertory, San Francisco Playhouse; upcoming at Syracuse Stage, Laguna Playhouse, The Keegan Theatre, among others), *The Art of Gaman* (Theatre503 in London, Relentless Award semifinalist) and *Unreliable* (Kansas City Repertory Theatre). Recent works include *Azaan,* a play for for Oregon Symphony, *In Braunau* for Playwrights Horizons Theater School and contributions to *You Across from Me* (Humana Festival, Actors Theatre of Louisville). She was a Hodder Fellow at the Lewis Center for the Arts at Princeton University, the inaugural Shakespeare's Sister Playwriting Fellow, and is a current Venturous Fellow with The Lark for her play *Passing*. She's a proud alumna of Ars Nova's Play Group, Soho Rep's Writer/Director Lab, the WP Theater Lab, the Dramatists Guild Fellows Program, the Ma-Yi Writers Lab, the Geffen Playhouse Writers' Room and is a new member of New Dramatists. She is under commission from South Coast Repertory, Manhattan Theatre Club and Barrington Stage Company. For television, Guha has written for projects in development at AMC, the series *Sneaky Pete* and is currently writing for *Black Monday* on Showtime. She earned her undergraduate degree at University College London, won a Frank Knox

Memorial Fellowship to Harvard University, and has an MFA from the Yale School of Drama under Paula Vogel.

Brian Otaño is a bicoastal playwright and screenwriter. Full-length plays include *The Dust, Dolores Slayborne, Tara, Zero Feet Away* and *The Dooley Street Trilogy*. His plays have been performed, developed and workshopped by Actors Theatre of Louisville, New York Theatre Workshop, Roundabout Theatre Company, Page 73, Ars Nova, Atlantic Theater Company, New Dramatists, INTAR, LAByrinth Theater Company, The Lark, The Amoralists, Judson Memorial Church and SPACE on Ryder Farm. His first short film *Call Me Daddy* (directed by Amanda DeSouza) is a two-time award winner (Best Narrative Short, The Women's Film Festival and Best Comedy at The Official Latino Film Festival). Residencies/Fellowships: NHMC Television Writers Fellowship, Geffen Playhouse Writers' Room, Center Theatre Group L.A. Writers' Workshop, Page 73's Interstate 73 Writers Group, New York Theatre Workshop 2050 Fellowship, New Dramatists Van Lier Fellowship, and Ars Nova's Play Group. Education: BFA, Dramatic Writing (SUNY Purchase).

Jason Gray Platt's work has been produced and developed around the country by Actors Theatre of Louisville, Denver Center Theatre Company, The Flea Theater, Round House Theater, TheatreWorks, The Institute of Contemporary Art/Boston, The Playwrights Realm, Prelude NYC, Page 73, and Red Bull Theater, and through residencies at The MacDowell Colony and Yaddo. He received a Helen Hayes Nomination for The Charles MacArthur Award for Outstanding New Play in 2013 and won Playing on Air's 2019 James Stevenson Prize. Originally from Arizona, Platt now lives in Los Angeles. He is a Core Writer of the Playwrights' Center. BA: Vassar College; MFA: Columbia University.

ACKNOWLEDGMENTS

You Across from Me premiered at the Humana Festival of New American Plays in March 2018. It was directed by Jessica Fisch, and performed by the Acting Apprentices of the 2017–2018 Professional Training Company:

Andrea Abello, Calum Bedborough, Bear Brummel, Sergio Caetano, Satya Chavez, Nayib Felix, Brandon Fox, Rigel Harris, Alaina Kai, Emily Kaplan, Emily Kleypas, Jerardo Larios, Joseph Miller, Tim Peters, Marika Proctor, Omer Abbas Salem, Jack Schmitt, Suzy Weller, Karoline Xu and Jenna Zhu.

with casting for specific pieces as follows:

The Prologue by Jason Gray Platt..........................Jack Schmitt

A Date with the Family, Part One by Dipika Guha
RADIO ANNOUNCER................................Bear Brummel
DAUGHTER...Emily Kaplan
MOTHER..Suzy Weller
FATHER..Joseph Miller
JUNIORS ....Tim Peters and Jack Schmitt

the origin of the cheese by Jaclyn Backhaus
REMBRANDT..Nayib Felix
JURGENS..Brandon Fox
THE CHEESE..Karoline Xu

~~Diversity~~ Inclusion by Brian Otaño
CHRISTINE..Marika Proctor
QUINN...Rigel Harris
HAMISH...Jerardo Larios
ABDULLAH..Tim Peters
MATEO..Calum Bedborough
HELEN...Jenna Zhu
ASHLEY...Alaina Kai
RAYFORD...Omer Abbas Salem

A Date with the Family, Part Two by Dipika Guha
RADIO ANNOUNCER................................Bear Brummel
JUNIOR..Tim Peters
DAUGHTER...Emily Kaplan
MOTHER..Suzy Weller
RACHEL...Andrea Abello
FATHER...Joseph Miller

Olive by Brian Otaño
PAMELA ....Satya Chavez
GEORGE.. Sergio Caetano
VLADIMIR..Brandon Fox
NATALKA...Emily Kleypas
NURSE ....Jenna Zhu

Mabel and Clare by Jason Gray Platt
MABEL..Marika Proctor
CLARE .... Nayib Felix

Just Right by Jason Gray Platt
A... Andrea Abello
B... Bear Brummel
1 ....Emily Kleypas
2 ....Joseph Miller
3 .... Karoline Xu
4 .... Alaina Kai

Mother's Blessings by Dipika Guha
BOYS ....Jack Schmitt, Nayib Felix,
                Omer Abbas Salem, Sergio Caetano,
                Tim Peters, Jerardo Larios and Bear Brummel
WOMAN ....Rigel Harris
MAN...Calum Bedborough

A Date with the Family, Part Three by Dipika Guha
RADIO ANNOUNCER.. Bear Brummel
MOTHER ....Suzy Weller
FATHER...Joseph Miller
DAUGHTER.. Emily Kaplan
JUNIORS ....Tim Peters and Jack Schmitt

The National Foosball Championships by Jaclyn Backhaus
conceived with The Ensemble
JUNIE... Emily Kaplan
CHIP ....Calum Bedborough
LILY-ANNE...Emily Kleypas
TRENT ....Joseph Miller
REF..Jack Schmitt
GREAT LAKES GUY..Marika Proctor
and The Ensemble

The Epilogue by Jason Gray Platt ....The Ensemble and the following production staff:

Scenic Designer	Arnulfo Maldonado
Costume Designer	Jessica Pabst
Lighting Designer	Isabella Byrd
Sound Designer	M. L. Dogg
Stage Manager	Katherine Thesing
Dramaturg	Jessica Reese
Fight Coordinator	Ryan Bourque
Dialect Coach	Rachel Hillmer
Properties Master	Heather Lindert
Directing Assistant	Jelani Cornick
Assistant Dramaturg	Meghan McLeroy

You Across from Me was commissioned and developed by Actors Theatre of Louisville.

Joey Miller, Jack Schmitt, Emily Kleypas,
Emily Kaplan, and Calum Bedborough
in *You Across from Me*

42nd Humana Festival of New American Plays
Actors Theatre of Louisville, 2018
Photo by Bill Brymer

You Across From Me

The Prologue
by Jason Gray Platt

THE PROLOGUE
followed shortly thereafter by

THE EPILOGUE

as spoken by M. _____ and dedicated to
HIS ROYAL BEARDNESS the DIRECTOR of ARTISTIC
Your Royal Beardness's
Most Humble
Most Obedient
And Most Faithful Servant

———————

Jason Gray Platt

The Twenty-Fifth of February
Year of our Lord Two Thousand and Eighteen

The prologue, spoken by M._____

Hello! And bienvenue mes chers amis
To our staging of *You Across from Me!*
First off—I'd be the basest of monsters
If I failed to thank our noble sponsors:
The Humana Foundation, for their zest
In supporting our hallowed new play fest,
The Kentucky Arts Council—those dear hearts—
Louisville's generous Fund for the Arts,
And the Roy Cockrum Foundation—Medici
To our Professional Training Company.
For your safety, keep aisles and exits clear.
During the show, should you need to disappear
Climb the aisle for a mezzanine egress.
Don't use doors on stage; you'll cause a hot mess.
At this time, please silence your devices;
Ringing phones prompt human sacrifices.

Before we play our dramatic vignettes,
I've been asked to send the playwrights' regrets.
They'd hoped to be here for tonight's debut
But... well, so, look—can I be real with you?
They'd hoped their show would be a luscious feast.
Joy and woe consumed, catharsis released.
The catch is—our playwrights can't cook for shit.
They think ribs are smoked in an orchestra pit.
All writers think about are their fables;
These four don't even own dining tables!
They'll eat off tables for foosball, chess, pool,
For surgery, drafting, one used a stool.
For them, tables are any flat surface,
But that misses the object's main purpose!
True tables forge feelings of unity.
Individuals become community
There, even just for an hour or two.
We hold back some ME to make space for YOU.
So if after these brutes' foul stage cuisine,
You must run to the critical—em—latrine,
I beg you: don't blame the apprentices
For foodborne viruses in these sentences.
The next time these playwrights grace our venue,
Don't be surprised if they're on the menu.

A DATE WITH THE FAMILY, PART ONE
by Dipika Guha

Darkness.

We hear the sound of static turning into iconic instrumental music from the 1950s.

Lights up on a classic American domestic scene from the 50s. A SON *and* DAUGHTER *wipe dishes clean together at a dining table complete with a decorative flower centerpiece, napkins, cups and plates.* No food. *A hat stand in one corner of the room, a radio. The music runs under the commentary of the* RADIO ANNOUNCER, *a male voice who has an omnipotent feel to him.*

RADIO ANNOUNCER V/O. This boy and girl look quite content. And why not? They're looking forward to an important date. <u>Dinner at Home with the Family</u>. What's the matter? Doesn't that sound exciting to you? Well, for them it's a special occasion. First of all Daughter has changed from her school clothes into something more festive.

(*The* DAUGHTER *does us a favor and makes a little spin so we can see her dress. It's gingham. It's pretty. So is she. The son,* JUNIOR, *runs offstage.*)

Dressing a little makes her feel and consequently look more charming.

(*Lights on* MOTHER *reading a newspaper.*)

Mother too changes from her daytime clothes.

(*She quickly puts it away and taps at her hair making sure it's perfect.*)

The women of this family seem to think they owe it to the men of the family to look relaxed, rested and attractive at dinner time.

(*She steps away from the scene and begins to apply lipstick. It's a subdued color.*)

Thank you Ladies.

(MOTHER *and* DAUGHTER *smile benignly, as though to say, why of course! Just then,* FATHER *enters, hat, briefcase, coat.*)

Father too looks forward to this date with his family.

He has had a hard day at the office.

(FATHER *wipes his brow. He hangs his hat and coat up.*)

But, right now he will relax at dinner with those he loves.

But where o where did Junior go?

(JUNIOR *runs back on eagerly. He's black. The tape stops. The family all stare at* BLACK JUNIOR.)

There appears to be a technical problem.

We're going to take a pause right here while we fix it. Don't go anywhere folks!

(*We go to dark.*

Then the same rousing instrumental music from the beginning of the piece. Lights up on WHITE JUNIOR *in the position* BLACK JUNIOR *was in prior to the blackout.* WHITE JUNIOR *resumes greeting his father.*)

RADIO ANNOUNCER V/O. Junior greets his Dad as though he is genuinely glad to see him.

(*The family do NOT acknowledge anything has changed.*)

Ahhh... dinner time.

(*The family make their way to the table.*

WHITE JUNIOR *runs ahead and pulls a chair out for* DAUGHTER.)

Junior seats his sister.

(*He runs around the table and seats* MOTHER.)

Then, helps Mother to her chair like he would his Best Girl.

The family all converse pleasantly while Father serves.

> (*The family all laugh merrily together on cue.*
> WHITE JUNIOR *goes to grab his fork, when* DAUGHTER *and* MOTHER *look at him pointedly.*)

No one starts eating until Father has served himself.

> (*As* FATHER *serves himself invisible food,* BLACK JUNIOR *runs in to take his place at the table.*)

This is the time for pleasant discussion in a thoroughly relaxed mood.

> (*They unfold their napkins more or less in unison.*)

Tell Mother how good the food is.

> (BLACK JUNIOR *sees* WHITE JUNIOR *in his chair.* WHITE JUNIOR *gives his mother a thumbs up.*)

It makes her want to continue pleasing you.

> (BLACK JUNIOR *circles the table in confusion.*
> BLACK JUNIOR *arrives at* WHITE JUNIOR*'s chair,* WHITE JUNIOR *stands up and then both* JUNIORS *go to sit at the same time. Both* JUNIORS *stand up again and look at one another in confusion, belligerence?*)

Back to the table Junior... come on... back you come.

> (WHITE JUNIOR *lingers, staring at* BLACK JUNIOR. RADIO ANNOUNCER*'s voice strains to sound normal.*)

You don't want to make Father angry now, do you Junior?

> (WHITE JUNIOR *and* BLACK JUNIOR *both shake their heads no.*)

Father doesn't like to do what he does when he gets angry, but he does it for your own good, you know that don't you Junior?

> (BLACK JUNIOR *and* WHITE JUNIOR *shake their heads yes as* FATHER *stands slowly, his shadow falling over them all.*)

Pleasant unemotional conversation helps digestion.

> (*Blackout.*)

**the origin of the cheese
an origin story**
by Jaclyn Backhaus

a dining hall in the olden days. a couple of rich kids pouring wine

REMBRANDT. check out my flagon

JURGENS. sorry sup?

REMBRANDT. yo check out my flagon
super full

(jurgens *looks in rembrandt's flagon. a great pour*)

JURGENS. wine bitch
drink it down

REMBRANDT. can i cheers u!

JURGENS. yes

REMBRANDT. ok i shall cheers u
we can cheers about the bountiful quantities of our plenty

JURGENS. yeah like cheers to all the meats and cheeses
former goats and pigs and cow milk that is now pieces of flesh
and also of fatty cheese
overstuffed in our larder
and on our dank tabe

REMBRANDT. i love riches

JURGENS. cheers

REMBRANDT. cheers
to feeling full

> (*they drink
> lip smackin*)

JURGENS. wine!

REMBRANDT. lip smackin.

JURGENS. mm
excess
delish

REMBRANDT. love excess

JURGENS. loooove excess

REMBRANDT. love. excess.

JURGENS. i'm a huge fan?
of excess.

REMBRANDT. mm yes

JURGENS. excess
excess

REMBRANDT. can you remember the first time you were ever like the first time you ever realized like
"oh
excess"
like
"i have excess"

JURGENS. like the first time i realized it?
or the first time i loved that i realized it?

REMBRANDT. or the first time that you realized that you realized it, and that you loved it
JURGENS. yeah yeah
probably the time when i was three and you were five
REMBRANDT. yas
loved that time
JURGENS. and you were like mummy mummy mummy
REMBRANDT. ya
JURGENS. you were like mummy mummy can i please have a pony?
REMBRANDT. "for christmas?" i was like
all like big eyes
"for christmas?"
JURGENS. "mummy can i please have a pony for christmas?"
REMBRANDT. big eyes all big eyes
little pray hands like
"mummy oh mummy?"
JURGENS. yeah and then like the next day in our front yard
pony parade
REMBRANDT. pony paRADE
ponies
circling the driveway of our courtyard
and then i got to keep like all the ones i wanted
JURGENS. i remember being like
three
and being like
this is way too many ponies.
REMBRANDT. (*nodding*) i kept eleven ponies
of fourteen
JURGENS. and then half of them died
because you were five and you didn't know how to take care of ponies
REMBRANDT. that
my sibling
is excess
JURGENS. muthafuckin excessssssssssssss
REMBRANDT. exceeeeeeeeeeeeeessssss
i want cheese
JURGENS. i want cheese
REMBRANDT. yo nab some hunks of cheese
JURGENS. love

cheese
REMBRANDT. excess? and
cheese
JURGENS. (*looking at the cheese, near to a trance*) hey rembrandt
REMBRANDT. sup jurgens
JURGENS. what's the opposite of excess
REMBRANDT. (*shaking head*) dont think about that
JURGENS. is it dexcess?
REMBRANDT. (*shaking head*) dont think about that
JURGENS. dont think about that?
REMBRANDT. nah sib
dont think about that
dont think about that
dont think about that
JURGENS. (*trance broken*) aight
REMBRANDT and JURGENS. *don't think about that!*
REMBRANDT. flagons up!
JURGENS. flagons up BRAH
> (*they cheers*
> *they drink*
> *they nab some hunks of cheese*
> *they take a bite*
> *a blinding light*
> the cheese)

THE CHEESE. see here
a vision from our collective past
these euro bros
whose descendants
dutch-settled in a land anew
an eulogy for me
i am the cheese
used
abused
the cheese
undermined
exploited
the cheese
eaten by monsters
the cheese
and here

a scene
of my death
by the hands and mouths
of these privileged two
my last wish:
that i
could choke
them

    (the cheese *does a little fragmented dance*
    the siblings look a little queasy)

and as i am swallowed

    (*they begin to choke*)

could it be
though i am dying
i attain my wish

    (*choking bros*)

in my last dying breaths
as i am torn apart
i can say i was a martyr
to a greater cause

REMBRANDT. the cheese—
is bad—
bro?

JURGENS. it's bad cheese bro—
bro!

REMBRANDT. bro?

JURGENS. bro!!

REMBRANDT. BROOOOO?!?!?!

JURGENS. BROOAOAOAOAOAOAOAOOAOAOOAOAOAOAOAOAA

BOTH BROS. ABAOASBAOSBOOAOABOASOAISAJSOSJOJOJOAIJOSJOAI-
SJOASJ

    (*the siblings choke*
    gluttony death
    the cheese)

THE CHEESE. in death
lodged in two throats
i take one last look
at the pantheon upon which i was once cast

    (the cheese *looks at the table*

meats wine mold grapes dead birds candle wax decrepit fruit butter crispy bread.

meats
wine
mold
grapes
dead birds
botulism garlic
candle wax
jars of ____
decrepit fruit
butter
crispy bread
and me. I am the Cheese.
we are the forgotten ones
the ones trod upon in unmerciful world
do not underestimate
that which you devour

~~Diversity~~ Inclusion
by Brian Otaño

<u>The Finalists</u>

MATEO – *an unflappable optimist, fresh out of graduate school. The youngest in the room.*

CHRISTINE – *cool, serene and continental.*

ABDULLAH – *a shark, ambitious, charming, hyper-observant. A gay man.*

QUINN – *the eldest of the bunch, a boldly sardonic, wicked jokester.*

All of the finalists should be played by white actors and swap roles when indicated in the text.

<u>The Executives</u>

ASHLEY – *Her smile never reaches her eyes. Has an emotional support animal. Played by an African American woman.*

HELEN – *Unkempt, but doing her best. Played by an Asian American woman.*

HAMISH – *Bright, peppy, always smiling. The newbie. Played by a Latino.*

RAYFORD – *A brick wall, with a razor-sharp gaze. Someone's nephew. Played by a Middle Eastern man.*

Setting:
Now.
Burbank, California.
Lights up on a conference room.

MATEO *practices smiling. He's a ball of nervous energy.* CHRISTINE *paces, rehearsing responses to questions.* QUINN *sits at the table and stares at* MATEO, *perhaps a little annoyed.* HAMISH *ushers* ABDULLAH *into the room.*

HAMISH. In you go! Good luck!

ABDULLAH. Thank you!

(*Oozing charm, glad-handing the others.*)

Hi, everyone, I'm Abdullah, I'm thrilled to meet you all.

CHRISTINE. I'm Christine, hello, hi, enchanté.

MATEO. (*Giving him a big bear hug.*) I'm Mateo! We made it! The final four! I'm so excited!

ABDULLAH. Wait… Are you not the executives?

CHRISTINE. No, we're the other finalists.

ABDULLAH. (*Sitting, freezing over.*) Oh… Hello. I didn't know this would be a group interview. Did you?

QUINN. Yes. I've been a finalist once before, back when this used to be called a "diversity" initiative.

ABDULLAH. How many slots are there this year?

QUINN. One. They only need one of us to be considered diverse.

CHRISTINE. I don't mind a group interview. You can sit back if you need to, or you know, pick up the cues everyone else throws out there.

QUINN. Plus, you have the added comfort of watching as your competitors say something untoward and drown as it happens right before your eyes. *That's* always helpful.

CHRISTINE. …Right.

(RAYFORD, HELEN *and* ASHLEY *burst into the room. They tote notebooks and pens.* ASHLEY *carries a small plastic cage with a hamster in it.*)

HELEN. (*Sing-songy.*) Finalists! Today's the day!

ASHLEY. Good morning, all. Oh… You're all so beautiful—

RAYFORD. (*To Abdullah.*) Get out of my chair.

(HAMISH *takes up the rear, carrying a mop and pushing on a cart covered in a red sheet. The finalists line up before the executives as they sit.* ASHLEY *pulls the hamster out of its cage and pets it.*)

ASHLEY. Firstly, the network is thrilled to be building a more inclusive work environment and you all represent a massive step forward. Kudos all around.

(MATEO *claps. His enthusiasm wanes when no one else follows suit.*)

Yes, by all means, give us a hand.

(*They all clap.*)

HELEN. You guys, three thousand writers applied for this diversity—

ASHLEY/RAYFORD. *Inclusion*—

HELEN. —inclusion program, and we've winnowed the competition down to you four.

ASHLEY. We had to make some really hard decisions. We'd love to take all of you, but we just, we *can't*. But you should be proud—.

RAYFORD. Great, right. Icebreakers. Full name, hometown, what you ate for breakfast. I'll start. Rayford Lee Etherton V, Hoover, Alabama, three McGriddles and a whiskey.

(*To* ABDULLAH.)

Go.

ABDULLAH. Uh—. I'm Abdullah Al Rahim. I'm from Silver Springs, Maryland, and nothing. I had nothing for breakfast.

(*To* RAYFORD.)

I *love* your pocket square, by the way. Very sharp.

RAYFORD. Thank you?

MATEO. I'm Mateo Rodriguez, I had Cheerios for breakfast and I'm from the Bronx.

HAMISH. (*Throwing up a gang sign.*) What-what! Biggup to the Bronx!

MATEO. Oh, are you from the Bronx, too?

HAMISH. What? No, I just—.

ASHLEY. Don't hurt yourself. Hello. I'm Ashley, I'm from Champaign, Illinois and I had coconut water and a Parliament Light for breakfast.

(*Holding up the hamster.*)

This is Gwyneth Paltrow, my emotional support animal. She was the smartest in her litter and she's vegan—for mostly moral reasons.

(*To* CHRISTINE.)

Hi.

CHRISTINE. I'm Christine Jenkins, I've—.

ASHLEY. Your hair is beautiful, Christine Jenkins.
>   (*Touching* CHRISTINE*'s hair.*)

Can I touch it?

CHRISTINE. Ok…
>   (*Pulling away gracefully.*)

I've had a lot of hometowns—.

ASHLEY. Foster care? Teenage runaway?

CHRISTINE. Oil brat, actually. I've lived in Cairo, Rio De Janeiro, Houston and Perth before I settled in Paris for boarding school.

ASHLEY. Oh. Huh. Good for you.

QUINN. Hello! I'm Quinn. I'm from San Francisco. I had eggs and toast for breakfast and washed them down with the blood of a small child.
>   (*The executives laugh.*)

ASHLEY. I like her.
>   (*To* QUINN.)

I like you.

QUINN. What's the mop for?

HELEN. We'll touch on that later. Greetings, everybody. I'm Helen Shires. I hail from Walla Walla, Washington, and you guys? I was so bad. I ate a fistful of gummy bears and warm Diet Coke for breakfast, if we're truth-telling.

HAMISH. I'm Hamish Hellman. I had Raisin Bran for breakfast. And I'm from Rye, New York. Westchester in the hizzy!

RAYFORD. Great. Now. We want to know what's *not* in your submission materials.

HELEN. Dazzle us.

ASHLEY. But don't try too hard.

HELEN. And have fun!

RAYFORD. But keep it brief. We've gone over your resumes, so how 'bout we *not* trot out all your credentials and your Ivy League Master's Degrees, mmkay?
>   (*Giving* HAMISH *the floor.*)

New Guy… Take it away.

HAMISH. Mateo Rodriguez! Where are you from?

MATEO. The Bronx.

HAMISH. But where are you *from*? Like, where were you *born*?

MATEO. Also, the Bronx.

HAMISH. Okay, as a Latinks. Latin-ex? How are we—? A *Latin*. As a Latin, what is it about this diversity—.

ASHLEY/RAYFORD/HELEN. Inclusion.

HAMISH. Sorry— How does this *inclusion* program speak to you?

MATEO. America is a melting pot, truly, and I think it's great that Hollywood wants to reflect that and open its doors to people who disrupt the "norm"—.

ASHLEY. Mateo, relax. This isn't a pageant. Breathe.

HAMISH. Pretend it's check day back in El Barrio and we're all here to party. Helen and Ashley are doing each other's hair on their front stoop.

ASHLEY. Rayford's bouncing a toddler on his knee—.

HAMISH. Is it his? Who can say? Ha ha ha! Try it again. Just be your normal, *spicy* self.

MATEO. (*With a pained grin.*) I don't know, uh—. Can you come back to me, actually?

RAYFORD. Alright, moving on... AbdullAH—. AHBdullah? Ah—you know what? Doesn't matter. ABE. Hi. So, you're a gay. We get it. And that's great. But I guess the question is: given your very *specific* lifestyle choice and perspective, how do you think your voice would resonate with our audience? With, you know, normal people.

ABDULLAH. My submission script was about drone pilots with PTSD, it wasn't exactly *swishy*—.

RAYFORD. When did you *know*? That you were gay, I mean.

ABDULLAH. I figured it out pretty early on.

RAYFORD. And that was okay? I mean, culturally? You weren't living in fear of being shunned by your family or being stoned to death?

ABDULLAH. No When I came out to my parents, they took me to Jamba Juice and bought me Spice Girls tickets. It was fine—.

MATEO. I didn't come out until after *college*. It was... a struggle. I—

HELEN. Wait, what?

ASHLEY. You're... *also* a gay?

HAMISH. Can one of you explain Grindr to me?

RAYFORD. This is a monumental fuck-up.

ABDULLAH. Why? Do we cancel each other out or something?

RAYFORD. Dun.

ASHLEY. Not necessarily... So, Christine. Brown undergrad? Yale grad? Oil brat? You're very... poised? You've got a very *calm* vibe...

CHRISTINE. Thank you. You sound surprised.

ASHLEY. Sure but... *Intrigued* would be the better word...?

CHRISTINE. Did you have a question for me?

HELEN. No, I think we're good. Quinn! Hi, there. You submitted a crime dramedy about pot farmers. So, I'm confused.

QUINN. Why would that be?

HELEN. I'm just—. I don't know, it seems out of character.

QUINN. I'm a perfect stranger to you, what would you know about my "character"?

HELEN. Well, I guess what I mean to ask is… *culturally,* what do you think you bring to the table?

> (*A shift.* HELEN *and* QUINN *swap identities.*)

HELEN. I'm not quite sure what cultural boxes I'm supposed to be checking off for you, but I'm not a submissive naif, a femme fatale or the product of tiger parents. But… I'm aesthetically versatile. You could cut a diamond with my dialogue. And I'm good in a room—.

QUINN. If you're so good, then why do you need to break into Hollywood through this program?

HELEN. This is just as viable a way into the business as any, right?

QUINN. Sure but… we're trying to fill a diversity slot—.

> (HAMISH *and* MATEO *swap identities.*)

RAYFORD/ASHLEY. An *inclusion* slot.

QUINN. Because we want to appear more / inclusive.

> (RAYFORD *and* ABDULLAH *swap identities.*)

RAYFORD/ABDULLAH. / We are—

ABDULLAH. Inclusive of multiple cultures, as evidenced by this program's existence.

> (*The executives exchange looks. It's awkward.* CHRISTINE *and* ASHLEY *swap identities through the following.*)

CHRISTINE. I just want to say—.

ASHLEY. It would be great if you could find room for all of us. I think leaving one spot open for a person of color is a great *start,* but I think we can do better.

CHRISTINE. Thank you for that input. We're trying. Really. This is so hard. Normally, the decision is mine to make when all is said and done, but this year, we're trying something different. In keeping with the "inclusivity," we're putting the power in your hands.

ASHLEY. Really? But how—?

CHRISTINE. Well, you can leave now or…

ABDULLAH. (*Unveiling the weapons.*) Choose your weapon. The last person standing wins.

CHRISTINE. (*To* MATEO.) Be sure to mop up the carnage when it's over. And Gwyneth Paltrow's cage needs new cedar chips.

(CHRISTINE *hands* MATEO *the cage and leaves.* MATEO *finds a poncho somewhere and puts it on.*)

ABDULLAH. I want to watch.

QUINN. (*Shoving* ABDULLAH *out of the room.*) You're all great! You're all winners! Good luck! May the odds be ever in your favor!

(*The finalists are left alone with the weapons. Despair. Resignation. Hunger. Rage.*
HAMISH *reaches for a weapon. Before he can grab one,* HELEN *flips the cart over.*)

HAMISH. What are you doing?

HELEN. We're not doing this.

HAMISH. I... I really need this job and they've only got room for one of us—.

ASHLEY. *That's* bullshit.

RAYFORD. It *is* bullshit, but what do you suggest we do about it?

HELEN. (*With an eye on* MATEO.) Take a hostage and negotiate.

(HELEN *picks up a knife and advances on* MATEO. *He cowers.*)

MATEO. Please, no, don't hurt me!

(HELEN *grabs the hamster cage from* MATEO.)

HELEN. I wasn't planning on it.

RAYFORD. Yes! Leverage Gwyneth Paltrow! There are so many more interns where he came from.

HAMISH. Is this really the way we're solving this?

HELEN. She gave us the option to leave. Go now if you're going.

HAMISH. I guess I'll stay if you're staying. Just don't hurt Gwyneth.

ASHLEY. You were ready to kill us all for this job two seconds ago. But now you're worried about the chinchilla. Okay, I see you.

RAYFORD. That's a hamster, by the way.

HELEN. (*To* MATEO.) Go get the executives.

(MATEO *leaves. With the knife in one hand,* HELEN *removes Gwyneth from her cage. From offstage—*)

ABDULLAH. That was fast. Ten bucks says it's the homo.

CHRISTINE. WHICH ONE?!

(*They enter laughing.* CHRISTINE *gasps at the sight of* HELEN *and the finalists.*)

GWYNETH! DON'T YOU HURT HER!
HELEN. (*Stepping forward.*) So… Welcome back! Now, let's talk about that one slot…
(*Blackout.*)

A Date with the Family, Part Two
by Dipika Guha

Same domestic scene from the 1950s. A BOY *and a* GIRL *wipe dishes clean together at a dining table, decorative flower centerpiece, napkins, etc. Hat stand, radio.*
RADIO ANNOUNCER V/O. This boy and girl look quite content. And why not? They're looking forward to an important date. <u>Dinner at Home with the Family.</u> What's the matter? Doesn't that sound exciting to you? Well, for them it's a special occasion. First of all Daughter has changed from her school clothes into something more festive.
(*The* GIRL *does us a favor and makes a little spin so we can see her dress. It's pretty. So is she. The* BOY *runs offstage.*)
Dressing a little makes her feel and consequently <u>look</u> more charming.
(*Lights on* MOTHER *reading a newspaper. She quickly puts it away and taps at her hair, making sure it's perfect. She looks all around surreptitiously. When she's sure no one's looking, she begins to apply some very red lipstick.*)
Mother too changes from her daytime clothes.
(MOTHER *turns the radio off.* DAUGHTER *continues to set the table as* MOTHER *undresses in front of us, throwing off her apron and gingham dress for something else. What? A witch's cape? A pirate outfit? A doctor's white coat? It might be any of those or something else so long as it's entirely different.* MOTHER *loses herself in her reverie. She forgets to see that* DAUGHTER *is now watching her.*)
MOTHER. It's not uncommon for women like me to yearn for a kitchen.
A kitchen where every day could be laundry day if I had a machine.
A machine where I could watch how dry the clothes inside were getting
By the positioning of the
Knobs.
(MOTHER *looks to her right and a window appears. She looks out the window searchingly.*)
Rachel… Mrs. Adams across the street has a George, I mean, a kitchen

The kitchen, yes, but the George, the George I suppose gave her the kitchen
    (*Suddenly* RACHEL *appears at the window. She locks eyes with* MOTHER; *sympathy, love and desire all wrapped in one.*)
Because he saw for himself
The look on her face
The sensuous delight of her fingertips caressing the
Toaster
Her lips brushing against the cool buttery cream from the electric
Blender
Her eyes
Her eyes, well
Her eyes say it all
When they glance in the direction of the
Fridge with its cool...
Ice cubes
I can't imagine how a woman like her must feel
Knowing that her husband lov—*knows* her well enough to to
Anticipate
The eyes, lips and finger-
Tips
Of his
Wife, her chores diminishing, hourly!
    (FATHER *enters the house, hat, briefcase, he does not see* MOTHER.)
Buying her another hour to look, gaze, search
Into the trees outside
    (MOTHER *looks back towards the window but* RACHEL *has vanished. In her place is now a tree.*)
To penetrate their thin leaf veins
Their sticky, prickly undersides
Their crackly core
Their gristled hide
Made hard from time
Too much time
Another hour not to sweep
But to *see*
    (*She stops.*)
What a gift.
To be seen.
    (*She turns the radio back on.*)

OLIVE

by Brian Otaño

Characters:

PAMELA – *Late 20s, a successful professional with a messy private life. The Alpha-sibling. A Nuyorican.*

GEORGE – *Early 20s, sensitive, a serial monogamist. The Beta-sibling. A Nuyorican.*

NATALKA – *22, works at a cellular phone store. A Russian immigrant.*

VLADIMIR – *21, a student. A Russian immigrant.*

NURSE – *20s, female-identifying, salty, with a thick New York accent.*

Lights up on the Hospice Lounge at Bellevue Medical Center in New York City.

PAM sits in a corner of the lounge, an icepack pressed to her cheek. GEORGE sits across from her, picking at a muffin.

NATALKA sits in a far corner of the lounge, eating food out of a Tupperware container. VLADIMIR stares down at a textbook in the seat across from her.

PAM. Will you quit dicking around with that muffin? *Comelo, ya, coño!* [Eat it, already. Fuck!]

GEORGE. You've got a problem with the way I'm eating now?

PAM. You're picking at that thing like a little bitch. Why did you even buy it?

GEORGE. It was the only thing in the pastry carousel that looked appetizing.

(PAM *sits back in her chair and sighs.*)

PAM. It's almost four a.m. She's gonna go over her time. I know it.

GEORGE. Had you kept your hands to yourself, we wouldn't be visiting Dad in shifts.

PAM. She started it.

GEORGE. She bumped into you.

PAM. Fuck outta here, that was a shoulder check.

GEORGE. Potato, potahto, woman. You're regressing to your old middle school shit at warp speed. You should know better than to throw hands at a freaking hospice. *Maleducada.*

PAM. Look, she put hands on me, she got dealt with.

(*Flexing her jaw.*)

Do you think this'll bruise?

GEORGE. Yeah. Probably.

PAM. It better clear up before the funeral.

(GEORGE *wilts at the mention of a funeral. He looks over at* VLADIMIR.)

What do you think they're in for?

GEORGE. Their mother. Brain cancer.

PAM. *Pobrecitos* [Poor things], they're practically babies.

GEORGE. He's been staring at that same page for two days. He's kinda cute.

PAM. Queen, you're out here trying to catch a dick in a hospice but I'm the *maleducada*. Okay. I see how it is.

GEORGE. Hey, it's not like I was trying to blow him in the linen closet. He just… He looks sad.

PAM. You're hopeless. You're drawn to broken people.

GEORGE. Marc isn't broken

PAM. Marc is a bike messenger who spells his name with a "c." He's not the one.

GEORGE. The bike messenger gig just keeps his lights on and his thighs on point. Marc's chosen profession is "mime artist."

PAM. I rest my case. Also, have you seen him eat? Every time he takes a bite, his tongue unfurls down past his chin. It's not Christian.

GEORGE. He's had nothing but nice things to say about you. Look, he's not like us. He's warm.

PAM. He's weak.

GEORGE. He's sensitive. You need to get your shit together, you're lashing out at everyone—.

PAM. I am not.

GEORGE. You're picking on Marc. You just rumbled with our stepmom—.

PAM. Hold up. Stop. Myra is *not* our stepmom… Matter of fact, she's lucky we're letting her see Dad at all. Mom and Dad never divorced. Myra's got no legal rights—we could have her ass booted out of this place in an anime minute.

(NATALKA *begins to cry.* VLADIMIR *comforts her. After a moment, he hands her an olive. She eats it.*)

George, listen, you and Marc aren't dating in a bubble. When we take boyfriends and husbands, we're bringing these people into our lives, into our family. You have to consider what they bring to the equation.

GEORGE. Every guy you've ever brought home has been a complete waste of skin, including your ex-husband. So—.

(PAM *and* GEORGE *notice* NATALKA *crying. Awkward silence, pins and needles.* PAM *stares at her nailbeds.* GEORGE *steals glances at* NATALKA *and* VLADIMIR. PAM's *phone buzzes. She looks at it.*)

PAM. Titi Margie just invited us to see the new Tarantino tomorrow.

GEORGE. *Tonight* tomorrow or *tomorrow* tomorrow? Either way, we shouldn't go.

PAM. …It's probably not going to happen tomorrow. They said he had a week.

(*A lull. A shift in gears.*)

GEORGE. I wish Dad had tried to integrate Myra into our lives. We're living through this fucking nightmare alongside a stranger.

PAM. Dad approached me about Myra when they moved in together. I went to the house. It was just me and Dad, she was at work. You could still smell the carpet glue, it was that fresh. The dining room table was completely bare, no junk mail, no textbooks, no ring stains from glasses left on the bare wood. The whole place had "fresh start" written all over it. He said, "Myra's the woman in my life. You two should know her." I said, "When you can hang with George and one of his boyfriends, I'll have coffee with you and that heifer."

GEORGE. Pam, what is wrong with you?

PAM. What? I was sticking up for you.

GEORGE. Why? Being gay and being an adulterer aren't exactly on the same moral ground. And… Had we gotten to know Myra, we could've had more time with him. He wouldn't have had to split his time.

PAM. I didn't realize the clock would run out so quickly. I'm sorry. I mean, could you imagine? Us, Mom, Dad and Myra. And *Marc!* At dinner? Thanksgiving dinner?!

(GEORGE *falls down a rabbit hole over the thought of Thanksgiving.*)

PAM. What?

GEORGE. Nothing… Just… Thanksgiving.

(GEORGE *begins to weep. He buries his face in his hands.* PAM *doesn't know how to comfort him. A few moments later, a* NURSE *walks into the lounge.* PAM, GEORGE, NATALKA *and* VLADIMIR *all look up. The nurse points to* PAM.)

NURSE. You. Your sparring partner just left. I guess it's your turn.

PAM. (*To* GEORGE.) You coming?

GEORGE. (*Clearing his throat.*) I need a minute.

(PAM *pats his arm and leaves. The* NURSE *smiles and nods at the others and follows* PAM *out.* GEORGE *sits alone in his corner.* NATALKA *holds out a container of olives to* VLADIMIR *and gestures toward* GEORGE. *He takes them over to* GEORGE *and offers them.*)

Oh. I'm good, thanks.

(VLADIMIR looks over at NATALKA.)

VLADIMIR. *On ne khochet iku.* [He doesn't want them.]

NATALKA. *Prosto dayte.* [Just give them to him.]

(VLADIMIR *holds out the container of olives again.* GEORGE *takes one.*)

GEORGE. Thank you.

(VLADIMIR *puts a small pack of Kleenex down in front of* GEORGE *and returns to his seat.* GEORGE *looks at it and looks over at* NATALKA *and* VLADIMIR. *They each hold up a hand—a wave? A show of solidarity?* GEORGE *isn't sure. He returns the gesture. Blackout.*)

MABEL AND CLARE
by Jason Gray Platt

The play goes something like this:

A small, four-person table with four chairs.

A modest apartment.

Upbeat instrumental music.

MABEL *enters. Late 20s, excited, anxious.*

Dressed for an occasion.

She methodically sets the table.

Shakes out her best tablecloth and delicately flattens it atop the table.

Drops two place settings across from one another, everything at exact right angles.

Places cloth napkins, glasses, and silverware on the place settings.

Makes small adjustments to the silverware arrangement.

Makes even smaller adjustments.

Until it is all just so.

Then MABEL *exits briefly and returns with a centerpiece—a large vase full of flowers, with a card attached.*

She reads the card. Treasures the words. Inhales deeply the fresh fragrance of the flowers.

The bounties of life can be truly great.

A fly buzzes out of the flowers, dissolving her revelry. She swats at the fly and it buzzes off.

She places the vase on the table.

The table tilts.

MABEL *is sure she must have imagined this.*

She lifts up the vase.

The table springs back.

MABEL *lowers the vase.*

The table tilts.

This is unacceptable! Everything will be ruined!

She pushes down on the opposite end from the tilt.

The table springs back up and splashes water from the vase everywhere.

MABEL *is horrified.*

But just then, the doorbell rings.

MABEL *wants to fix the table but has to answer the door.*

She exits, and in a moment returns with CLARE—*also late 20s, also excited and anxious.*

He presents a bottle of wine that he has brought. How thoughtful!

They share a moment of charged anticipation. Anything could happen tonight.

MABEL, *embarrassed, apologizes and explains the table situation then says she'll be right back.*

She exits.

CLARE *reads the card he sent along with the flowers.*

God, he's good with words. He brushes a little dirt off his shoulder for a job well done.

MABEL *returns with another cloth napkin and a corkscrew.*

She hands the corkscrew to CLARE *then ducks under the table to investigate the situation.*

As MABEL *searches for the faulty table leg,* CLARE *uncorks the wine and pours them both a glass. Then tops off the glasses because, after all, it is a special evening.*

MABEL *has located the culprit, so she folds up the napkin and stuffs it under the leg.*

She starts to stand and smacks her head against the underside of the table.

A little woozy, she stands, assuring CLARE *that she is perfectly fine.*

She has to test her napkin shim first, so she presses down on the table.

The table tilts even more dramatically than before, now spilling the full glasses of wine.

Chaos!

MABEL *apologizes; no,* CLARE *apologizes.*

MABEL *runs offstage and immediately runs back on, trailing a full roll of paper towels that unspools behind her like the tail of a comet.*

They split the paper towels and furiously begin mopping up the spilled wine.

While on the ground, MABEL *shoves wads of paper towels under all four table legs—that oughta do it! The legs are now resting on giant clouds of paper towel.*

MABEL *starts to stand and again smacks her head against the underside of the table.*

MABEL *stands, distraught, semi-concussed; the night is a total loss!*

CLARE *comforts her; these things happen, it's not even very good wine, he's just enjoying spending time with her.*

They share a moment of kindness, their bodies near enough to sense the warmth of each other's skin.

Bells begin to peal. Do they both hear it? It's like a movie. Like a message from heaven. Oh wait, no—that's the timer she set for dinner.

MABEL *exits, at which point* CLARE *takes out his cell phone and uses the camera as a mirror to double-check his hair. It's on point.*

MABEL *returns, gently balancing two enormous bowls of steaming soup.*

CLARE *takes his bowl from her hands, and together they gingerly—* GINGERLY—*place the soup on the table.*

The table remains level.

A sigh of relief.

They reach for their spoons.

But wait! CLARE *wonders if they should say grace first.*

Sure, why not, says MABEL.

*They carefully—*CAREFULLY—*place their elbows on the table to say grace.*

The table remains level.

The paper towels are working.

They close their eyes and CLARE *begins to say grace.*

All of a sudden the fly returns to buzz around them.

MABEL *swats at her ear.*

She opens one eye and begins tracking the insect like a psychopathic entomologist.

The fly buzzes, and MABEL *waits.*

The fly buzzes toward them and lands on the table.

MABEL *SMACKS THE FLY*

Hitting the tabletop so violently that it tilts like a windmill and sends soup soaring up out of the bowls, coating the table and its guests.

CLARE *gamely draws a finger across his cheek and tastes the spilt soup. It's delicious!*

This time MABEL *is not embarrassed, only burning with volcanic rage. She storms off, leaving* CLARE *to retrieve another roll of paper towels from the kitchen.*

He does so, and begins to mop up the soup as MABEL *returns carrying a handsaw and a spirit level.*

CLARE *sees her intentions, pleads with her to let it go so that they can just enjoy the rest of their night.*

But MABEL *will give no quarter—she shall have her pound of wood.*

MABEL *puts the level in* CLARE'S *hand, and with maniacal glee she sets to sawing off the bottom of the offending table leg.*

She saws and saws, as CLARE *decides this might be his cue to leave. He props the level on the table, makes a call on his phone, grabs the bottle of wine, and walks off drinking straight from it.*

MABEL *is alone, sawing.*

After a moment she has achieved her goal.

She jumps up, victorious, to test the table.

It is perfectly even. Not even a hint of tilt.

She calls to CLARE *to share her conquest, and for the first time realizes that he is not there.*

She looks off to the left.

She looks off to the right.

But CLARE *is gone.*

MABEL *returns to the table, crestfallen.*

She takes the card from the flowers to read it again.

MABEL *sits in one of the chairs.*

The chair collapses underneath her.

End play.

JUST RIGHT
by Jason Gray Platt

Characters

The Interview Committee – 1, 2, 3, and 4
The Applicants – A and B
The composition of the ensemble should reflect the world outside the theater.

Text Notes

A dash (–) means the speaker has stopped themselves.
A backslash (/) denotes a point of overlapping or interruption by the following dialogue.
Text in parentheses (text) is spoken sotto voce.

A conference table.
1, 2, 3, and 4 sit on one side.
A and B on the other.

B. Like winning the lottery /
3. It's a steal /
A. And we feel so fortunate for the opportunity /
1. I thought she could have gotten more for it.
A. Don't tell her that!
1. Oh no of course not.
But all that natural light?
A. With those original built-in cabinets?
B. It's such a relief because the process is so stressful
when you're buying
and you think
this is going to be my home for the next, what
fifteen, twenty years /
4. It's an investment in your future.
B. Yes, which you also want to make responsibly.
But with what we were looking to spend
most of the places we considered were in neighborhoods that were–
A. Undergoing a lot of transition.
2. It's happening across the country.
A. The way people's lives are being uprooted is tragic.

And we really had to ask ourselves
do we want to contribute to the disintegration of a neighborhood
of a community
just to have 100 extra square feet?
We wouldn't feel right.

B. Because community–
we want you to know–
being active in our community is so important to us.

3. Well we always like to hear that /

A. Yes, we want to take the time to know our neighbors
we want to support local businesses /

4. Careful what you wish for!

B. But that is a gift, isn't it?
To be a member of a close-knit /

A. Such a gift.
And we feel so fortunate to have–
fingers crossed–
to have the opportunity to live in the building.

2. We do feel here–
and I say this as one of the newest residents who is so appreciative that this is the case–
we do feel like this building is its own little community.

1. We're like a tribe.

B. You can sense that.

2. The most important thing
in any small community
is that everyone gets along.
Everyone feels
comfortable.

B. That's so important.
And I want to say
apropos of that
that we really appreciate how diverse the building is.

A. One of the reasons we're so excited about this opportunity
even though it's a bit of a stretch for us financially
is that we're thinking about children.
And when I imagine the environment I want for my child
a big part of that is growing up in a diverse community.

1. There's simply no other way.

A. The fact that even the interview board has this range of perspectives.

It's so reassuring.

4. We take pride in knowing that everyone has an equal opportunity when they apply.

2. What matters most, though
is that the community can exist in a state of harmony
and isn't infected by anyone who is too–
How would you describe it?
Too /

3. Extreme.

2. Too extreme, yeah.

B. ...

A. What do you mean by "extreme"?

3. Are you familiar with the Goldilocks principle?

A. Goldilocks?

B. As in the fairy tale?

3. You remember the basic–

A. Little blonde girl
three bears
porridge.

3. Exactly.
Goldilocks enters the bears' house, tries to find a chair to sit in.
One is too hard, one is too soft, one is just right.

B. And doesn't it break?

3. It breaks, so she moves on to the bowls of porridge.
One too hot, one too cold, one just right.
Then the beds.
One is too hard, one is too soft, and the third?

B. Just right.

3. Just right, there you go.
Eventually this arrangement came to be known as the Goldilocks principle.
It means that dynamic systems
tend to work best under conditions that are in a comfortable middle range.

B. That makes sense.

3. We find that the principle works just as well for people.
The best way for a community to get along
is to avoid including anyone who might be
outside the zone of moderation.

A. I'm not sure I'm following–

2. Politically.

(*Beat.*)

B. You
want to know what our politics are?

A. Are you legally allowed to ask that?

3. Yes.

4. Don't misunderstand–
It's not that we want people to be apolitical.

A. I would hope not.

4. Actively participating in the political process is the foundation of a healthy democratic society.

1. The issue is that people who are on the extremes?

2. They have trouble with boundaries.

4. That's right.

2. And our feeling–
correct me if I'm wrong–
but our feeling is that this building is a home.
So it needs to be a safe space
where residents don't have to worry that their private lives will become fodder for some
political grudge match.

B. You're saying that everyone who lives here is in perfect agreement on every political issue?

3. It's not about agreement.

1. Even the four of us don't see eye to eye on everything.

3. It's about being able to disagree respectfully.

B. Oh, well, that's–
Admirable.

3. How would you describe your politics?

B. Uh.
I think we'd say we're–

A. Hard to boil it down /

B. Open-minded?

A. Liberal /

B. Not FAR left /

A. Well
not FAR far left /

B. Maybe when we were younger–
I mean in college / isn't everyone

A. The country has drifted so far to the right the past few decades / so historically

B. But you get older and you gain a little more perspective.

1. You've grown up.
It was the same for me.
When I was in school
all I wanted was for someone to hand me a rifle
and send me to man the barricades.

2. The barricades at Harvard?

1. You're supposed to be idealistic at that age.
You want to believe the world can really change
if you throw yourself against its walls hard enough.
Eventually you realize the only thing you're breaking down
is your own body.

B. I know the feeling.

3. For the record, then.
You'd place yourself somewhere near the center?

A. Out of curiosity—
How do you define extreme?

4. It comes down to your neighbors being comfortable.

3. Using the Goldilocks tale as a model
something that's extreme
if it's much too hot or much too cold
that's going to make you uncomfortable.

4. With the world today as uncertain as it is
we like to think that providing people with a little comfort
is in its own way a moral act.

2. And that idea of comfort informs every aspect of the building.
The white noise in the hallways
the seasonal rotation of flowers.
We recently brought in experts to install more soothing lighting.

B. Is that what the glow is?
Because walking into the lobby is like taking a Xanax.

A. So all you want is people to keep their private and public lives separate?

3. Well
no.

4. Separate implies different.

1. And we don't want people pretending to be something they're not for our benefit.

That would be unfair.

3. We want the public and the private to match.

1. Which is why in the lease agreement
you'll be required to list your social media handles.

A. I'm sorry?

2. That way we're able to keep track of what you post
to check for anything that might fall far off-center.

A. People don't find that a little
invasive?

4. They recognize that it's for their own safety.
In the current political climate–

ALL. Awful / What's happening / I know / Disgraceful

4. People are being assaulted
literally killed
for their beliefs.
If one of us in the building
if the man who lives next door to you
is involved in something that invites an attack or abuse
that leaves you vulnerable as well.

1. The Building Block Watch monitors everyone's online presence
just to give us a chance to protect one another.

2. Plus it's a great way to get to know your neighbors.

B. We would be on the Block Watch?

2. All residents take turns on the digital stuff.
And once you've stared at someone through a security camera for a few hours
it's hard to stay a stranger.

B. I can't imagine a Block Watch is very busy in this neighborhood.

3. Not at all.
Though you can thank them for your apartment being available.

A. Did something happen in that unit?

1. Oh, no, nothing bad.
We were just forced to evict the woman who had lived there.

4. Finally.

A. What did she do?

4. She had begun to
associate
with the wrong kind of people

A. Wow, ok.

You do realize she broke in, right?
4. Who?
A. Goldilocks.
In the story.
She breaks into the bears' cottage.
2. Nooo–
She was wandering through the forest /
B. She was just wandering, honey /
A. Sure, but just recounting the series of events–
She trespasses in a stranger's house
damages their property
takes their food
soils their sheets
and runs off.
    (*Beat.*)
B. I guess they should have called it Goldilocks and the three strikes law.
3. What an
unusual interpretation.
A. It just occurs to me that
you've said you use this
"principle"
to maintain the stability of the community–
But it's about a sociopathic five-year-old on a crime spree.
4. You side with the animals?
A. I'm not taking / sides
4. Over the little girl?
The human?
A. They make porridge and sleep under quilts
they aren't exactly savage beasts.
3. I can't remember anyone defending the bears before.
At least not anyone who lives here.
B. If I could just–
What they are, actually?
Is a family.
So I think what my wife is saying is that the COMMUNITY in the story
is really the bears /
1. Ohhhh /
B. And because Goldilocks disrupts the–
The equilibrium

of that community?
She should be punished.
A. Yes.
4. I see I see.
She's an anarchist.
A. An / extremist
1. All children are anarchists.
B. I can see why she says that
takes the side of the family
because for some time now
we've been talking about how one of the best ways to genuinely have an impact
on the world
might be to have a child.
Right?
A. We have.
B. To raise a thoughtful, considerate daughter or son.
And if everyone simply took care of that
when a new generation of pioneers comes of age
there might even be hope.
Of course we want to provide the best home possible for that child
which is why we're here.
A. Yes.
It is.
B. Even if it may
cost us
a little more than we had planned.
3. Can we say the story means both things at the same time?
Your version and ours.
A. ...
There's never one right answer.
2. So everybody gets what they want.
B. Which is how it should be.
3. We're all on the same page then?
In terms of the board's concerns–
B. I know I am.
It's just such a great opportunity.
1. The view from that living room alone /
B. Over the park?

It's paradise.

2. And wait 'til you get a look at the school system.
If you're thinking about kids–

3. (*To* A.) Yes?

A. To be honest–

...

You know the more I think about it?
It really is a great opportunity
Not the apartment itself
but because, so often we isolate ourselves?
We end up living someplace where we're surrounded by people who are echoes of our own beliefs.
And to be in a building where there is a spectrum?
Where people are bridging those political gaps just by occupying the same space?
That's a positive example to set.

B. Especially for children.

A. Yes, to show that we can come together.
That's the real opportunity.

B. Once in a lifetime opportunity.

A. Once in a lifetime.
And any time you build community
it means sacrificing a little self-interest.
But there's a balance there that is–

B. It's just right.

(*End play.*)

MOTHER'S BLESSINGS
by Dipika Guha

A very long dinner table. It is so long we can't see the end.
A boy comes in.
Then another.
Then another.
Then another.
They greet each other with nods and fist bumps
Another rushes in
Then another
Then another

>*They sit around the table.*
>*Someone whispers to someone else*
>*Who laughs loudly*
>*Soon the whole table of boys are laughing.*
>*A* WOMAN *enters.*
>*The laughing stops.*
>*The boys all stand.*
>*A* MAN *enters behind the* WOMAN. *The* WOMAN *sits at the head of the table.*

WOMAN. Be seated.
>(*The boys all sit and* MAN *sits in a chair whispering distance behind the* WOMAN. *There are so many boys. More than we thought.*)

Who will say grace?
>(*A hand shoots up from the boys. The* MAN *whispers something quickly we can't hear into the* WOMAN*'s ear. It must become increasingly evident that she's blind.*)

Please begin.

BOY 1. In the heat of burn
The world is turn
Crickets in night
Stirs the fright
Mother is all
All her good grace
Blessings.

WOMAN. Blessings.

ALL. Blessings!
>(*This goes fast. It's roll call.*)

WOMAN. B

BOY 1. Present.

WOMAN. R

BOY 2. Present.

WOMAN. K

BOY 3. Present.
>(*The* WOMAN *senses something.*)

WOMAN. Straight yer shirt.
>(BOY 3 *does hastily.*)

Wing

BOY 4. Present ma'am.

WOMAN. Low
BOY 5. Present and attention.
WOMAN. Only one.
BOY 5. Attention.
WOMAN. Good.
Gin.
BOY 6. Present.
    (*A small twitch from the* WOMAN, *a sensing.*)
WOMAN. Up.
    (BOY 6 *straightens his back.*)
Look straight—
    (BOY 6 *adjusts his gaze.*)
Howl.
    (*Silence.*)
Where is...
    (BOY 7 *charges in.*)
BOY 7. Present!
WOMAN. Where?
BOY 7. Late.
WOMAN. Sit.
BOY 7. Attention!
    (WOMAN *rings a bell.*)
WOMAN. Begin!
    (*The* BOYS *begin to eat hungrily.* WOMAN *watches, she whispers with the* MAN *out of earshot of the* BOYS.)
Boys be restless
MAN. Boys be boys
WOMAN. Idle hands—
MAN. Och no, no devil here—
WOMAN. My skin pricks
Shadows stick.
    (*The* MAN *touches the* WOMAN*'s chair wistfully.*)
I'll tear out my womb 'fore I give up my chair.
Attend—
    (*She rings the bell. Eating stops at once.* MAN *steps up. His tone is now businesslike.*)
MAN. Cars are driving

ALL. Oooh me! Me! Pick me! Pick me!

    (MAN *raises his hand*.)

MAN. Ah ah ah. Shhhh.
God don't like noise.

ALL. (*More hushed*.) Me... pick me! Pick me! Pick me!

MAN. Cars are driving
Rain is driving
Wet is slip
Who will drivin'?

BOY 7. I will!

MAN. Late.

BOY 7. Tsk.

BOY 6. I will.

    (BOYS *all turn to* BOY 6.)

WOMAN. Gin will.

BOYS ALL. Gin will? Gin?? Gin will?

WOMAN. Gin will drivin'.

BOY 5. What about the slip?

WOMAN. Slip's how it 'tis.
Today slip
Tomorrow sun
'Tis how 'tis
Fast
Or else

BOY 5. Gin can't—

WOMAN. What?

BOY 5. He can't...

WOMAN. What who's speaking?

BOY 5. It's me, Low.

WOMAN. Repeat yerself.

BOY 5. (*Loses nerve*.) Uhm...

BOY 4. (*Bravely*.) Gin can't see.

    (*Everything stops*.)

WOMAN. What?
Can't see?
What's he—

MAN. Can't ye see Gin?

BOY 6. ......

WOMAN. State ye truth.

BOYS ALL. STATE YE TRUTH
STATE YE TRUTH
STATE YE TRUTH

WOMAN. Hush boys.
Gin?

BOY 6. Can't see.

WOMAN. Ye've bin wheating
Without eyes
Wellin' water
Without eyes
Tractorin' even
Without eyes

BOY 6. Half can

WOMAN. Which half?

BOY 6. Ma'am?

WOMAN. Top or bottom half?

BOY 6. Can't—

WOMAN. Speak up

BOY 6. Half not bad
Is all

WOMAN. Inside.

BOY 6. No!

WOMAN. Inside fer you.

BOY 6. Girls are inside!

(*The table stops again.*)

WOMAN. What?

BOY 6. Kitchen's fer girls..

WOMAN. Girls in my kitchen
Over my dead
Girls be in fightin' front
That's how 'tis
Teeth for blades
Nails for claws
Eye for eye
She devil for devil
Understand?

BOY 6 (*Small.*) Yes.

WOMAN. K?

BOY 3. Here ma'am.

WOMAN. Take him.
Sweeps
Mops
Drapes
No tractorin'.

BOY 3. Permission to speak?

WOMAN. Permission.

BOY 3. Sun got down
Still-like
In far
Shape-like

WOMAN. What shape?

BOY 3. Big.
Legs long
Horse like

WOMAN. What is this?

MAN. Don't hardly know—

BOY 3. Sun laid down
Had two
On back
Like hills
Like horse
With hills
And horns

BOY 2. Lies.

WOMAN. Done.

BOY 3. Not done!
I tell ye
It's close

WOMAN. Done I say!

BOY 3. Like a hole
Suckd light
From ye
From all ye!

    (WOMAN *turns to* MAN.)

WOMAN. What's this?

MAN. Sit down son.

BOY 3. I'm 'feared.

Up River's wet wit dead girls—
Hair tearin' skies
Tears drivin' wind south
Can't breathe for the sad
It's a storm.
It's comin'!

ALL BOYS. (*Terrified.*) It's coming???

WOMAN. Falsehoods!

BOY 4. Ain't a lie.
I feel it too.

ALL BOYS. He's feel it! He's feel it!

    (WOMAN *puts a knife into the table. A gasp from the* BOYS.)

WOMAN. SILENCE!
Only din be mine
Eventide rabble
Be mine
Monsters are for stories
Not for this workin world
Mother's blessings

ALL. Mother's blessings

    (*As* WOMAN *speaks, the stage slowly begins to darken as an enormous shadow begins to fall on the scene. The* BOYS *begin to get restless.*)

WOMAN. Man be the only monster
I ever known
Sheddin' dark on the table
Leechin' light from night
Spreadin' sick in tins
Eatin' us inside out

    (*As the shadow grows, the* MAN *steps back away from the scene, menacingly quiet.*)

Two thousand and thirty moons
Man sat in this chair
Cuttin' his hair
Knifin' this bread
His wretched day is done sons
I slain more Men than I slain monsters
Didn't spill warm blood
To welcome dark days again
At my table

    (*The shadow begins to darken the stage.*)

BOY 6. Is it me? I can't see!

BOYS ALL. Can't see! Can't see!

> (WOMAN *stands up to face the shadow—as she does, we see she carries a cane, she feels round the table and we realize she too is blind.*)

WOMAN. Boys?

> (*The shadow begins to swallow them all.*)

BOYS ALL. Mother!

> (*The* MAN *grabs the knife from the table.*)

WOMAN. Who are ye?

> (*Lights out.*)

A DATE WITH THE FAMILY, PART THREE
by Dipika Guha

Same scene; dining table, the flower centerpiece is broken, napkins, cups and plates are all in place. The RADIO ANNOUNCER *talks at regular speed but the family move in slow motion.*

MOTHER *stands where we left her, holding a newspaper in one hand; a bloodied gash on her head drips blood onto the floor.* FATHER *lies dead in a huge pool of blood.* DAUGHTER *holds a piece of broken china dripping blood on the floor while both* WHITE JUNIOR *and* BLACK JUNIOR *cower by the radio.*

RADIO ANNOUNCER V/O. (*Desperately.*) This family looks quite... <u>CONTENT.</u> And WHY NOT?? ...As you can see they're looking forward to an important date. <u>Dinner at Home with the Family.</u> What's the matter? Doesn't that sound exciting to you? First of all, Daughter has changed from her school clothes into something more festive.

> (DAUGHTER *wipes the broken piece of china absentmindedly on her dress, staining it.*)

Dressing a little makes her feel and consequently <u>look</u> more charming.
Mother too changes from her daytime clothes.

> (MOTHER *puts her apron on and lies down slowly next to* FATHER *on the floor over the* ANNOUNCER'*s next lines.*)

The women of this family seem to think they owe it to the men of the family to look relaxed, rested and... *attractive* at dinner time.
Father too looks forward to this date with his family.
He has had a hard day at the office...

> (MOTHER *strokes* FATHER'*s face.*)

WHITE JUNIOR *goes to leave.* BLACK JUNIOR *grasps* WHITE JUNIOR*'s shoulder.*
DAUGHTER *starts to walk slowly towards* BLACK JUNIOR.)

This is the time for pleasant discussion in a thoroughly relaxed mood.

(BLACK JUNIOR *and* WHITE JUNIOR *look at each other.* DAUGHTER *has reached* BLACK JUNIOR. *She presses the piece of china into* BLACK JUNIOR*'s hand.*)

Back to the table Junior... come on... back you come.
You don't want to make Father angry now, do you Junior?

(BLACK JUNIOR, WHITE JUNIOR *and* DAUGHTER *shake their heads no.*)

Father doesn't like to do what he does when he gets angry, but he does it for your own good ..

(WHITE JUNIOR *now takes* BLACK JUNIOR*'s other hand.*)

You know that don't you Junior?

(BLACK JUNIOR, DAUGHTER *and* WHITE JUNIOR *look up.*)

Pleasant unemotional conversation helps digestion.

(*Slow fade to black.*)

THE NATIONAL FOOSBALL CHAMPIONSHIPS
by Jaclyn Backhaus
conceived with The Ensemble

notes

montage quality:
large BUZZER SOUNDZ between each moment, commentator giving us time after each buzzer
to keep us abreast of where we are in game
very important game! we gotta defeat some mens rights activists yall
headbands yall
the coaches
sideline reporters

characters

junie
chip
trent
lily-anne
coaches (2)
ref

>   ball boy
>   fans
>   concessions guy
>   cheerleaders

>   *a woman. putting on a fresh blazer. a sea of opportunity awaits her*

JUNIE. i used to sit out on my granddad's porch and look up at it
the orange night sky
wonder if the star lights would shine down on me
the way they shined down on my brothers
Toby was hockey
Hank was baseball
Pete was swim team
i went to every game
proud sister, basking in the light

in high school
i went on a dinner date with Freddy Evans
varsity soccer star
and i told him how much i loved sports
he laughed
i told him i wanted to be a commentator
play by play, i said,
i want to convey the intricacy of every play to the viewer
he chuckled and said, "if i was watching a game on tv
and i heard a girl's voice trying to tell me what was happening
i would change the channel."

today,
i put on my commentator's blazer for the first time.
this one's for you, Freddy Evans
you marvelous fuckhead.
cos i got a date with foosball baby
FOOS BALL
BAE BEEEEEEEE

>   *(she puts on her blazer*
>   *airhorns. flashing lights*
>   *she dances toward her podium*
>   *she takes her proverbial seat at the table*
>   *in the commentary booth*
>   *as a literal table*
>   *enters the center space*
>   *time shifts again and players, coaches, ball boys enter the space*

*frantic energy, excitement
the air is ripe!*)

CHEERLEADERS. who's got that foos?
u got that foos u got that foos
who's got that ball?
u got that ball u got that ball
u got that foos u got that ball
u got that FOOS BALL BAE BEE

(*chip, the fellow announcer, joins* junie *in a little pump up dance they begin!*)

CHIP. WELCOME EVERYONE TO THE 42ND ANNUAL NATIONAL FOOSBALL CHAMPIONSHIPS
hosted by the NATIONAL FOOSBALL LEAGUE
broadcasting LIVE from Louisville, Kentucky,
home of the hot brown.
I'M CHIP AMBLEWORTHY
AND JOINING ME HERE IN THE COMMENTATORS' BOOTH
FOR THE FIRST TIME
IS JUNIE CARSON-WEATHERS

(*meanwhile in the stands*)

JUNIE. IT'S A GREAT DAY FOR FOOSBALL
HAPPY TO BE HERE CHIP

CHIP. HAPPY TO HAVE YOU JUNIE

JUNIE. today's NFL competitors are fighting for the title of best foosball player in the nation

CHIP. it's the culmination of a heated and very DIVISIVE tournament in which players seem to be fighting not only their competitors, but their competitors' souls junie?

JUNIE. fighting for the championship title today
we have
LILY-ANNE "THE BUTTERFLY" GERALDINO
of bayonne, new jersey
Lily-Anne is only the second woman ever to make it to the National Foosball League Finals.
If she wins today, she will be the first woman to ever hold the trophy
the players are entering the arena
Lily-Anne is playing today
against heralded mens rights activist and long-time National Foosball Leaguer

CONCESSIONS GUY. Spuds
Git yer spuds
git yer french fries
git yer tater tots
git yer mashed
git yer home fries
git yer fingerlings
git yer scalloped
git yer pommes frites
git yer au gratin
git yer hash browns
git yer baked spuds
git yer chips—Spudz Chips
$49

TRENT SPUDNIK
of lower cheeses, north dakota

CHIP. Trent is the fifth lower cheeses resident to make it to the foosball finals making it a hallowed local tradition up there in north dakota

JUNIE. we are sure to have a strong viewership tuning in from lower cheeses

CHIP. as well as a strong presence of SPUDFREAKS in the stands here today

(*a loud roar from the audience*)

JUNIE. Lily-Anne "The Butterfly" Geraldino is foosing today for her mother, Miriam Geraldino, who Lily-Anne has said "is the rock that taught me everything I know about foosball." Miriam, notably banned from the sport in her youth because she was a woman. You played against Miriam in some of your college matches, didn't you Chip?

CHIP. I did Junie, before I went pro.

(trent *and* lily-anne *are prepping*)

JUNIE. and the ref has signalled for the traditional
over-the-table handshake
Lily-Anne Across From Trent
Lily-Anne extends her hand, ready to shake

CHIP. and TRENT FAKES HER OUT
DOES NOT ACCEPT THE HANDSHAKE
FRIENDS, THIS IS GOING TO BE AN UGLY ONE

JUNIE. the rejection of the handshake is really not a proper way to start a match
have we ever seen anything like this chip?

CHIP. we have not, junie, not in the history of foosing
such an action signals, in trent, a dismissal of everything lily-anne stands for and everything she identifies as

JUNIE. well we shall have to see how he takes it when he loses

CHIP. aup!

(*a little aside*)

Junie. First rule of play-by-play—stay impartial

JUNIE. (*aside*) Trent has exhibited hateful behavior all tournament!

CHIP. (*aside*) if you don't stay impartial, producers will give me the go-ahead
i'll take over play-by-play right there on the airwaves
got it?

JUNIE. stick to the amusing anecdotes and catchphrases Chip
I got this.
and here, we have the ref's hand in the air, holding the ball
the players have their hands splayed

ready to grab the knobs as soon as the ball enters the playing space
the air is tense
and the ref drops the ball!
and they're off now, folks
Trent and Lily-Anne, their fingers fly from knob to knob
twiddling their players
readying their men for the all important shot

CHIP. it's a best of three match
so whomever wins this first ball will have crucial advantage

JUNIE. Trent seizes a Straightliner to the Loop but it is blocked by Lily-Anne's Left Sideswipe
she gains control of the ball
her Center Line takes a Liontap
and it Straightaways into the goal!
POINT ONE, LILY-ANNE GERALDINO

CHIP. She turns to the stands and celebrates with her signature BUTTERFLY
her fans silently stand, flapping their wings in return
of course, the SPUDFREAKS boo in response
always ready to shut down a noninvasive party
with their signature invasiveness

JUNIE. the players return to their corners, where they run through some signature cooldown moves with their coaches.

CHIP. it's important to keep the digits moving
to avoid cramping and spastic twitching

JUNIE. Lily-Anne's coach, Tammy Owens "T. O." Frampton, is a legend in foosball—the first woman to play for the NFL and the only other woman to ever reach the Championship Match
the players are back at the table
the ref drops the ball
and they're off folks

CHIP. TRENT and THE BUTTERFLY matching each other move by move in a tete-a-tete of foosplay

JUNIE. the ball flies from one side of the table to the other
a classic Tete-a-Tete BacknForth

CHIP. will this play ever end?
will this play ever end?
will this play ever end?
YES IT WILL

JUNIE. trent using his corner dibber for the dib that sends the ball dribbling into lily-anne's net it's a one all game folks

CHIP. i'm sure you're heartbroken there junie

JUNIE. i'm stayin impartial chip

CHIP. seems like it's hard for you

JUNIE. (*aside*) i didn't commentate the NCAA hackey sack championships for three years for nothing, CHIP
i play by the rules

CHIP. the producers are worried

JUNIE. what are they talking in your earpiece?

CHIP. they are indeed, Junie

JUNIE. well have fun talking to them
I'm gonna go ahead and DO MY JOB
Lily-Anne, back at the table ready for the third set
here as Trent finishes a bowl of Lucky Charms

CHIP. is he being spoonfed by his coach?

JUNIE. he sure is Chip
Trent's coach, Marvel Weathers, is better known to our audiences by his nickname: ManBaby

CHIP. ManBaby is wiping the milk off of Trent's chin
with a nice soft towel
and we're ready for the third set

JUNIE. ref drops the ball in
and WHOA—TRENT
for a Zingaling Straightaway
the score is 2-1

CHIP. a very aspirational ball boy has endeavored to bring the ball back to the table

JUNIE. he's gonna go far in this sport

CHIP. lily-anne looks shocked
Trent Spudnik's victory is only one championship point away
it would be a humiliating setback for all womanhood, right Junie?

JUNIE. Well as the great yogi berra always said
You Can Pry My Feminism from my Cold Dead Hands.
Lily-Anne the Butterfly Geraldino and Trent Spudnik
are heading back to the table

CHIP. once again, Trent is playing for Championship Point

JUNIE. the players at the ready and
OHP! Trent Spudnik

twiddling his knobs before the start of play
and there's the ref's flag
CHIP. That's gonna be a false start for Spudnik
Let's review the play
  (*slow mo false start*)
JUNIE and CHIP. no question/definitely a False Start/it's undeniable/here's the ref with the call
REF. False Start—Spudnik
Penalty Foos—Geraldino
JUNIE. and TRENT SPUDNIK has engaged in a False Start, which means he will have to stand the
requisite three feet from the board as Lily-Anne takes a single shot at the goal
SPUDFREAKS. MENS RIGHTS MENS RIGHTS
JUNIE. what are they shouting
CHIP. it sounds like "mens rights"
JUNIE. Trent's coach ManBaby is thrashing his arms at the ref, spit flying from his foamy privileged mouth
CHIP. looks like the ref is having none of it now
ladies and gentlemen MANBaBY is ejected from the Championship match
JUNIE. it takes four officials to hold ManBaby down and forcibly eject him from this arena
CHIP. i am not partial in this match and it was definitely a false start
JUNIE. Lily-Anne The Butterfly Geraldino
looks ready to make her comeback
the ball is dropped
and it's a stealthy, smooth shot right through center goal
CHIP. Friends, this game is tied 2-2!!!
SPUDFREAKS. DEATH TO WOMEN
DEATH TO WOMEN
JUNIE. The chanting has changed now to something much more dangerous
CHIP. the men must be feeling threatened
JUNIE. Are you making excuses for them?
CHIP. Junie
the producers have asked that you stay impartial
JUNIE. I'm impartial, Chip—
Are you?
Are you a mens rights activist, Chip?

CHIP. No no no no Junie no

JUNIE. Then say it, Chip. On the air.

> (chip *gives the smallest nod to* junie
> *he turns out to the camera and*)

CHIP. the producers in my ear are telling me to stay silent, but listen here, viewers:
I don't condone the behavior of the Spudfreaks in the Arena today.
It does not reflect the majesty of foosball—my favorite sport
I'm Chip Ambleworthy and I approve this message.
Back to you Junie.

JUNIE. thanks, Chip. Trent is reeling, his fans are spiraling, and Lily-Anne maintains her butterfly poise.
We are here, friends, at Championship Point.
IT. ALL. COMES. DOWN. TO. THIS.
The ref drops the ball
and they're off! both sides furiously twiddling every knob,
Spingliders and Sideswipes at every turn
this is anyone's game folks

CHIP. the ball is moving so fast I can barely see it

JUNIE. Swizzle Linedrives and Tiny Soccerkicks
Control of the ball from Lily-Anne to Trent back to Lily-Anne

CHIP. it is anyone's game

JUNIE. Back to Trent and—wait—could it be?
FOLKS, Trent Spudnik, in his haste, sent the ball into his OWN GOAL

CHIP. The ref has confirmed—that makes Lily-Anne our National—but wait—
Lily-Anne seems to be refusing the point

JUNIE. Lily-Anne Geraldino is refusing the point

REF. "Point Refused. Match Point Reset"

JUNIE. It seems Lily-Anne wants to win this game on her own terms

CHIP. Viewers, this is unprecedented
Back in my pro days this would be considered foolish, but today it seems heroic

JUNIE. Match Point, Round 2
the ball is dropped
Trent with a FLASHZOINK into the Corner
STOPPED DEAD by Lily-Anne's Lil Goalie
She Revs up for a 360 Spinglide
that Boardcrosses STRAIGHT INTO TRENT'S GOAL

JUNIE and CHIP. LILY-ANNE THE BUTTERFLY GERALDINO IS OUR NATIONAL FOOSBALL CHAMPION!!

CHIP. trent spudnik is racing off the court crying, his fans filled with toxic rage
he seems to be permanently ostracized from his signature hate-filled community

JUNIE. Let's go to Lily-Anne

LILY-ANNE. thank you for this trophy. i hope for more days like this when we can judge women
based on their skillsets and personhood
where women feel valued for their contributions to society
and where they are supported in their dreams.

    (*the fans do the butterfly.* lily-anne *gives a thumbs up to* junie.)

JUNIE. a great day for foosball indeed.

ALL. FOOS BALL BAE BEE

    (*end of play*)

EPILOGUE
by Jason Gray Platt

Before all the post-game analysis
Lulls you into psychic paralysis
We offer you, in tonight's leitmotif,
No epilogue, but a small digestif.
A stiff drink helps fight off bacteria,
In case of theatrical listeria.
As kind guests will pity a humble host
Who served cold soup or undercooked the roast,
You'll no doubt show us the same compassion
If you found fault with your thespian ration.
On one point I hope we can all agree:
What matters most is each other's company.
Fellowship is the finest nutrition
For this ravenous human condition.
Since our ancestors tamed the first wild fire,
We have met as a hungry, broken choir
To feed both stomach and soul 'round its light.
There's grace revealed in our raw appetite:
Some crave bread, some justice, some connection
But no one is spared hunger's subjection.

As long as communal fires are burning,
We can unite in our separate yearning.
Help us keep these shared flames from falling dark;
The striking of hands casts the sweetest spark.

End of Play

www.ingramcontent.com/pod-product-compliance
Lightning Source LLC
Chambersburg PA
CBHW071225230426
43668CB00011B/1314